Siberian Huskies
FOR DUMMIES®

by Diane Morgan

Wiley Publishing, Inc.

Siberian Huskies For Dummies®

Published by
Wiley Publishing, Inc.
111 River Street
Hoboken, NJ 07030
www.wiley.com

Copyright © 2001 by Wiley Publishing, Inc., Indianapolis, Indiana

Published by Wiley Publishing, Inc., Indianapolis, Indiana

Published simultaneously in Canada

For general information on our other products and services or to obtain technical support, please contact our Customer Care Department within the U.S. at 800-762-2974, outside the U.S. at 317-572-3993, or fax 317-572-4002.

Wiley also publishes its books in a variety of electronic formats. Some content that appears in print may not be available in electronic books.

Library of Congress Cataloging-in-Publication Data:

Library of Congress Control Number: 00-107689
ISBN: 0-7645-5279-1

Manufactured in the United States of America
10 9 8 7
1B/QT/QV/QU/IN

About the Author

Diane Morgan is an Adjunct Professor of Literature, Religious Studies, and Philosophy at Wilson College in Chambersburg, Pennsylvania. In addition to her books about Siberian Huskies, Basset Hounds, Poodles, and Beagles, she writes about Buddhism, Taoism, Hinduism, Tennessee Williams, and pigs. She also writes the Dummies Daily eTips for Cats and Dogs (go to www.dummiesdaily.com for more information or to sign up to get tips from Diane every day). She is a founding member of Basset Rescue of Old Dominion.

Diane lives in Williamsport, Maryland, where she shares her home with eight dogs, two cats, and a variety of goldfish, none of whom can pull a sled. She has never been to Siberia.

About Howell Book House
Committed to the Human/Companion Animal Bond

Thank you for choosing a book brought to you by the pet experts at Howell Book House, a division of Wiley Publishing, Inc. And welcome to the family of pet owners who've put their trust in Howell books for nearly 40 years!

Pet ownership is about relationships — the bonds people form with their dogs, cats, horses, birds, fish, small mammals, reptiles, and other animals. Howell Book House/Wiley understands that these are some of the most important relationships in life, and that it's vital to nurture them through enjoyment and education. The happiest pet owners are those who know they're taking the best care of their pets — and with Howell books owners have this satisfaction. They're happy, educated owners, and as a result, they have happy pets, and that enriches the bond they share.

Howell Book House was established in 1961 by Mr. Elsworth S. Howell, an active and proactive dog fancier who showed English Setters and judged at the prestigious Westminster Kennel Club show in New York. Mr. Howell based his publishing program on strength of content, and his passion for books written by experienced and knowledgeable owners defined Howell Book House and has remained true over the years. Howell's reputation as the premier pet book publisher is supported by the distinction of having won more awards from the Dog Writers Association of America than any other publisher. Howell Book House/Wiley has over 400 titles in publication, including such classics as The American Kennel Club's *Complete Dog Book,* the *Dog Owner's Home Veterinary Handbook, Blessed Are the Brood Mares,* and *Mother Knows Best: The Natural Way to Train Your Dog.*

When you need answers to questions you have about any aspect of raising or training your companion animals, trust that Howell Book House/Wiley has the answers. We welcome your comments and suggestions, and we look forward to helping you maximize your relationships with your pets throughout the years.

The Howell Book House Staff

Publisher's Acknowledgments

We're proud of this book; please send us your comments through our Dummies online registration form located at www.dummies.com/register/.

Some of the people who helped bring this book to market include the following:

Acquisitions, Editorial, and Media Development

Project Editor: Elizabeth Netedu Kuball

Acquisitions Editor: Scott Prentzas

Technical Editor: Paulette Jones

Editorial Manager: Pamela Mourouzis

Editorial Administrator: Michelle Hacker

Cover Photo: © Kent and Donna Dannen

Production

Project Coordinator: Leslie Alvarez

Layout and Graphics: Amy Adrian, Clint Lahnen, Jill Piscitelli, Brent Savage, Jacque Schneider, Jeremey Unger

Proofreaders: Laura Albert, Valery Bourke, Corey Bowen, Andy Hollandbeck, Nancy Price

Indexer: Ty Koontz

Special Help
Carol Strickland

Publishing and Editorial for Consumer Dummies

Diane Graves Steele, Vice President and Publisher, Consumer Dummies

Joyce Pepple, Acquisitions Director, Consumer Dummies

Kristin A. Cocks, Product Development Director, Consumer Dummies

Michael Spring, Vice President and Publisher, Travel

Brice Gosnell, Associate Publisher, Travel

Suzanne Jannetta, Editorial Director, Travel

Publishing for Technology Dummies

Andy Cummings, Vice President and Publisher, Dummies Technology/General User

Composition Services

Gerry Fahey, Vice President of Production Services

Debbie Stailey, Director of Composition Services

Dedication

To the Chukchis

Author's Acknowledgments

It's impossible to write a book like this one without incurring a lot of debt. And I owe so many people so much that I'm glad they didn't charge me. First of all, my heartfelt thanks to all the people at Wiley who made it happen: Amanda Pisani, my friend and editor extraordinaire, who thought of me for this book; Dominique De Vito, who trusted me to carry it though; Scott Prentzas for handling a tough project in transition (and for finding the pictures!); and Elizabeth Kuball, my Project Editor, for her skillful work in making this book a pleasure to read.

To all the members of Sibernet, the online group with all the knowledge, experience, and kindness to answer all my questions, I owe my deepest appreciation.

To Paulette Jones, who took the time and trouble to explain the thrills of sled racing, and most of all for her expert technical editorship. Any errors in the text are mine, not hers.

To Peg Wheeler, for her love of and dedication to this beautiful breed. Many Siberian Huskies owe her their lives.

To my beloved companion John Warner, for his sage advice, staunch support, technical help, and careful reading of many drafts of this book. He kept me sane, sort of.

Cartoons at a Glance

By Rich Tennant

The 5th Wave — By Rich Tennant

"Actually, sitting on top of their dog house during inclement weather is normal for a Husky. Catching snowflakes on the tongue, however, seems unique to our particular pet."

page 5

The 5th Wave — By Rich Tennant

Shoot, that ain't nothin', watch this— Roll over. Rusty. C'mon, roll over! Roll over!

page 135

The 5th Wave — By Rich Tennant

"Okay, okay— maybe it's not a good idea. I just thought since Huskies were bred for winter weather, part of the grooming process might include having them flocked."

page 31

The 5th Wave — By Rich Tennant

ALONG WITH BEING VERY GOOD SLED DOGS, HUSKIES ARE KNOWN TO BE EXCELLENT SHOPPING CART DOGS

page 197

The 5th Wave — By Rich Tennant

"OK, I'LL LET HIM PLAY AS LONG AS YOU STOP SAYING, 'YOU CAN'T TAKE AN OLD DOG'S NEW TRICKS'."

page 59

The 5th Wave — By Rich Tennant

CHASING STICK

GOOD DOG   BAD DOG

BOWL DRINKING

"Okay, let's get into something a little more theoretical."

page 213

Fax: 978-546-7747
E-mail: richtennant@the5thwave.com
World Wide Web: www.the5thwave.com

Table of Contents

Introduction

T he Siberian wind is a mute wind; there are no trees to make it roar, no grasses to let it sing or whisper. It rushes on, cold and silent, over the endless miles of tundra.

But there is sound, nonetheless. A haunting cry rides the wild wind, a cry chiseled out of frozen air, etched in darkness. Perhaps it is a wolf, for wolves abound here, following the vast herds of reindeer. But maybe not. Perhaps the cry is fuller than the howl of a wolf, sweeter, and more burdened with loneliness. Perhaps it is the song of the first Siberian Husky ever born.

Welcome to the world of the Siberian Husky. If you've ever wondered why your Siberian is different from all the other breeds, this book will tell you. You discover what made your Siberian the way he is, and how you can get the most out of your relationship with this engaging, unique, and totally original breed. This is a book that will make your life — and your Siberian's — richer, more satisfying, and a lot more fun.

How This Book Is Organized

Siberian Huskies For Dummies is divided into six parts. Each part dives into one aspect of Husky ownership, covering everything from finding a Husky to training the one you have.

Part I: Getting to Know Siberian Huskies

In this part, you'll find out where Huskies came from, how they got to America, and what they are like today. To fully understand the Siberian, and to appreciate his many fine qualities and needs, we have to look at his exciting origin.

Part II: Looking for Your Soul Mate

In this part, you discover how to get a Husky and how to prepare for your new dog's arrival.

Part III: Living with a Siberian Husky

In the chapters in this part, you get lots of useful tips for getting your Husky used to his new home, socializing him with other animals and people, training him to be a well-behaved member of the family, and avoiding common problems.

Part IV: Keeping Your Husky Healthy

In this part, you get the lowdown on everything from grooming and nutrition, to choosing a veterinarian and dealing with general health problems.

Part V: Bringing Out the Sled Dog in Your Siberian

Here you find out about the thrills of mushing. And you get the scoop on Husky Nirvana — the Iditarod.

Part VI: The Part of Tens

This wouldn't be a book ...*For Dummies* without The Part of Tens. Here you'll find short bursts of information on everything from reasons to have a Siberian to tips for raising one.

Icons Used in This Book

Throughout this book, you'll find cute little pictures in the margins next to certain paragraphs. But these aren't merely for your amusement; they actually serve a purpose. And I explain the purpose here:

When you run across this icon, you know you're in for a useful bit of information on how to do things with or for your Husky.

This eye-catching icon alerts you to potential hazards or problems that you need to watch out for.

When you see this icon, you're sure to find some very useful information that's bound to impress your friends at the next neighborhood get-together. But it isn't essential that you pay attention to this stuff if you're just looking for the basics.

Some things are so important they bear repeating, and when I repeat myself, I try to remember to mark it with this icon.

When you see this wagging tail, you're sure to find products or services that are particularly helpful for Husky owners.

This icon points out fun tidbits of information that are great to know about Huskies — stories that will make you laugh or, at the very least, bring a smile to your face.

Where to Go from Here

You may not know much about Siberians, but the fact that you've picked up this book shows that you care and want to have a good relationship with your dog. In this book, you have all the information you need to get started on a lifetime of enjoying your Siberian Husky.

Part I
Getting to Know Siberian Huskies

The 5th Wave   By Rich Tennant

"Actually, sitting on top of their dog house during inclement weather is normal for a Husky. Catching snowflakes on the tongue, however, seems unique to our particular pet."

In this part . . .

This is the place to turn if you're looking for background information on Siberian Huskies as a breed — everything from the characteristics of a Husky to the breed's fascinating history. If you're just starting to think about adopting one of these wonderful dogs, look no further.

Chapter 1

What Is a Husky?

In This Chapter

▶ Telling the difference between a Siberian Husky and a wolf or a Malamute

▶ Knowing the Siberian Husky breed standard

Many people mistake Siberian Huskies for other animals, such as wolves or Malamutes. So in this chapter, I give you the scoop on what differentiates a Husky from these other animals. And I let you know what exactly a Siberian Husky is, by filling you in on the American Kennel Club (AKC) breed standard. Not sure quite what a Husky is? Read on!

The Difference between a Husky and Other Similar-Looking Animals

Many people think that wolves, Siberian Huskies, Malamutes, and "Alaskan Sled Dogs" are all pretty much the same thing. But they aren't. In fact, the original breeders of the Siberian Husky did little to alter his wolf-like appearance, other than his size. They wanted a smart, strong, domestic animal, who could run fast and would not bite his owners. They paid little attention to nonessential, purely aesthetic factors, which is one reason that the odd and fanciful features of some breeds, like the Sharpei's wrinkles, or the floppy ears of the Irish Setter, never developed in Huskies. (Their blue eyes must be purely serendipitous.)

Alaskan Malamutes

Despite the fact that the Alaskan Malamute and the Siberian Husky bear a superficial resemblance to each other, the Alaskan Malamute has an entirely different history from the Siberian. Malamutes were developed by the Eskimo people known as the *Mahlemiut,* whose dogs became much in demand as freighting animals during the Alaska Gold Rush of 1896. They are larger, slower, and more powerful than Huskies, and they never have blue eyes. Malamutes can also have a more difficult temperament than the merry, easy-going Siberians. Today, Malamutes are frequently used for pulling.

"Alaskan Huskies"

Another breed you may have heard about is the so-called "Alaskan Husky." Like Malamutes, these "Huskies" come from Alaska, but they do not comprise a distinct breed. They are mixes, bred specifically for sled dog competitions. Alaskan Huskies are purely sled dogs and do not make good house pets. Other sled dog breeds include the MacKenzie River Husky and the Chinook.

Wolves and wolf-hybrids

Some people find it "macho" or "cool" to keep a *wolf-hybrid,* a wolf crossed with a Siberian, Malamute, Akita, or German Shepherd. But keeping a wolf-hybrid is definitely a very bad idea. Wolves, wolf-hybrids, and wolf mixes make dangerous pets.

Some wolves or wolf-hybrids may appear tame, but no wolf or wolf mix is ever truly domesticated. Many wolf mixes are obtained by crossing Huskies with wolves, possibly under the mistaken impression that the resultant puppies will inherit the Siberian's happy disposition. But this is simply wrong. Instead, a wolf/Siberian mix combines the worst features of both species. The crosses behave more like wolves than dogs, combining fear and aggression in an extremely unpleasant way. In many places, owning such an animal is illegal, and even where it isn't, it's just asking for trouble. The same applies to dog-coyote mixes, another unsavory trend.

Wolf-hybrids cannot be trusted around human beings. They have a bad track record of killing people, especially children. Wolves in the wild rarely kill human beings, by the way. That's because completely wild animals have a sensible fear of people and stay well away from them. The wolf mix or hybrid has no fear of humans, and he shows it. Still, a few people continue to keep children in homes where a wolf-hybrid is present, with predictable and sometimes fatal results.

The Siberian Husky Breed Standard

The original breeders of Siberian Huskies were more concerned with function than form, so early Siberians came in a bewildering mix of shapes and sizes. Some were lean and leggy, some stout and thick-bodied. To be able to breed true, dedicated breeders in this country began to develop a conformation standard. (Animals *breed true* when similar parents consistently produce offspring who look like themselves.)

The American Kennel Club recognized the Siberian Husky as a breed in 1930 and placed the breed in its Working Group. The Working Group is a diversified bunch of dogs that also includes Akitas, Great Danes, Newfoundlands, and Rottweilers. The Siberian Husky is a *Spitz-type* dog, a word that recalls its northern breeding (Spitzbergen is a group of islands in the Arctic Ocean north of Norway). Akitas, Samoyeds, Malamutes, and even the little Pomeranian are all Spitz-type dogs.

The first registered Husky was a bitch named Fairbanks Princess Chena, who was born September 16, 1927. Her father was named Bingo. The first Siberian Huskies to become AKC Champions were Pola in 1931 and Northern Lights Kobuk, from the Northern Lights Kennel in Fairbanks, Alaska, the following year.

The Siberian Husky breed standard was first published in 1932; it has changed little since that time. The Husky is a dog built for both speed and endurance. He is one of the smallest of the Working Dogs but also one of the quickest. The Husky is also, pound for pound, the strongest of all the sled or draft dogs.

The Siberian's smooth combination of grace and strength makes him a star wherever he goes. Today, he ranks 18th in popularity among all AKC breeds, which is a good position. (Too high on the popularity scale invites dangerous overbreeding, whereas too low can indicate a too-small gene pool.) The keys to a good Siberian are balance, proportion, coat, and temperament. Males should be masculine, not coarse; females should be feminine, not frail. The Siberian Husky standard represents the ideal show dog, the goal toward which breeders strive. No Siberian is perfect, but seeing how close a dog can come to the standard is always interesting and sometimes amusing.

Don't worry if your own Siberian doesn't match the standard; many of the best obedience, racing, and companion dogs would bomb out in a show ring.

Check out Figure 1-1 for an illustration of the external features of a Siberian Husky, and refer back to it as you read about the Husky's different body parts in the following sections.

Size

Males, referred to as *dogs* in the dog world, should stand between 21 and 23½ inches at the shoulder and weigh 45 to 60 pounds. *Bitches* (the term used to refer to female dogs) average slightly smaller — 20 to 22 inches at the shoulder and between 35 and 50 pounds. Weight should be proportionate to height.

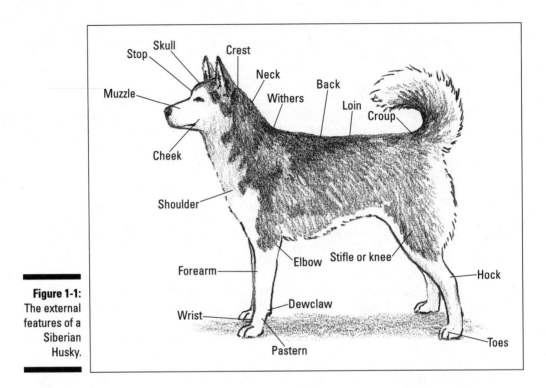

Figure 1-1:
The external
features of a
Siberian
Husky.

Animals taller than the standard would be excused from the show ring as being oversized; however, the extra inches don't affect a pet's quality at all. Within the standard, judges don't give any preference to dogs at either end of the spectrum; a larger dog is as likely to win as a smaller one, and vice versa. There is no minimum height listed in the Siberian Husky breed standard.

Body

A good Siberian should present a rectangular rather than a square body profile, meaning that the length of the dog from the point of the shoulder to the base of the tail is longer than the height to the shoulders. The ribs should be neither absolutely flat nor oversprung. Olaf Swenson, arctic explorer and Siberian Husky aficionado, believed that a good flank provided energy for long pulls. That idea has remained in the standard. Swenson also said that dogs with great stamina have vertebrae that are higher than those of the average dog, with deep depressions between the knobs. This advice is great to keep in mind.

The *topline* (or back and rump) of a Husky is level from *withers* (shoulders) to *croup* (rump). The Siberian's body is also a bit longer than his tail. The croup slopes away from the spine at an angle.

The chest should be deep, because it contains the heart and lungs, but not too broad. The shoulder is set at a 45-degree angle to the ground; a straight or loose shoulder is a fault.

Front view

The Siberian Husky's legs should be straight and parallel, moderately spaced, with the elbows close to the body.

Back view

The Husky's hind legs should be parallel and moderately spaced, with well muscled upper thighs. Rear dew claws should be removed, because they are of no use and easily get caught in the dog's normal movement, hurting the dog.

Neck

The neck is of medium length, and should be well-arched. A good neck is very important in the Husky world, because many muscles controlling the front pass through it.

Skull

The head should be medium-sized, slightly rounded at the top, and gradually tapered from the widest point to the eyes. The muzzle should be straight; the point of the muzzle should be neither pointed nor square. The dog should have a pronounced *stop* (the place where the muzzle meets the forehead), and the head should present a clean-cut appearance. A heavy, clumsy head is a fault; so is a too-thin muzzle.

Teeth

Siberian Huskies are expected to have a *scissors bite,* which means that the top teeth fit closely over the lower teeth. A scissors bite is most efficient for catching and devouring prey. A level bite, where the teeth meet evenly, top and bottom, is considered a fault in this breed.

Expression

Siberians are well known for their keen, mischievous expression, which exudes intelligence and a love of life. They wear a perpetual smile. The black markings around the eyes, nose, and ears are a distinctive characteristic of the breed.

Eyes

The Siberian's eyes may be of any color — brown, blue, or part blue and part brown all in one eye, referred to as *parti-colored* (or *speckled, pinto,* or *split*). The eyes may also be green or amber. The Siberian breed standard accepts dogs with *bi-eyes* (one of each color). The standard does not prefer one eye color over another, and most breeders don't either, although many owners have a penchant for ice-blue eyes.

Whatever the color, the eyes should be almond-shaped, and set at a slightly oblique angle; eyes set too close together are a fault. Most experts agree that brown eyes are dominant over blue or green. This means that blue- or green-eyed parents will produce puppies with like-colored eyes.

Puppies who are born with dark blue eyes usually have brown eyes as adults. Those born with light blue eyes, however, will probably retain that color through adulthood.

Except for white and copper Huskies, the rims of the eyes should be black. (The eye rims of white and copper Huskies may match their coats.)

Ears

The Husky's strongly erect, medium-sized ears are triangular with slightly rounded tips, set high and not too far apart. They should be well covered with fur, both inside and out. Furry ears are not only cute, but of paramount importance in an arctic dog.

Feet

Like the ears, the toes should be well supplied with fur. (In the arctic regions, the fur is needed to keep the extremities warm.) The feet are oval-shaped and neither too small nor too large. Good feet are absolutely critical in a dog bred for sled pulling.

Tail

The Husky has a *fox tail,* which means it is full and bushy. While in repose, walking, and pulling a sled, the Siberian usually carries his tail low, but in times of high excitement, the tail often curls over the Husky's back. The technical term for this carriage is *sickle tail.* The sickle tail should not bend either to the left or right but remain curled (not too tightly) over the center of the dog's back.

Both the curl and furriness of the tail is typical of arctic dogs in general. Both serve a practical purpose, allowing the animal to sleep in a curled position with his sensitive nose buried in the thick warm tail fur, protected from the bitter arctic night. This is the famous *Siberian swirl.*

Coat texture

Huskies have what is called a *double coat,* which is a soft dense undercoat, with an outercoat of *guard hair.* The under- and outercoats have contrasting textures. The guard hairs should lie straight and fairly smooth. A silky or harsh outercoat is considered a fault. The hairs are medium in length, and should not obscure the Husky's profile. (All other northern breeds have long hair.) Conformation (show) dogs sometimes have longer hair than working dogs.

Color

Huskies may be of any color — or any combination of colors — from pure white to pure black. No preference is given to any particular color.

Color is a complicated topic. For one thing, no single gene is responsible for causing a dog to be any particular color. Scientists have identified at least ten genes for dog hair color patterns, as well as color type, distribution, and intensity; genes are also responsible for the characteristic Siberian mask. In Siberians, the undercoat and top coat of guard hairs may be of two different colors or shades. In addition, colors appearing on young dogs may change over time. Masks appear and disappear. Coats may change from dark to light, or vice versa. Some even change from dark to red. I have a friend whose Husky changes shade with every shed!

A good dog is a good color

Siberian breeders go by the old maxim, "A good dog is a good color." This is a lesson that even the arctic explorer Olaf Swenson had to learn. When he first went to Siberia to buy dogs, he decided that he wanted a striking-looking ensemble of dogs. He made up his mind that he would have an all-white team, composed of especially large, fine, well-matched animals, with handsome red harnesses and red sleds.

The native Siberian people, the Chukchis, were amused at the notion, but they obligingly hunted up the dogs for Swenson, and he finally obtained his white team. It looked splendid, and Swenson noted that it would have made the most impressive Christmas exhibit any department store could contrive. But as a sled team, the dogs were useless. There were a few good dogs in the team, but before long Swenson replaced half the team with new dogs who had stamina, speed, and intelligence. For years, the Chukchis joked with Swenson about that infamous white team, but he took it with good spirit.

Most dog breeds have particular colors or patterns associated with them. Dobermans, for example, are black and tan, and Labradors are yellow, black, or chocolate. Not so for the Siberian.

A Husky who has individual hairs all of one color is called a *monochrome* dog. This is true even if some of these individual hairs are white and some are yellow. In a monochrome dog, the individual hairs are not *banded* (covered with white or yellow), even though one dog may have hairs of several different colors. Monochrome dogs may be white, copper, or black. Other colors, like gray, sable, and agouti, are never monochromes. The opposite of a monochrome is a banded coat.

Both skin and coat color are determined by the amount of melanin produced by certain skin cells. How much melanin is produced is a complex matter of genetics. The Husky genetic code allows the Siberian to appear in a gloriously wide array of colors and banding patterns, including *piebald,* in which the coat is predominantly white, with irregular patches of another color, usually black or brown, sometimes only on the ears. Some breeders do not consider piebalds to be acceptable for showing, so they may be available for a very reasonable price. This attitude may be changing, however, as several piebalds have recently received championships.

The Board of Directors of the Siberian Husky Club of America approves the following color descriptions: Black and White, Gray and White, Red and White, Sable and White, Agouti and White, and Solid White. In ordinary parlance, the word *white* is left off when referring to a dog's color, unless, of course, the animal is solid white.

✔ **Black and White.** Black and white Siberians come in the following shades:

- **Jet black:** The guard coat is solid black, and the undercoat is black, charcoal, or dark gray. This is known as a *monochrome* coat. These hairs are not banded, although occasionally a single white hair or two pops up. Most jet black dogs also have black pigment on their pads and the roofs of their mouths.

- **Black:** The black guard hairs may be banded and some white may appear near the roots. The undercoat is a lighter color than that of the jet black dog; in fact some buff-colored hairs may appear.

- **Dilute black:** The guard hairs have a whitish banding, but the tips are black. The undercoat has a whitish cast and the longer hairs on the back and head are black. The shorter white hairs of the undercoat give the flanks a silvery cast.

✔ **Gray and White.** Gray and White Siberians come in the following shades:

- **Silver gray:** The guard hairs are banded with various tones of white. The undercoat is whitish, giving the dog a silvery aspect, with a little darkening along the spine. This silvery tone is called the *chinchilla factor.*

- **Gray:** The guard hairs are banded with cream or buff tones with black tips. The undercoat has a beige or yellow tone, giving the dog a yellow/gray cast.

- **Wolf gray:** The guard hairs are banded with buff near the roots and are tipped with black. The undercoat is cream, giving the dog a warm brown/gray cast.

✔ **Red and White.** Red and white dogs are sometimes called *copper.* In copper dogs, no black hairs are evident. The guard hairs are banded with various shades of solid colors other than black. Red and White Huskies always have liver-colored *points* (eye rims, ears, noses, and lips). If two copper Siberians are mated, the puppies are almost certainly copper. Copper Siberians may have eyes of amber or blue, but never brown.

✔ **Sable and White.** Guard hairs are banded with red near the roots but are tipped with black. Sable and White Siberians always have black points and black tipping on the fur. The entire dog has a reddish cast. This is a rare color.

✔ **Agouti and White.** The guard hairs are banded with black at the roots and tips with bands of yellow or beige in the middle of the hairs. The undercoat is charcoal. The saddle area of the dog often has a grizzled look to it. *Agouti* is defined as the "wild color." The Siberian Husky Club goes on to note that this is the color "most frequently seen in wild rodents," but I don't know that they actually needed to say *that.* (Technically, they're correct, though. An agouti is a tropical South American rodent, about the size of a rabbit. It has barred hairs, resulting in distinctive alternating light and dark bands.) For some reason, the agouti color is seen more often in racing lines than in other Siberians. Agoutis usually have very black whiskers and black toenails.

✔ **Solid White.** The guard hairs are either pure white or banded with very pale cream at the roots, although an occasional black hair may be present. The undercoat is solid white or silver, and the points may be either black or liver-colored. Most Siberian Husky lovers prefer that White dogs have black points, although there is no rule about this. White is a recessive color in Siberians; if two white Siberians are bred, all the puppies are white as well. Many breeders think, however, that the best color (Solid White with black points) comes from breeding a dark parent (which carries a white gene) to a Solid White. In this case, 50 percent of the puppies are Solid White.

Nose

The Siberian's nose should be black for gray, tan, or black dogs; liver for copper or red dogs; and flesh-colored for white dogs. A pink-streaked *snow nose* is also allowable. The snow nose may be seasonal, disappearing in the summertime. (Actually, the whole nose doesn't disappear, just the pinkish color.) The appropriately named snow nose is quite common among Siberian Huskies.

Gait

The Siberian should stride out in a smooth and effortless movement, showing good reach in the front and good drive in the back. The head is carried slightly forward when the dog is trotting. A short, prancing gait is considered a fault. Crabbing or crossing is also penalized.

Temperament

The Siberian was developed as a team dog. Consequently, his temperament should be alert and friendly; aggression is severely penalized. Siberians welcome everyone, including strangers. I think the best word to describe the Husky's temperament is *exuberant.*

Chapter 2

Husky History 101

As everyone knows, Siberian Huskies come from Siberia. But they weren't found just running around wild there. The Siberian is of a pure and very ancient lineage, dating back perhaps 4,000 years or more. The Siberian breed was developed by the Chukchis, an ancient Siberian hunting people.

In this chapter, you'll find one history lesson you're sure not to sleep through. The history of Huskies is a fascinating one, full of heroism and adventure. And in the following pages, you get the inside scoop.

It All Started with the Chukchis

The *Chukchis* are a semi-nomadic, reindeer-hunting people of extreme north-eastern Siberia. Today, the Chukchi population totals about 16,000; there is evidence that, in the past, the population was greater. Both the climatic and political oppression they have endured over the centuries have given the Chukchis the nickname "Apaches of the north." Of course, they don't call *themselves* that. They call themselves the *Luoravetlan,* which means "the genuine people," possibly implying something negative about the rest of us.

The word *Siberia* is almost synonymous with "cold," but the earliest Chukchis probably enjoyed a milder climate than they do today. In those warmer times, they apparently relied on dogs primarily for help in hunting the plentiful reindeer. About 3,000 years ago, however, the climate changed drastically for the worse. The reindeer had to travel farther and farther to find food, and the deer-dependent Chukchis had to travel with them, taking their entire households along.

During this same period, the Chukchis engaged in a series of struggles with the Eskimos for control of the Bering Strait region. The Chukchis lost, and consequently, they were pushed even farther back into the interior, far from the seal-rich seas.

It was in this way that the Siberian dogs added sled hauling to their list of accomplishments. These animals were so highly prized that only very young, very old, and very sick Chukchis were allowed to ride in the sleds as passengers. The sleds were mostly used for hauling goods; the people walked. Sometimes the Chukchi women and children pulled the sleds also — right along with the dogs.

Chukchi land, officially known as the *Chukchi Autonomous Region,* is a place of almost unbelievable hardship. It is mostly tundra, a vast and treeless plain, with permanently frozen subsoil. The forested tundra had plenty of rugged mountains, however, alternating with lowlands and many small lakes, with swampy *taiga* along the coast (taiga ends where the tundra begins). The rivers are mostly mountain streams, which flood heavily and rapidly. When they're not flooding, they're frozen. That's just the way it is in Chukchi country. The winter lasts up to eight months, and even the summer isn't what you'd call balmy.

Although the Chukchis were an illiterate people, they gave birth to a rich and complex culture. They created portable art in the form of ritual dances and tambourine music. They developed an elaborate, monotheistic religion based on shamanistic healing, and conceived of a heaven whose gates were guarded by a pair of their Chukchi dogs. Furthermore, the Chukchis believed that anyone who mistreated a dog would not be allowed into Chukchi heaven. (Maybe other religions should adopt this idea.)

After a while, the Chukchis learned to domesticate the reindeer they had previously hunted. It was a whole lot easier than chasing them around over the tundra. As a result, the Chukchis became a little less nomadic; they taught their dogs to herd the deer instead of killing them. Reindeer meant everything to the Chukchi people. They used them for food, tents, transportation, and clothing. They burned reindeer fat in their lamps. Thread for sewing came from reindeer sinew.

The Chukchis bred their dogs for multi-purpose work: hunting, herding, and hauling light loads. Because the Chukchis had their now domestic reindeer to pull the heaviest loads, they placed a premium on developing their dogs for speed, endurance, and agility, rather than brute strength. It paid off. No other breed in the world can haul a light load as fast and far as the Siberian Husky — and on so little food.

There's a difference of opinion as to whether the original dogs of the Chukchi were the same dogs as the Siberian Husky of today. What genetic traces of those long ago and far off times lie in the present-day Siberian Husky is impossible now to determine. We have no photos and no written contemporary records.

Many authorities believe that originally there were two separate breeds, perhaps developed by two separate groups — one for sledding, and one for herding. Others think the earliest Huskies did it all — pulled, herded, and hunted. They may have even eaten their "owners" from time to time. Whatever the case may have been, today's Husky is used for sled pulling only, although if left unchecked, they will occasionally kill deer. (They won't herd them though.)

Chukchi sleds

The first sled frames were made of whalebone or driftwood. If they could obtain it, the Chukchis preferred hickory wood for the sleds' tapered runners, because hickory is one of the hardest woods. These hickory runners ranged in length from 5 feet to more than 30 feet, with the average about 12 feet long. In preparing for a trip, the Chukchis would dip the runners in water, and let them freeze. They repeated this operation several times, until the runners became encased in several thin layers of ice that would glide easily over the snow.

The sled baskets were composed of hides. The whole sled was then lashed together with rawhide, which gave it a flexibility and tensile strength that cannot easily be matched, even by modern materials. In cases of extreme emergency, the Chukchis reportedly carved themselves sleds out of ice cuttings.

Chukchi dog harnesses

The Chukchis used three different methods of harnessing their dogs to the sled, depending on terrain, weather conditions, and sled load. When the load was not heavy, the Chukchis harnessed the dogs alternately along a single tow line. To pull a heavier load, the Chukchis harnessed their team in pairs, on both sides of a line attached to the front of the sled. The problem with these methods was that too many dogs could be lost as the sled shot over snow-covered crevasses and cliffs. A safer way was a *fan* style of harnessing — all the Huskies hitched in a fan-shaped arrangement to draw the sled. This prevented everyone from falling into a crevasse, but one scraggly little tree in the path could really tangle things up. It was practicable only over wide-open tundra, where it is sometimes still used.

Chukchi kennel management

Apparently, the Chukchis kept only the leader of the team unneutered; the rest of the male dogs were castrated with an iron knife. Castrated dogs tended to be more amicable with the rest of the team. They were also easier to train and kept their weight on better than unneutered males in that bitter climate. Thus, only the best dogs, with proven pulling and leadership abilities, were bred. It is rumored that at least some of the Chukchis may have cut the tails off their sled dogs, erroneously believing that this would increase their speed. Dogs with temper problems had their teeth dulled or removed.

The origin of dogs

Dogs were domesticated at about the same time all over the world, perhaps 20,000 years ago. (Scientists don't agree about the exact timeframe; the earliest undoubted dog fossils found so far are only about 12,000 years old.) The first ancestors of dogs, however, may have split off from the parent wolf branch more than 100,000 years ago, just about the time modern humans emerged. Dogs and people grew up together, so to speak.

Many scientists think that all dogs were developed from one wolf-like species. Candidates for this "Mother of All Dogs" include the Arabian and Indian wolves, which are small subspecies of the Gray wolf found in southern Asia. According to this scenario, the Husky is genetically no closer to the wolf than is the Mexican Hairless. Other scientists believe that domestication occurred at numerous times and at several locations. In their view, different species or subspecies of wolves were involved. An older idea, that jackals or foxes may have been involved in producing the modern dog, is pretty much discredited today.

So why do Huskies look like wolves and Mexican Hairless don't? Well, a couple of reasons have been suggested. One possibility is that northern dogs, after their evolution into domesticated animals, may have been crossed more or less frequently with the Gray (or Timber) wolf found in northern Asia and North America. Cross-breeding with these northern wolves could account for the appearance of Siberians and other northern dog breeds, which certainly look like wolves and share several wolf-like characteristics, such as pack behavior and howling.

Other people point to an environmentally driven reason for differences between Huskies and, say, Afghans. They maintain that the reason a Siberian Husky looks more like a wolf (Canis lupus) than does an Afghan Hound may be simply that the Siberian was domesticated in an area similar to the northern wolf's native habitat. (Afghans were bred in the desert.) The Husky's looks are an adaptation to a northern climate, just as the Gray wolf's are. But wolves and Huskies, despite surface similarities, are very different creatures.

For instance, closer study reveals that the Siberian's brain capacity, muzzle-length, and bite-power are less than that of wolves. And Huskies, like all dogs, come into heat twice a year, rather than only once (like wolves). Certainly a Husky's temperament is that of the thoroughly domesticated dog. Plus, no wolf has blue eyes, a common characteristic in Siberians.

DNA testing has revealed that dogs should be regarded as a subspecies of wolves. Both belong to the same genus, Canis, but wolves are designated Canis lupus, and dogs, all dogs, are now called Canis lupus familiaris — the familiar wolf.

The Chukchi women took on the primary responsibility of selecting the puppies and breeding the adults. They even nursed orphaned puppies themselves. This feminine influence may have played an important role in breeding Siberians who were good family members, as well as reliable sled dogs. Chukchi dogs began learning to pull when they were only a few months old. Often entire litters were trained together, with their mother as the teacher. On average, sled dogs worked for about seven years.

The Russians Are Coming!

The Chukchis were always a sharp thorn in the side of the Russians, even before the Communists took over. For one thing, they declined to surrender during the 1700s when the Russians had conquered every other Siberian people in their effort to control the fur trade. So the Russians kept fighting the Chukchis, and beating them every time, but the Chukchis still refused to give up and starve. They'd just pack up their things and move farther on, making the Russians chase them some more. Sometimes, the Chukchis moved their entire settlement onto an iceberg and floated away.

The Russians finally had enough, and in 1742 they declared an all-out war, vowing to destroy every man in Chukchi land. As for the women and children, the Russians threatened to redistribute them all over Siberia until every last Chukchi was either dead or assimilated. To do their dirty work, the Russians hired a bunch of Cossacks, who were always available for that kind of thing. Most of the time, however, the Cossacks just couldn't manage to find any Chukchis. When they did run across some, they killed the men as ordered, but the Chukchi women ruined the Cossacks' fun by killing their own dogs, their own children, and finally themselves, to avoid being taken captive.

Pavlutskiy plays Custer

Finally, a Russian general named Pavlutskiy decided he could handle the Chukchis. In an incredibly stupid move, Pavlutskiy plowed into a narrow ravine to finish them off. Of course, the Chukchis were just sitting there in ambush, not daring to hope that the Russian general could possibly be dumb enough to trap himself in this way. But he was. The surprised Chukchis then killed the Russians, including Pavlutskiy, and confiscated their guns. Although the Chukchis did not have a clue how to use their newfound weapons, they did have the foresight to capture some disaffected Russian serfs, who gladly passed along their firearms lore. The serfs didn't like the Russian army or the Cossacks any better than the Chukchis did.

By this time, the Russians finally decided that it would be smarter all around just to leave the Chukchis alone. They "conquered" Chukchi land by merely proclaiming they had conquered it, and that was that. This was sufficient for their purposes, apparently, because no one bothered to check. For their part, the Chukchis didn't care what the Russians proclaimed, especially because the 1837 treaty they negotiated stated that no Russians could enter the country and that the Chukchis were excused from paying any taxes.

The Communists versus the Huskies

During the height of the Stalinist era, in the 1930s, the Communists, not satisfied with nationalizing Russia's industry, such as it was, decided to go after the dogs. They put forth a major effort to destroy every vestige of traditional, non-Soviet culture, including the native dog breeds. Although such policies seem counterproductive and shortsighted today, the early Communists probably thought they were doing everyone a good turn. They decided sled dogs were bourgeois and outdated creatures anyway, and that they all should be replaced by up-to-date motorized vehicles. At least that's what they thought until they actually got to Chukchi land and found that all their up-to-date motorized vehicles got stuck in the snow.

At that point, even the pet-phobic Communists were compelled to admit the dog's economic, if not spiritual, usefulness. But instead of doing the sensible thing and leaving the Chukchis and other native peoples in peace to breed dogs most suitable to their lifestyles, the Soviets decided to reorganize the dozens of existing northern breeds under four artificial headings: sled dogs, reindeer herders, big game hunters, and small game hunters. This worked for a while, at least for the Russians. There's no evidence that the Chukchis paid any attention to it.

In 1947, the Russians had yet another reorganization attack. The Soviet Congress, which apparently had nothing better to do, decided that the Workers' Paradise really didn't need any sled dogs or reindeer herding dogs after all, and they reclassified the hunting dogs into four new subdivisions, none of which corresponded to any real breed.

The dog we now call the Siberian Husky was left out of all these classifications; the Soviets, in their infinite wisdom, decided that they were too small to pull anything, even though they had been hauling sleds all over Siberia for the past few thousand years or so.

The Siberians were indeed much smaller than the other Arctic breeds, topping out at around 50 pounds, which is why the Russians sneered at them. But the Chukchis didn't mind. They knew that nothing could surpass their native dogs for long-distance sledding. When the Chukchis needed more power, they simply hitched up more dogs. And because of the Siberian's super-excellent temperament, as many as 18 or 20 dogs could be hitched to a single sled. And there was no fighting. This kind of cooperation was simply not possible with the other, more short-tempered Nordic breeds.

Besides, Siberian Huskies had other advantages, which made them unlike most of the other northern breeds. Because they had been raised in a family setting, and not left out to fend for themselves, they could be trusted with children, and they could run faster, longer, and on less food than any other breed in the world. All this is still true of the Husky today.

Olaf Swenson Saves the Day

Sadly, there may be no pure Siberian Huskies left in the land of their birth. They disappeared during the Stalinist purges (along with most of the Chukchis and a few million dissident Russians). Happily for us, however, some Huskies were exported to North America first; the last of them made the trip in 1929. These had been purchased by the Arctic explorer and fur trader Olaf Swenson, some at the then exorbitant price of $150. (Despite his Scandinavian name, Swenson was born in Manistee, Michigan.) Swenson had cultivated friendly relationships with the Chukchis for many years. Indeed, he was the only outsider ever willingly allowed into Chukchi territory.

Swenson admired both the friendly temperament of the Siberians and the gentle treatment the dogs received from their Chukchi families. He understood that the two factors were intimately related. Many of the other northern breeds received nothing but brutal treatment at the hands of their owners, and in time became brutal themselves.

There was one dog in particular Swenson coveted. In his fascinating 1940 memoir, *Northwest of the World: Forty Years Trading and Hunting in Northern Siberia,* he recounts how he spent two years trying to buy a certain Billkoff (Snowball). He was always rebuffed, no matter how much he offered. Finally, Swenson stopped bidding on the dog because he could see how deeply attached the Chukchi owner was to his animal, and what a terrible internal conflict Swenson was instigating by his extravagant offers. Besides, Swenson admired the man greatly for his loyalty to the dog. A little later, Swenson says, he went out of his way perform a "small favor" for the Chukchi. Swenson did not see his friend for a year, but when he visited him again, his Chukchi friend seemed uncommonly glad to see him. Going over to Billkoff, he took the dog by the collar and led him over to Swenson. Then he placed his hand on the dog's head. "Your dog," he said solemnly. The man refused to take a penny for him.

Denial ain't a river in Egypt

By 1971, the Soviets had gone completely around the bend and were claiming that the Siberian Husky, along with several other native, ancient, and extremely pure breeds, had never even existed. But Soviet proclamations did not change the truth. Altogether, at least seven aboriginal sled dog breeds continued to thrive in the lonely outreaches of the arctic, far from political machinations. Each breed was designed for somewhat different purposes, and lived in a different climate.

As he had suspected, Billkoff proved to be the finest lead dog Swenson had ever owned. No matter what the conditions, Billkoff could cope. Even the most recalcitrant dogs on the team would follow his lead. This was a critical advantage.

From the team's point of view, the lead dog may be even more important than the driver. After all, the driver has no reins to guide the team — they are following the lead dog.

Knowing that the unique Siberian Husky was in great danger of disappearing forever, Swenson had some of the finest Chukchi dogs shipped directly to America. Some went to Maine; others were shipped to Quebec. Still others were bred to the dogs of the legendary Leonhard Seppala. It is an interesting footnote to history that the two outsiders who knew the Siberian Huskies the best were the same two men who brought them to America, thus preserving for all time one of the truly great dog breeds of the world.

The All Alaska Sweepstakes Race

In 1909, the Russian fur trader William Goosak showed up in Nome with his nine Siberian Huskies to enter the All Alaska Sweepstakes Race. This famous race had been first run the year before in 1908 — a 408-mile dash from Nome to Candle. It was a vicious marathon that took in every hideous variety of weather and landscape that its architects could devise, including forests, tundra, narrow declivities, and a glacier or two.

The first prize for the All Alaska Sweepstakes Race was $10,000 dollars; that was a lot of money back in 1909, even if you did have to win a 408-mile race to get it.

Few people in Alaska had seen Siberians at that time, although there were plenty of other dogs around. The rugged Alaskans were not particularly impressed with the newcomers.

Most Alaskans scoffed at the idea that the slender, 50-pound Siberians could be a match for the heavy-boned bruisers competing against them. They seemed too refined — and too short legged. The Nomers cheerfully dubbed the Huskies "Siberian Rats." Undeterred, Goosak hired a musher named Louis Thrustrup to pilot his team. Thrustrup then proceeded to come in third — at odds of 100 to 1. He probably would have won, had he not made a serious tactical blunder by not properly resting his dogs.

All sorts of nasty things were said about race-fixing and the like, but none of it was ever proved. Besides, if one were going to fix a race, it seems as if one would fix it to *win*. At any rate, it's probably a good thing the Siberians didn't win after all, for it was claimed that if they had, the Bank of Alaska would have gone broke, considering the number of bets laid against them. (The Bank of Alaska didn't have all that much money in 1909.)

Watching the race (and suitably impressed with the Siberians' performance) was Fox Maule Ramsay, a young Scottish businessman. He had come to Alaska interested in mining possibilities but became entranced with the Huskies instead — so much so, in fact, that he chartered a schooner to Siberia and bought 60 of the best racing stock he could find. By the time of the 1910 All Alaska, Ramsay entered the race with not one but *three* teams. Ramsay's teams placed first and second, and suddenly everyone was talking about the little dogs with the big hearts — which is still true today

The Influence of Leonhard Seppala

The greatest name in Siberian history has to be that of the Norwegian Leonhard Seppala. Seppala, who had been born in the fishing village of Skyjaevoy, 250 miles inside the Arctic Circle, was no stranger to bitter weather. He kind of liked it, actually. When he emigrated to America in 1914, he naturally chose Alaska for his new home. He began by working in the gold-fields and driving freight dogs, but soon he, too, got bitten by the racing bug.

To begin his new hobby, Seppala bought some young racing Huskies from a certain Jafet Lindeberg. Lindeberg had originally intended to sell the dogs to the famous Norwegian adventurer Roald Amundsen, for an attempt to reach the Pole, but Amundsen had had to abandon the try when World War I broke out. So, Seppala got to run his new team in the 1914 All Alaska Sweepstakes Race, but he was badly defeated. He got lost in a whiteout blizzard and came within a few feet of a 200 foot precipice. Only the immediate responsiveness of his native Siberian lead dog, Suggen, prevented complete tragedy. Undeterred by his scary experience, Seppala simply made plans to try again the following year.

Seppala went on to a brilliant racing career with his Huskies, winning the All-Alaska Sweepstakes in 1915, 1916, and 1917. (The races had to be halted when the United States entered World War I.) Seppala won races not just in Alaska, however, but also in New England and all over the east coast of the United States. Seppala proved the Husky's ability to race at all distances — not just the marathons. Today, Huskies excel at so-called *middle distance racing*, 30 to 60 miles. Well, it's middle distance for them, if not for us.

Seppala won so often than he was accused of being a "Superman," and of "hypnotizing" his opponents. Yet never, in all his years of racing, did Seppala ever strike his team. Only once did he even crack his whip — and that was in order to get the dogs up quickly after a short rest. Today, it is against the rules for mushers to even carry whips in sanctioned sled dog races.

The Great Serum Run: Mission of Mercy

Leonhard Seppala's greatest feat had nothing to do with the sport of dog racing. It was January 1925. A raging diphtheria epidemic had overtaken Nome, and two Eskimo children had already died. The fear was that the native population, who had had little exposure to the disease, could be wiped out entirely if help did not arrive at once.

The city's small cache of 6-year-old serum had been used up, and the nearest supply was in Anchorage — almost 1,000 miles away. The Alaska Railroad could take it as far as Nenana, but Nenana was still 658 miles from ice-shrouded Nome. There were only three airplanes in all of Alaska — and the three people who knew how to fly them were very sensibly spending the winter elsewhere. Furthermore, the planes were in Fairbanks, out of commission. Although three unqualified pilots gamely volunteered to fly the rickety planes to Anchorage and thence to Nome, the 80 mph winds and raging blizzards made the authorities wisely decide to attempt a more traditional transport. (They worried about a plane crash. They didn't care so much about the pilots dying; the fear was that the precious serum would be lost, too.)

Only Huskies could save the day. A 20-pound package of diphtheria serum, a supply of 300,000 units, was relayed from Nenana to Nome. Under the able leadership of Leonhard Seppala, 20 expert drivers and over 100 dogs were recruited for the grueling trip. The drivers included men with names like Wild Bill Shannon, Tommy Patsy, Myles Gonangnan, and Jack Screw.

To make things even more difficult, the mushers had to stop periodically in order to warm the serum, because nobody knew if it would still work if frozen. (Reindeer skin, quilt, and canvas were used for insulating the serum containers.)

Almost beyond belief, the dogs ran 658 miles in five and half days, sometimes through blizzards and snowdrifts that were waist high. It was snowing so hard that the drivers literally could not see the dogs in front of them. At times, the temperature plunged to 62 degrees below zero. Two dogs actually froze to death in harness; their musher, Charlie Evans, took their place and, along with the surviving dogs, pulled the sled himself the remaining miles of his run.

Leonhard Seppala himself drove 340 of those miles. Seppala's 12-year-old lead dog was the great Togo, a dog bred by Seppala himself; in fact, he was the son of the resourceful Suggen. Togo was therefore a first generation American. At first, Togo seemed an unpromising specimen; he ran away from home, bit the other dogs, and allowed no one but Constance Seppala (Leonhard's wife) to handle him. Gradually, however, he came around, and to everyone's surprise, became one of the greatest racing dogs in history.

Togo was a little dog (weighing only 48 pounds) and not much to look at by today's standards, but he could lead a team like no other dog. Altogether, Seppala estimated that Togo had run over 5,000 miles during his distinguished career. Fittingly, the great Serum Run was his last appearance. Aging and injured on the trip, the old hero was permanently retired afterward. He died in Poland Spring, Maine, in 1929, at the age of 14 or 15.

Strangely enough, Togo's stuffed remains took on a peripatetic life of their own. For a while they were stored at Harvard's Peabody Museum in Cambridge, Massachusetts; then they were sent to the Shelbourne Museum in Vermont; finally they were transferred to the Iditarod Headquarters in Wasilla, Alaska, where you may go look at them yourself, if you want to.

The final leg of the serum relay, however, was run not by Seppala and Togo, but by Gunnar Kasaan, who reached Nome on Groundhog Day. Kasaan was driving Seppala's second string of dogs, using a dog named Balto as the lead dog. In Seppala's considered opinion, Balto was a second-rate dog. For once, Seppala was wrong.

Balto, who had suffered bad press as "just a freight dog," surpassed himself in the Great Serum Run. When Kasaan became lost on the ice of the Topkok River, it was Balto who scented out the right trail (in 50 mph winds) and brought the team in safely. If it had been left to Kasaan, the entire team would have plunged through the ice.

Kasaan staggered into Nome at 5:30 a.m. on February 2, 1925. His dogs were cold and exhausted, their feet torn and bloody. But the serum was delivered. Kasaan handed it over to the only physician in Nome, Dr. Curtis Welch of the Public Health Service. And then he began to pull the ice splinters out of his dogs' feet.

Within five days of the arrival of the serum, the diphtheria epidemic was halted. It was the last major outbreak of the disease in North America. And so, out of the Great Race of Mercy to Nome, was born the modern sled race we call the *Iditarod*.

During his travels in the east, Seppala left some of his animals with Harry Wheeler of Quebec, who began breeding them. All currently AKC-registered Huskies can trace their ancestry back to this foundation stock.

As far as Kasaan's team went, the musher took the dog on a nationwide tour. Then Balto and company were sold to a movie producer named Sol Lesser, who made a film called "Balto's Race to Nome," eulogizing the dog. Afterward, the entire team was sold again and put on exhibit as a kind of curiosity show. The poor dogs were abused, neglected, and forgotten until a Cleveland businessman named George Kimbal, with the help of Cleveland school children, bought the six remaining dogs for the then astounding sum of $2,000. They raised the money in two weeks.

The dogs were brought to the Cleveland Zoo and lived out their lives in peace. When Balto died in 1933, he was stuffed and put on display in the Cleveland Museum of Natural History. Most of the time, he's still there. (Every once in a while, Balto's remains make a trip to the Iditarod Headquarters in Wasilla. But they always come to back to Ohio.) Check out Figure 2-1 for a photograph of Balto, taken after the Great Serum Run.

Figure 2-1:
Balto, after
the Great
Serum Run.

Carrie M. McLain Memorial Museum

Balto

In New York City's Central Park stands a bronze statue of Balto, paid for by penny collections from children. Many Siberian aficionados resent the fact that it was this dog, rather than Seppala's beloved Togo, whose likeness is sculpted. But it doesn't really matter. The statue symbolizes the boundless courage of all the dogs who made that tremendous journey against the greatest of odds. Togo or Balto — he faces north, forever dreaming, perhaps, of his immortal run in the service of humankind. The inscription reads, "Dedicated to the indomitable spirit of the sled dogs that relayed anti-toxin six hundred miles over rough ice, across treacherous waters, through arctic blizzards from Nenana to the relief of a stricken Nome in the winter of 1925. Endurance. Fidelity. Intelligence."

The Development of the Siberian in the United States

Siberian Husky fanciers owe a debt of gratitude to the inimitable Leonhard Seppala. Not only did he develop a great racing dog, but he also worked to standardize the breed. Traveling across the continent with his teams, he introduced Huskies and the sport of sled dog racing to thousands of people. The Ricker/Seppala Kennel he helped to establish in Poland Spring, Maine, set the benchmark for the breed's characteristic looks and temperament.

Equally legendary were two famous New Hampshire kennels: the Chinook Kennels in Wonalancet, and the Monadnock Kennels in Fitzwilliam.

Chinook Kennels

The Chinook Kennels took a roundabout and independent road to breeding Siberians. The original Chinook was a big yellow lop-eared "MacKenzie River Husky," who was purchased for three bags of flour in Dawson, Alaska, in 1898. His new owner, Arthur Walden, took him home to New Hampshire, and established a famous line of racing sled dogs, naming his kennel Wonalancet Farm.

As you may expect, the big Chinooks became rivals of the Siberians for honors in the world of sled dog racing. Although the Siberians appeared to be no match for the oversized Chinooks, Seppala beat them soundly race after race. Spectators were also impressed by the uniform good looks of the Siberians, their amiable nature, and their ability to thrive on very little food.

Walden and Chinook went off on an Antarctic adventure with Admiral Byrd. Sadly, Chinook himself never returned from that journey. During his absence Walden left his kennels in the capable hands of Eva "Short" Seeley and her husband, and on his return, Walden sold his kennels to her.

"Short" Seeley renamed the kennels after Chinook. Despite this token honor, however, she abandoned the breeding of "Chinooks" per se and worked hard to help develop the Siberian Husky standard, with the help of some of Leonhard Seppala's dogs. The Seeleys also helped develop the breed standard for the Alaskan Malamute. (Chinook dogs are still around, by the way, but they are not recognized as a breed by the American Kennel Club.)

The Chinook Kennels provided Admiral Byrd with dogs for his second and third trips to the South Pole. Later, Chinook Kennels trained Huskies as search and rescue dogs for the United States Army Air Transport Command in World War II. Chinook dogs were used in Labrador, Greenland, Alaska, and Italy. They were also employed in rescuing the wounded during the Battle of the Bulge.

Monadnock Kennels

Monadnock Kennels, also located in New Hampshire, used a more conventional breeding strategy, and employed Seppala's dogs as foundation stock. They developed Siberians for every purpose: show, sled, and companion dogs. In a breeding program that lasted over 40 years, the Monadnock dogs set the standard for Husky good looks and fabulous temperament.

Today, the Siberian has truly become a worldwide breed. Important Siberian Husky breeding programs are currently underway in Canada, England, Finland, Switzerland, France, Belgium, Holland, and Australia. Thanks to the work of these and thousands of other dedicated Siberian fanciers, the Siberian Husky today is healthy, beautiful, and for many, the ideal family pet.

Part II
Looking for Your Soul Mate

The 5th Wave   By Rich Tennant

"Okay, okay— maybe it's not a good idea. I just thought since Huskies were bred for winter weather, part of the grooming process might include having them flocked."

In this part . . .

So you've decided a Siberian is for you. Now that you've made that important decision, you're probably eager to find your soul mate in Siberian form. In this chapter, I guide you through the important process of finding the *right* place to get your Husky and let you know what to look for in a pup. I also get you ready to bring that puppy home, letting you know what to have on hand the moment that four-legged friend walks through the door.

Chapter 3

Finding and Choosing a Siberian

- -

In This Chapter

▶ Figuring out whether a Husky is right for you

▶ Locating a good breeder from whom to get your puppy

▶ Picking out a puppy

- -

*T*he Siberian Husky is an incomparably beautiful dog. And that's probably part of the reason why you want one. Or maybe you saw Sergeant Preston and King on TV when you were a kid. Or you've heard about how wonderful Siberians are with children, how intelligent they are, and what terrific jogging partners they make. Someone may have mentioned something to you about their lack of "dog smell." All these things are true. But it's also true that not everyone should have a Siberian Husky.

So in this chapter, I start by helping you figure out whether you and a Husky would make a good match. Then I guide you through the process of finding a good breeder and choosing the right pup. Don't skip that all-important first part of the chapter, though. You owe it to yourself and your dog to be sure you're choosing the right breed.

Determining Whether a Husky Is Right for You

If you are a well-adjusted, happy person, in a stable family situation, you may be the perfect Siberian owner. On the other hand, if you are living in a contentious, unhappy household, you can expect your Siberian to pick up a lot of that tension.

If you expect your new Siberian to act the way your old Labrador did, you may be in for a little shock. Huskies are more free-spirited (and free-ranging) than many other popular breeds.

Huskies also require an enormous amount of attention. They are strong-willed animals, and most of them do better with an experienced dog owner. This does not mean that you can't have a Siberian for your first dog; it *does* mean you should know what to expect. (You've already taken a step in this direction by buying this book.) Some people consider Siberians stubborn, but it is more accurate to say that they are determined and persevering — necessary qualities in a good sled dog.

Sadly, many people do not sufficiently understand enough about the background of the breed they choose to own. The so-called "bad" qualities of Siberians were necessary components of dogs raised in an arctic environment for a particular purpose. The very elements that make Siberians great sled dogs can sometimes be inconvenient when Huskies are transported to a very different kind of life.

As a prospective Siberian owner, your responsibility is to understand your dog's heritage, and make the necessary accommodations to it. If you harbor any doubts at all about owning a Siberian (or getting a dog at all), don't get one.

Huskies are adaptable to many situations. They are not one-person dogs but enjoy the company of the entire family, particularly children. They like strangers, too. In fact, if you are looking for a watchdog, get a Chihuahua. Huskies not only like burglars as well as they like anyone else, they seldom even bark at trespassers. They prefer to stand around silently wagging their tails while the thief makes off with the silverware. If you own a whole pack of Huskies, the non-dogwise miscreant may stay away from your house, on the hunch that Siberian Huskies are dangerous. But he'd be wrong.

Because a Siberian is family dog, be sure that everyone in your family wants a dog, and that everyone agrees that the Husky is the right dog for your family. Siberians often live 15 years or more; so make sure you get a dog with whom you are willing to forge this lifelong bond.

In the following sections, I cover some important factors to consider when getting a dog.

Children

Most Siberians are good with and for children; a very few are not. A lot depends on the nature of the children. Careless and cruel children (and there are a lot of them) do not deserve a pet of any kind. Never buy a pet to teach a child responsibility. You are the adult; *you* have the responsibility of caring for the pet.

Certainly, having your child help with pet care is wise; you may even want to make it the child's job to feed, groom, or walk the dog. But the dog is ultimately the responsibility of adults. If the child forgets to feed the Siberian, then *you* must. If you yourself are not willing to undertake the care of the dog when the child forgets, rethink owning any animal. If your child gets bored with the dog, then he becomes yours. Many dogs who are fine for older children are not suitable for children under the age of three, and a young child should never be left alone with a pet, for both their sakes.

Because many children are allergic to dog hair and dander, I strongly advise prospective Husky owners to get their kids allergy tested before bringing home this shedding breed.

Financial considerations

Siberians can be expensive, but perhaps not in the way you imagine. The initial cost of your dog, whether you spend $100 for an adoption fee or $800 or more for a show-quality Siberian, is the cheapest part of sharing your life with a Husky. Your new friend needs high-quality food and medical attention throughout his life. You are responsible for these costs. And they can be considerable.

Boarding fees, crates and other equipment, high-quality food, regular medication like heartworm preventive, and training classes cost more than you think. The first year, when you are buying the crates, barriers, dog bowls, and beds, will be the most expensive. In fact, *Dog Fancy* magazine estimates that the annual expenses for a small dog will be about $1,800 dollars a year; for a medium-sized dog like a Siberian, add another $500. And that's *just* for the necessities.

Many people become so attached to their pets that they purchase collars and leashes with their pet's name inscribed, orthopedic beds, special treats, toys, and other accoutrements. They buy books about their pets (like this one); subscribe to breed magazines; they join clubs and Internet groups. You may become addicted to showing or racing your Siberian. Besides, you may eventually want to get a second Husky as company for the first. Those costs add up quickly.

Your house

Meticulous housekeepers may not be happy owning a Siberian. These dogs shed a lot and have a reputation for destructive behavior. Much of this reputation is undeserved, but it's fair to warn you that if an extremely clean house is very important to you, owning a Siberian will add stress to your existence.

Despite their shedding, Siberians are exceptionally clean. They do not have the doggy odor typical of many breeds. They are clean eaters, as well.

Climate

Unfortunately, climate is an important consideration that many people overlook. Although you can certainly keep a Siberian if you live in South Carolina, you will need to take extra care and precautions in the summer. As a general rule, the colder it is, the better Huskies like it. If you live in Minnesota and like the winter, the Siberian is the dog for you! However, if you can't take the cold yourself, you may want to match up with a less arctic animal.

Time

Siberians are supposed to be independent, but in truth they crave the human touch. The more time you spend with your Siberian, especially when he's young, the happier and better adjusted he will be as an adult. Don't consider getting a puppy if you will be away from home for long hours every day. It's not fair. An adult dog or two may be just the ticket, however.

Exercise

Siberians need a lot of exercise — every day. If you want a Husky, you need to be willing to provide your pet with the high level of activity he requires to keep him happy and healthy. These activities can include regular jogging, playing, swimming, or best of all, sledding. One Husky can keep several members of the family in top condition. Be honest with yourself about how much exercise you can give your dog. If you are not willing or able to give your dog a lot of attention, consider a breed with lower activity level needs.

A Siberian Husky must be fenced in, or at least exercised vigorously several times a day. Most communities have containment laws, and even where there are none, Siberian Huskies cannot be allowed to roam free. They have a habit of chasing and killing cats, rabbits, and even lambs or calves.

Legal considerations

Make absolutely certain your lease or covenant agreement will allow you to have a dog. You don't want to have to make an uncomfortable choice later on. And whether you are an owner or a renter, you should carry liability insurance if you have an energetic dog. In today's litigious society, even a playful nip can mean big lawsuits.

If your Husky escapes and kills the neighbor's chickens, you will be held responsible for the damage.

Commitment

Who will be primarily responsible for the care of your new Siberian — financially, emotionally, and in charge of day-to-day activities like walks or feeding? Splitting these chores among different members of the household is okay, as long as everyone knows and agrees to his part. Too often, people complain that "I'm not the one who wanted the darn dog in the first place, and now I'm stuck with feeding/exercising/taking him to the vet." Decide on these things in advance, and delegate responsibilities.

Finding a Puppy and a Breeder

Before you can choose a dog, you must know what you are looking for. Do you want to do recreational mushing, racing, showing, tracking, or just have a nice family pet? If you want a healthy, genetically sound Siberian you should get your dog from a reputable Siberian breeder. Some breeders specialize in one type of dog, but beware of breeders who say that they just breed pets. These dogs may not be of good quality. The best pets are often those who didn't make the "cut" as show-quality puppies. This would be an excellent break for you, because you can purchase a well-bred puppy at a very reasonable price.

It's an axiom in the dog world that a good dog comes from a good breeder, a reputable breeder. But how do you know who is reputable and who isn't? Check out the following sections for help.

Get recommendations from reputable sources

Ask around to get recommendations for good breeders in your area. Check with your local Siberian Husky Club. Members will be happy to refer you to a good source. The American Kennel Club (AKC) can provide you with the phone number for a breeder referral representative from the Siberian Husky Club of America. Breed magazines also advertise upcoming litters. You can visit the AKC Web site at www.akc.org for more information. Or you can write to the AKC (see Appendix C for contact information).

Go to dog shows

If possible, attend a few AKC dog shows. This experience will give you a good idea of what a quality Siberian Husky looks like. You may also get a chance to speak with a few exhibitors who can give you information about good local breeders and may know about a forthcoming litter. This can be tricky, though. Most people show up for their own breed class (say at 10:00 a.m.) then pack up and go home. You'll need to call in advance to find when the Siberians are showing, or come at 8:00 a.m. and hang around all day. Exhibitors may be busy at dog shows and may not have the time to talk. However, they may be available *after* the show or may be willing to give out their phone numbers so you can contact them later.

If you shell out the money for a show catalog (which usually costs about $5) you can see the names and addresses of the exhibitors. If you notice a dog whose looks you especially like, don't hesitate to contact the owners after the show. They should be pleased with your effusive compliments and be happy to point you along the path toward getting your very own Siberian.

You may get really lucky and be able to view one of the few *benched shows* left in the country. A benched show is one in which all the dogs in competition are on display (although not necessarily actually on a bench) all day. Breeders hate these shows, because they're hard on the dogs and themselves, but spectators love them. The most prestigious All-Breed Shows are benched, which is why exhibitors continue to subject themselves to them. These shows include the legendary Westminster Show, and five others — two in Chicago, and one each in Detroit, Philadelphia, and San Francisco.

Interview a breeder before deciding to buy a puppy from him

Check out the breeder personally. Here are the marks of a quality breeder:

- ✔ **A quality breeder specializes in only one or two breeds.**

- ✔ **A quality breeder has puppies for sale only occasionally, not every day of the year, and especially not specifically for the holidays.** Many breeders will not even sell a puppy around the holidays, precisely because people tend to buy pups as presents for people who may not be prepared to care for them.

- ✔ **A quality breeder makes her kennel areas available for viewing.** The kennels should be clean, comfortable, and odor-free. The puppies should be kept safe in a *whelping box,* like those shown in Figure 3-1.

Jeanette and Dominic DiBalsi

Figure 3-1:
These healthy Siberian puppies are kept safe in a whelping box.

✔ **A quality breeder has developed a breeding plan with the goal of producing high-quality Siberians.**

✔ **A quality breeder has well-socialized dogs and puppies.** The dogs and puppies interact well with you and with each other.

✔ **A quality breeder does not sell inexpensive dogs.** A good pet-quality puppy will cost in the range of $450 to $500. If you think you may like to show your dog, expect to pay even more.

Remember that choosing a pup for show purposes is always a gamble. No one, not even the sharpest-eyed breeder on earth, can accurately predict which puppies will "make it." This works both ways, however. I once purchased a puppy as a pet, who turned out to be a winning show dog much to everyone's surprise, including mine. The breeder should be able to explain to you exactly why she undertook this particular breeding, and what she expected from it. Her response can give you some idea of whether the dog would be good for showing.

✔ **Quality breeders have people waiting in line for their dogs.** Six months or more is not an unreasonable time to have to wait for a puppy. Just think how much you can learn about Siberians in that period.

✔ **Quality breeders will not sell puppies before they are at least 9 weeks old.** Breeders who are showing or racing may keep puppies longer, because they are trying to evaluate the litter for show or sled potential.

✔ **Quality breeders have healthy puppies.** The puppies should have been vet checked and vaccinated. The *sire* (father) and *dam* (mother) should have been screened for genetic diseases. In particular, they should be certified by the Orthopedic Foundation for Animals (OFA) with a minimum rating of "good." They should also have had recent eye checks and be certified by the Canine Eye Registration Foundation (CERF) or the Siberian Husky Ophthalmologic Registry (SHOR), with a rating of "clear." The eye checks are very important in Huskies. Make sure you see this paperwork; don't just take the breeder's word for it.

✔ **Quality breeders are actively engaged in showing or racing, and they should have the ribbons to prove it.** They are involved in their local Siberian Husky Club. If you don't have a recommendation, ask for the name and phone numbers of other people who have bought puppies from the breeder. Then call them to see how their dogs turned out.

✔ **Quality breeders provide an AKC registration paper, often referred to as a *blue slip*.** A pedigree is the family history of your puppy. It should go back three generations, but you can apply (for a fee) for a longer one, if you want.

✔ **One or both parents of your puppy should be champions or winning sled dogs.** If they aren't, find out why. If you are buying a sled dog, find out what his parents have accomplished. (The AKC does not currently provide titles for sled dogs, so it won't be recorded on the pedigree.) The Siberian Husky Club of America, however, does grant titles: SD for Sled Dog, SDX for Sled Dog Excellent, and SDO for Sled Dog Outstanding.

The initials *Ch.* in front of a dog's name means it is an AKC champion. *CD* (Companion Dog), *CDX* (Companion Dog Excellent), or *UD* (Utility Dog) after the name means the dog has an obedience title. If you see a *UDX* (Utility Dog Excellent) in the family history, be very surprised. Only a handful of Siberians have achieved that level. *TD* (Tracking Dog), *TDX* (Tracking Dog Excellent), and *VST* (Variable Surface Tracking) are tracking titles. *NA* (Novice Agility), *OA* (Open Agility), *AX* (Agility Excellent) are just a few of the agility titles that a dog can earn. Sledding titles are not part of a dog's AKC registration.

Having both parents on the premises is not necessarily a sign of a good breeder. It may just mean that the seller owns two dogs of opposite sexes; it's no guarantee of quality. Breeders frequently outcross to a particular sire who may live across the country. Some of the best bred dogs are the result of artificial insemination or a long-distance liaison. The breeder should be able to provide you with a photo of the sire, however. (The dam should obviously be on the premises.) Take a good look at her, but don't be alarmed if she's a bit bald. Sometimes the hormonal changes that come with pregnancy produce this effect. The puppies should all have hair, though.

- ✔ **Quality breeders will interview you.** Although you may find some of the breeder's questions intrusive, a good breeder is only trying to choose the best home for his puppies.

- ✔ **Quality breeders will have a purchase agreement for you to sign.** Don't be surprised if the breeder requires that you spay or neuter your Husky as part of the deal. That's the breeder's way of making sure that only his very top-of-the-line dogs will be out there propagating. Keep an eye on your growing Husky. If you think you may have a show-quality dog after all, call the breeder and ask her to evaluate him for you.

  For many AKC events, only unneutered/unspayed dogs can be shown.

  The purchase agreement should also provide a certain number of days for you to get your puppy checked by your veterinarian. The breeder agrees to replace an unhealthy puppy or to refund your money. Some contracts even require this. Make sure you get your puppy checked immediately. It may save you heartache.

- ✔ **Quality breeders will agree to take back a puppy who doesn't work out.** Discuss the details of this beforehand.

- ✔ **Most quality breeders raise their puppies in the household.** Although some show and sledding breeders keep their pups in a kennel, you're risking getting a dog insufficiently socialized with human beings. Don't do it if your primary interest is getting a good pet.

- ✔ **Quality breeders provide more information than you can absorb.** Most of them will chat on and on about their breeding goals. Learn what you can, but make sure anything really important will be given to you in writing.

- ✔ **A quality breeder will stay in touch, long after the puppy becomes yours.**

Good breeders often try to hang on to their puppies as long as possible. Some breeders who are looking for good show and working prospects often won't sell a puppy until close to the 12-week mark. If possible, you should arrange to get your puppy a little earlier — 9 to 10 weeks is ideal. After all, you want your puppy to bond with you, not with the breeder or the kennel help. If the puppies are kept in a kennel without much human contact, you should try to get your puppy as close to 8 weeks as you can. Dogs separated from their litters too early, however, may have problems adjusting to other dogs in the future.

Some people have had good luck buying from a distant breeder, possibly without even first seeing the puppy, and having the puppy shipped to them. I never recommend doing this. You really need to see your new puppy before buying him. Besides, dogs sometimes get lost on airplanes, just like your baggage does.

Choosing the Right Puppy

When you've decided on a breeder, you're ready to start thinking about what you want in a puppy. Being faced with a whole litter of adorable pups (like the 9-day-old little ones in Figure 3-2) can be difficult. They're all adorable. But be sure to look at the whole litter, not just one dog; you need to be able to make comparisons. Ask the breeder whether this is the first litter from this sire and dam, or whether the pair have been mated previously. If the latter is the case, ask to see photos of the grown up puppies from the first litter. (If the breeder has kept in touch with previous buyers, as she should, these should be available.) These photos are the best guess as to how the current litter will turn out.

General condition

The puppies should be active and plump, but not bloated. A bloated belly is a sign of roundworm. Although many puppies are born with roundworm, it shouldn't be evident at the buying stage. The stools should be fairly firm and well-formed. There should be no evidence of diarrhea or staining under the tail. Foul breath in a puppy may indicate problems, although many are blessed with a characteristic puppy breath, which smells a little like garlic. Male show-quality puppies must have two testicles, which should be detectable at a young age. (This is one of the things a vet will check if you're uncertain.)

Figure 3-2:
These 9-day-old Siberians aren't anywhere near old enough to go home with new owners, but they give you an idea of how hard it is to choose between several equally adorable pups.

Jeanette and Dominic DiBalsi

Size

Siberian puppies should be compact in build. Expect some differences in size, especially between male and female puppies. The biggest may not necessarily be the best; the biggest is just the biggest. In a show ring, a Siberian can be disqualified for being too big, so if you're interested in a show prospect, you may be better off not getting the biggest, especially if both parents are very close to the upper limit.

Sex

Female dogs tend to housetrain more easily, mature sooner, and be less dominant than males. Some people think they are more loyal. Females are less strong than their brothers, however, which may be a consideration if you will be doing serious sledding. For recreational sledding, either sex is fine.

Females are usually more loving (some would say demanding) and probably easier to train. Males are more physically impressive and stronger. They are probably more independent and challenging of human authority than females.

Some people claim that males have a better temper than females. If true, it may be because the female's heat cycle causes hormonal swings. In any case, unless you plan to be a breeder, you will have your Husky spayed or neutered, which eliminates these hormonal mood swings. In general, I recommend a female for families with small children, because they tend to be tolerant of children's mistakes.

Color

Most Huskies are born dark, except those destined to be pure white. The characteristic Siberian masks will be present in puppies, but their coat colors may change somewhat as they mature.

Eyes

The puppy's eyes should be bright and clear, no matter what color they are. Dark blue eyes may change into brown later on.

Ears

Most authorities agree that Siberians have some of the keenest ears in the dog world. Some Siberian puppies have floppy ears. Don't worry; they'll stand up later. The ears should have no discharge or unpleasant odor.

Sometimes a Husky's ears will revert to floppiness when he's going through his teething period.

Temperament

The puppy should be friendly and curious. A shy puppy will grow up to be a shy dog. Step a few feet away, crouch down, and call to the puppy softly and encouragingly. If the puppy toddles over to you, it probably means that he has a happy, friendly disposition.

Don't confuse normal boisterous play with a neurotic condition sometimes called *spinning*. Sometimes pups who have been confined in too-small kennel areas display a compulsive whirling round and round. Avoid these puppies. They have been severely traumatized and will never be normal.

Many breeders today do a temperament test on their dogs. These tests look for early signs of assertiveness, outgoingness, and so on. The results are usually given numerically. In one popular test, the Puppy Aptitude Test, the scores range from 1 to 5, with 1 leaning toward the dominant, aggressive, watchdog side, and 5 being very submissive or lethargic. For most pet purposes, you would like to see a puppy score close to 3. (Potential watchdogs score 1, show dogs 2, and so on.) Of course, these tests are not foolproof, but they can give you an indication of temperament when you have nothing better to go on.

Age

Puppies should be at least 8 weeks old when they are adopted. This is the legal minimum in many states. If you are planning on sledding, you may want to leave the puppy with his littermates for a longer period of time to increase his peer socialization skills. If your pup is destined to be an only dog, you want to get him closer to the 8-week mark, so that he will bond with you.

Don't be scared off from getting an older puppy, or even an adult dog. Siberians are not one-person dogs. They are able to form a bond with people at any age. Dogs often end up in rescue or an animal shelter through no fault of their own. With Siberians, it is usually because the first owner was unprepared to deal with the Husky's relentless energy or the shedding that comes with the breed. You will be doing a good deed, building good karma, and saving a life. What could be nicer?

Puppies are cute and charming, but they aren't housetrained, and are usually quite interested in chewing everything in sight. Besides, puppyhood doesn't last forever.

Older dogs are usually house-trained, and very grateful to have a new home. The older dog is often the perfect choice for older people as well. Considering that Siberians may live for 15 years, it may make more sense for an older person to choose a pet who will not outlive him! Besides, an older dog is quieter around the house and needs less exercise. I have an older friend who adopted a quite elderly female, saying that they could be old ladies together.

It may be difficult to housetrain an older dog who is used to being outside all the time. If your new older dog has been confined in a kennel for a while before you have adopted him for a house dog, expect that his housetraining skills may not be up to par. Prepare to teach him all over again. Siberians are extremely anxious to please in this regard. On the positive side, though, older dogs have bigger bladders than puppies, and they can hold it much more easily.

Exploring Other Sources for Getting a Husky

If you're willing to consider an older dog, you may be pleasantly surprised with the great dogs, like the one shown in Figure 3-3, who are available and in need of a loving home through shelters or rescue organizations. Check out the following sections for more information.

Shelters

Perhaps a young puppy is not for you, or maybe you would like to provide a loving home to a previously unwanted or neglected dog. In this case, try your local Siberian Husky Rescue, your county shelter, the Humane Society, or the American Society for the Prevention of Cruelty to Animals (ASPCA). Usually, adopting and acclimating an older dog is a much less time-consuming task than it is with a puppy.

Figure 3-3:
This beautiful Husky was rescued from a garage sale. After being given lots of love and affection by her new family, she makes a wonderful pet.

Jolie and Kimberly Runyan

Try to find out all you can about your prospective new family member. Play with him, take him for a walk. See how he reacts to children, cats, and other dogs. Find out if your local shelter does temperament testing before placing a dog on an adoption list. Sometimes you may also be able to contact the former owner to get more information about the dog and why he was given up. Get all his medical records if possible, and take him to the vet for a checkup as soon as possible.

It's usually a bad idea to give or take on a new dog at the holidays. First of all, the holidays are an extremely busy time of year with lots of people coming and going. There's a risk that the new family member will get either too much or too little attention, and he'll certainly be overwhelmed by the confusion of the company. A quieter season, when there's plenty of get-acquainted time, is better.

Never give a pet as a present. People should choose their own dogs. Even though you know that a Siberian is the best pet for Aunt Hilda, she may have her heart set on a guinea pig. Shelter and rescue groups are overwhelmed every February and March with the annual holiday "dump." Think of it this way: If the new pet does not work out, are *you* willing to adopt him into *your* family?

Pet stores

Buying your Siberian puppy from a private hobby breeder is really the best possible option, but if you see a pet store Siberian that you can't resist, you are forgiven. However, because some pet stores get their dogs from commercial breeders, you need to be extra careful. Dogs from commercial breeders may have health or temperament problems that won't become apparent for months.

Pet stores should charge no more for their puppies than a hobby breeder does in your area.

The pet store should be able to provide you with the contact information of the original breeder. Call that person up, and ask the same questions that you would of a hobby breeder. Be leery of anyone who will not forthrightly answer your questions. And be doubly wary if the puppies come from out of state. Your best bet is a pet store that deals only with local breeders. Ask for proof, and obtain the contact information. Then use it.

The puppy should come with a pedigree, a health record, and a guarantee. Demand to see CERF and OFA records just as you would with a private breeder. If the pet store cannot supply these, you should know that your puppy is at risk for eye problems and hip dysplasia. At the very least, you should be able to bring the dog to your vet for a thorough checkup before the purchase is finalized.

Because pet store puppies have already been weaned, you won't see the mother, which can be a disadvantage. Take the time to play with each puppy and check to be sure that they are playful, but not too aggressive. Use the same criteria to evaluate the puppy that you would elsewhere.

Although it may break your heart to walk away from a puppy, it hurts a lot worse if you make the wrong decision. Impulse buying is a very dangerous thing when it comes to dogs.

It is true that some people can rescue a sick puppy from an unhealthy situation. If this is what your heart tells you to do, then do it. People often take dogs from the shelter for the same humanitarian reasons.

Rescue organizations

Rescue organizations are one of best sources for a first-rate Siberian. Siberian Husky Rescue (`www.siberianrescue.org`) specializes in the breed, and usually has many available for adoption. Most rescue groups are choosy about whom they adopt to. Expect to fill out an application and to pay an adoption fee, usually of about $150. A house check or vet references may also be required. Shelter groups will often lower this fee for older or special-needs dogs. You may be able to get a retired sled dog or one who just didn't work out as a racer.

There truly is a dog for everyone. My friend Peg Wheeler, who operates our local Siberian Rescue, adopted out a three-legged Husky named Thumper to a loving home. The couple who adopted her had already had two previous three-legged Huskies; they had been looking everywhere for another one. They also decided to adopt another of Peg's rescues, thinking that Thumper needed some company. They named their new girl Bambi.

Chapter 4

Preparing for Your Puppy

Don't let your new Siberian come home to an empty house. You need to fill it with Husky paraphernalia. This chapter lets you know the basic necessities for life with a Siberian.

Collars and Leashes

Figure 4-1 shows a variety of collars that you may use for your Siberian Husky. You can buy either a rolled-leather buckle collar or the flat kind made of leather or nylon. The rolled collar leaves less wear on the neck. Some of these collars are adjustable, and many are equipped with a kind of quick-release system.

You may also want to consider using one of the new head collars, like the Gentle Leader or Halti head collar in addition to, or in place of, a regular collar. See Chapter 9 for more details.

I'm not a major advocate of the choke collar, to say the least. This collar can be useful at times, but if you train your dog correctly, right from the start, you probably won't need one. Most people don't know how to use a choke collar correctly. A choke collar works by putting pressure on a dog's windpipe. If correctly adjusted, the pressure is *not* great and self-corrects quickly. However, choke collars *do* work by making dogs uncomfortable or possibly even causing them pain. Most choke collars also tear out fur, although a fur-saving choke collar is available. An incorrectly applied choke collar can cause trauma, a collapsed trachea, or even death. Is it worth it? I don't think so. Besides, the best relationships are forged without applying pain. If you plan to use a choke collar, check out Figure 4-2 for the correct way to put the collar on your dog.

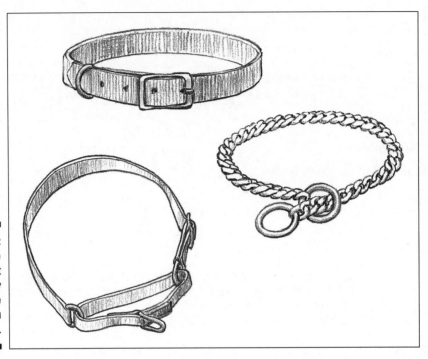

Figure 4-1:
Collars are
an important
safety
measure
when you
own a dog.

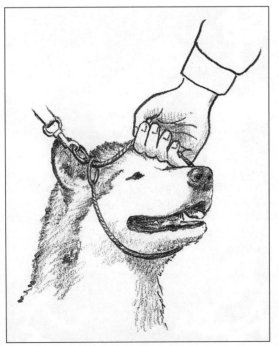

Figure 4-2:
The correct
way to put a
choke collar
on your
Husky.

You need a leash for taking your Husky on those long walks he'll require. If a leash is an unfamiliar item to your dog, allow him to drag it around the house or yard for a while as he becomes accustomed to it. Don't leave him unattended, however — your Siberian will certainly attempt to devour the thing. The leash may also get tangled up in the furniture or bushes and panic the dog.

Leather leashes are easy on your hands, but they're slippery when wet. Nylon leashes can give you rope burn if you're not careful. Dogs seem to prefer to eat leather leashes, but Huskies are fairly omnivorous in this regard.

The Flexi and other similar brands are great inventions. These leashes adjust to various lengths at the push of a button and come in lengths of up to 23 feet. They are perfect for long walks in the meadows.

ID Tags

Have your Siberian wear a collar with ID tags at all times. Some people fear that their dog's collar will get caught, but the collar is a real lifesaver. My friend Debbie was out of the house when fire broke out in her home. Because her Tibetan Terrier, Dalai, was wearing a collar, it was easy for the firefighters to capture him and lead him to safety.

Besides, any dog can escape or be lost, and Huskies are a lot better at this than most. A collar and some identification are the simplest way for you to be reunited with your delinquent pal. Even if you walk your Siberian on a choke collar, keep a buckle collar on him at the same time with his identification, license, and rabies tags. My dogs' collars have their names and our phone number sewn on them in big letters (available from pet catalogs), but you can accomplish the same thing with a laundry marker.

Don't leave a choke collar on an unattended dog. These are more likely than regular collars to get caught on something and, unlike a regular collar, can do some damage to the dog's neck.

Huskies are just clever at pulling out of a collar; you don't want to be caught standing with the leash *and* the collar in your hand. Ideally, collars with tags should be the reflective type; they help protect runaway dogs from cars.

If your Husky runs away, check the local animal shelter personally to see if your dog is there. Do not rely on a phone call alone. Believe me, I have learned from personal experience that many shelter workers don't know a Coonhound from a Cocker Spaniel. Go look yourself. Half the time, after you retrieve your Siberian, you'll get an incredulous, "Huh, whaddya know? We thought that was a Rottweiler/Dachshund mix."

You can register your dog with a lost-pet service, which may provide for tattooing or microchipping your dog. These procedures don't hurt and can be effective, but they should be used in conjunction with a collar, not as a replacement of one.

Keep some clear and recent photos of your dog handy. If your Husky gets away, you will want to make flyers with his picture on them.

Food and Water Dishes

The best pet food dishes are made of stainless steel or chrome. (You can buy weighted ones that your Husky can't push around so easily.) Some of them have tapered sides, to make cleanup easier. Stainless steel, dishwasher-safe bowls are much easier to keep clean than plastic ones. Plastic dishes can also develop tiny crevices from being chewed on by dogs. Heavy stoneware is usually acceptable, but even that can chip or develop minute cracks. These small fissures can become hiding places for all sorts of creatures you don't want in your kitchen or in your dog's digestive tract. There are enough awful things there anyway.

Outdoor dogs should drink from plastic or ceramic bowls in the wintertime. Their tongues can stick to metal ones.

If your Husky spends a lot of time outdoors in the winter, purchase a little immersible heater that will keep water temperature at 40 to 50 degrees. You can also get electrically heated food and water dishes. For bigger dogs, you can buy a heated 5-gallon flat-back bucket. Remember, too, that your outdoor dog needs more calories in the winter than in the summertime — up to twice as many.

Pet Doors

Although a pet door is not strictly necessary, it is a really desirable convenience. A high-quality pet door allows your dog to go from the yard to the porch or kitchen at will, and the best ones can be adjusted so they will let pets in but not out, or vice versa. If you're a working owner of a Husky, or if you just keep up with letting your dog in and out of the house five times an hour, then a pet door is a necessity in your life!

Outdoor Kennels

A kennel with a run is a useful item for Siberians, especially if you have no fenced yard. The minimum size should be 6-x-12 feet and 6 feet high. If you have a choice of shape, the best kennels are long and narrow rather than square. The long run encourages a kenneled dog to run and get exercise.

A concrete ground surface is easiest to clean, and it's also impossible for your Husky to dig out of. However, concrete can be hard on a dog's feet. Some people recommend filling the kennel area with pea gravel or sand, at least in the middle, in order to give the dog a digging spot. Make sure the run is shaded as well.

Grooming Tools

Grooming tools are a necessity for keeping your Husky healthy and beautiful. Here are the essentials:

- **Rake.** This is a wooden instrument with two rows of teeth. It removes dead hair and keeps the coat healthy.
- **Wide-toothed metal comb (also called a *Collie comb*).**
- **Slicker brush.**
- **Pin brush (ones made for people are fine).** See Figure 4-3 for an illustration.
- **Dematting tool.**
- **Spray mist bottle with water.**
- **Grooming table.** This item isn't necessary, but it's really nice.

Dog Beds

Your Siberian should have his own bed. More than most breeds, Siberians are content to sleep on the floor, but they deserve their own special place. I like dog beds with at least some cedar bedding inside; they smell nice and repel fleas. Unfortunately, a few dogs simply won't go near a cedar bed. You may have to experiment a little.

Figure 4-3:
Brushes and
a shedding
rake will
help you
keep your
Husky
healthy and
beautiful.

The Pet Butler Company sells an outdoor dog bed. This bed is made of vinyl coated synthetic yarn in an open weave construction, designed to dry fast. It is non-odor-absorbing and contains a fungicide to prevent mildew.

If you like making up your own dog beds from zippered liners and pillow cases, 25 pounds of cedar chips will make you about 7 Husky beds!

Gates

You can use a baby or doggy gate to keep certain rooms out of your dog's domain while you are home. Gates come in flexible widths and various heights. Don't use them as dog sitters, though. Some Siberians eat or jump over doggy gates with ease.

Crates

Unfortunately, some people who are not used to working with crates have an aversion to them. This may be because, to our human eyes, a crate looks like prison, and we do not generally acquire pets to keep them locked up. But this is looking through human eyes. For a dog, a crate is his den, a comfortable place to get away from it all. Dogs go into crates and dens naturally. Many people keep a crate, with the door open, in the house at all times, and when the dog turns up missing, there he is, snoozing peacefully away in his crate.

Crates have many advantages:

- ✔ **They are the ultimate house-training tool.** (I talk more about this in Chapter 5.)
- ✔ **They make transporting your pet safer and easier.**
- ✔ **Many motels will accept only dogs who are confined in crates.**
- ✔ **If your dog has an injury or any operation, it may be necessary for him to be kept quiet for a period.** A crate makes this possible.

So even if you don't plan to use a crate on a regular, day-to-day basis, you're doing a dog a tremendous favor by allowing him to have one. A crate is also an extremely useful tool for house-training, but it is only a tool. It should never become a prison — or a baby-sitter.

A full-grown Siberian needs a crate measuring about 36 inches long by 24 inches wide by 26 inches high.

Several types of crates are available:

- ✔ **Heavy-gauge welded wire mesh.** These crates allow excellent ventilation and provide better visibility for your dog, reducing the separation factor. I recommend them for Siberians, because Sibes, with their thick coats, need lots of ventilation.
- ✔ **Heavy-duty plastic.** These usually come in two pieces, with ventilation areas on the sides (see Figure 4-4). This is the kind airlines usually require. They are cozy and den-like. Make sure you get one that is very tough, because Siberians are addicted to chewing plastic.
- ✔ **A lightweight, fabric, portable crate that folds up like a tent.** Some kinds weigh under 6 pounds; you can stick them in your car or under your arm (as long as there's not a Siberian in them). A Siberian should be supervised while he is in this type of crate; he can hop across the floor in it. These are best for shows, motels rooms, and other activities where you are there to supervise.

Used correctly, your Husky will consider the crate his very own little den and go into it voluntarily when things get too much for him. Overuse of the crate, however, or using it for too long a period or as punishment, will not create the desired result. Make sure the crate has a water dish attached inside.

Figure 4-4:
A heavy-duty plastic crate is great for airline travel as well as everyday home use.

New crates can be expensive, usually over a hundred dollars. See if you can buy a secondhand crate from the classifieds or local yard sales. Or check with friends. It's amazing how many people have extra dog crates lying around their basements. You may even be able to borrow one, especially if you plan to use it only until your Husky is house-trained.

Chew Toys

If your Siberian is stuck in a barren house with little to entertain him, he'll make his own fun. This is when tension chewing starts. And because your Husky has no stamp collection of his own, he may start working on yours. Try getting him some of his own toys, and alternate them frequently so that he doesn't become bored with them. Use toys of different shapes, hardness, and textures.

The days of the simple squeaky toy are past. Some very creative and interesting dog toys are now on the market. Some toys make a variety of noises: They bleep, baa, snarl, honk, and roar. Most dogs find these things fascinating. (I do, too!)

Don't give your Siberian rawhide bones; they can cause digestive upset, and even pancreatitis, especially in dogs who manage to chew the things up in huge chunks and then swallow them.

Praise your dog for chewing appropriate toys. You can even play along with him when he chooses the right ones.

Never give your dog an old shoe as a toy, unless there is some way he can particularly identify it as his. You cannot expect him to be able to distinguish between old shoes and new ones. It is difficult enough for a dog to learn exactly what are his toys and what aren't, under the best of circumstances. Human toys are not acceptable for dogs either, because dogs are much rougher on toys than even the most destructive toddler. They simply won't hold up.

Socks never make good chew toys for dogs, because a dog can easily swallow a sock. The sock can become impacted in the digestive system, and the dog may require surgery to have it removed.

The best stuffed animal toys are made of acrylic fur and 100 percent polyester filling that washes easily. You don't have to make a habit of it, but when the mood strikes you, you can put them in a mesh bag and throw them in the washer with some dog towels for balance.

To entertain your Siberian in a handsome style, you may want to purchase a combination chew and toy in the form of Space Balls, Kongs, and related products. You can insert a treat in these bouncing toys, and your dog will have a delightful time, attacking and chewing the toy, rather than the furniture. Kongs are microwaveable, so for a special treat, you can melt a bit of cheese or peanut butter and dry dog food together inside it. It'll take your greedy dog hours to get all of it out. Be careful of very hard toys, though. They are the major cause of tooth breakage among dogs. Use your best judgment.

Never give your dog a ball so small that he can swallow it! (Siberians can crush and swallow tennis balls.) If a ball gets stuck in his throat, you'll need to open his mouth and reach in with pliers to get it out. And if you don't catch it soon enough, he could die.

Some people recommend letting the dog chew real sticks; I think this is fine when he's outside, but inside it's too much to expect your pup to know the difference between an oak branch and your Windsor chair. I can't always tell the difference myself.

Part III
Living with a Siberian Husky

The 5th Wave   By Rich Tennant

"OK, I'LL LET HIM PLAY AS LONG AS YOU STOP SAYING, 'YOU CAN'T TAKE AN OLD DOG'S NEW TRICKS'."

In this part . . .

Siberian Huskies make fantastic housemates, but you need to help them adapt to your home through proper training. And the only way you can do that is by learning how to communicate with your dog. In this part, you'll discover how to do exactly that.

You'll also figure out how to deal with problem behaviors and how to socialize your dog with people and other dogs.

Chapter 5

Welcome Home!

• •

In This Chapter

▶ Helping your puppy adjust to his new home

▶ Making it through the first night with your puppy by your side

▶ Figuring out whether your Husky will live indoors or outdoors

▶ Giving the outdoor Husky everything he needs to survive the elements

▶ Knowing how to house-train your dog

▶ Cleaning up after your new Husky when he has accidents of every kind

• •

*B*ringing a new puppy home is truly one of life's greatest joys. But it's not without its problems either. So, in this chapter, I give you all the information you need to make the transition easier for you and your puppy — everything from making it through that very first night to deciding whether your dog will live outdoors or inside.

If your ideal living room could be an advertisement for *Better Homes & Gardens,* reconsider your decision to get a Siberian. Dogs are messy. They shed, they chew, and they like to sleep on your best furniture.

You simply cannot keep a house in pristine condition after your furry bundle of joy bounds through the door for the first time. No matter how careful you are, accidents will happen. Something you treasure dearly will be eaten, peed on, clawed, or crushed by your pet. But, in this chapter, you'll find suggestions for ways to deal with the messes that come with the territory.

Surviving the First Day and Night

If possible, arrange for your new puppy to arrive in the morning, so you can have the whole day to become acquainted. Ideally, this should be a quiet time, with only the family present. Take your new puppy out for a walk right away, even before you bring him into the house. Walk him to the area you want him to use for eliminating, and praise him lavishly when he uses it. (Praising puppies often includes jumping up and down with joy like a crazed person.)

Feeding your new puppy his first meal

When you feed your Husky his first meal, give a bit less than he has been accustomed to receiving. He'll be nervous and excited, and too much food could make him sick. If he eats dinner without a fuss, you can give him a treat later on.

At first, feed your new puppy the same kind of food he was receiving from his breeder. He's just had a major change in his environment, so you'll want to preserve as much continuity in the puppy's life as possible. Abrupt diet changes can also cause stomach problems. If you want to change his diet, do so gradually over a week or so.

When your new puppy is eating, sit near him and handfeed him a treat or two. Practice taking away his food and returning it to him. This is one way to establish the fact that you are his master and in charge of the food. It will also help prevent food possessiveness later on.

Helping your pup adapt to his new family

The first few days will be strange and new for your Siberian, so make sure you give him plenty of nurturing and lots of hugs. At this stage, love is more important than play. Gently handle your puppy a lot and don't allow the kids to keep waking him up. You want your puppy to know that you are a safe haven from the vacuum cleaner, the mean cats, and any other household hazards he may encounter. (This doesn't mean you should feed his phobias, but you should be there to support him the same way you would a young child.)

Make introductions to the rest of the family gradually. Teach your children the correct way to hold your puppy — with both arms. Don't allow very young children to carry a Husky puppy around; sooner or later they will drop him on his head. Don't leave puppies and children together unsupervised; the trouble they can get into together is unimaginable. (I have a friend whose young child dyed their yellow Labrador Retriever pink. In this case, the "young" child was 15 years old.)

Reassuring your puppy on his first night

Letting your puppy sleep in your bedroom with you is the best option, especially during his first few nights. He'll be reassured by your presence, and you can tell if something is wrong or he needs to go out.

Even in your immediate presence, your new puppy may cry the first night. Never yell at him or punish him for doing so; if you do, he'll feel even worse. You can ignore his crying, after you've first made sure he's secure in his crate with a chew toy. (This takes nerves of steel, but it pays off in the long run.) Or you can give in and sleep near the puppy or just transport him to your bed. If you do this, he'll probably be there forever, though.

In rare cases, a dog interprets your allowing him onto your bed as meaning that you accept him as an equal. Obviously, this isn't a good plan. If you are the slightest bit doubtful about your ability to control Ranger, let him sleep quietly in his own bed at your feet.

Even during the daytime, your new puppy may cry when placed inside the crate, at least at first. Never let him out of the crate while he is actually crying, whining, or barking. That just teaches him that he can get what he wants by annoying you. Wait until he's quiet before you release him. On the other hand, he should regard his crate as a friendly place for relaxing and sleeping — not an all-day prison. Keep the door to the crate open, so he can go in and out at will. Feeding him there may be a good idea.

Deciding Whether Your Husky Will Live Inside or Outside

Siberian Huskies really enjoy being outdoors in the cold. In fact, they prefer the outside to the inside. Even young Siberians can be acclimatized to living outdoors; after all, they *are* arctic dogs. In the Iditarod, when temperatures routinely plunge to –65 degrees, the Siberians sleep comfortably, curled up in the snow. Their drivers, however, wearing heavy fur parkas, face masks, and mittens, frequently suffer severe frostbite.

Despite their love for cold outdoor weather, Siberians are extremely family-oriented. An outside Siberian must not be an *ignored* Siberian. Siberians suffer badly from loneliness. If you decide to keep your Husky outdoors, make doubly sure he is getting his share of love and attention.

The Husky's love of the cold outdoors created no conflict back in Chukchi country, where everybody lived outside, but it can be a problem today. Most well-loved Huskies nowadays are housedogs, simply because we want our pets close to us. You could always move outdoors with your dog.

Winter or summer, your Siberian will require a secure fenced yard. Never chain a dog outside. For one thing, it's dangerous. Dogs can get the chain wrapped around their necks or legs and be killed. Also, dogs who are chained out for long periods tend to become territorial and snappish. Dogs who are tied out temporarily need to be under supervision. Chains can be made much safer with a swivel, however, and using one of these is preferable when you need to tie out your dog (for example, when you're engaged in an outdoor activity with him).

Although Huskies handle cold weather remarkably well, they do need to become acclimatized to it. Do not constantly alternate between having your dog spend winter nights indoors and out. Sudden repeated fluctuations between warmth and cold is much harder on your Siberian than continued cold weather. Of course, when it's extremely bitter, you will want your Siberian inside with you.

If your Siberian does come in during cold, wet weather, don't let him out again until he is thoroughly dry. If he goes out wet, the wet hairs could freeze and give your Husky a bad case of *hypothermia*. Hypothermia is a fancy way of saying "subnormal body temperature." The symptoms include intense shivering and frostbite on a dog's toes, ears, and genitals.

If you acquire a dog who is used to sleeping indoors, and you wish to make the transition to outdoor accommodations, go slowly. Indoor dogs need time for their fur to thicken up. However, the worst problem you may encounter is a lot of very vocal complaining from your Siberian, a phenomenon your neighbors may not appreciate.

Even in the coldest weather, your Siberian needs fresh clean water. Water in metal dishes freezes quickly, so try switching to a heavy plastic dish that will conserve heat better. Metal dishes pose another danger as well — your dog's tongue could freeze to it in bitter weather. Ceramic or plastic is a better choice for the cold outdoors, and water in a deeper dish will stay liquid longer than in a shallow one. (It stays cooler in the summer also.) Choose a dark color for winter use, and use a lighter one in the summer.

You will probably find that as the temperatures plunge, your Husky's activity level rises. Even as you long to toast your toes before the fireplace, your dog will be urging you to come out and frolic with him in the subzero night. Strange creatures, aren't they?

Paying Attention to the Outdoor Husky's Special Needs

Even the heavily insulated Husky needs a house that provides protection from bitter winds, although he may go in it only rarely. Some Huskies prefer sleeping on *top* of their homes, while the wind whips through their fur. It's a weird sight.

Giving your Husky his own abode

Good doghouse materials include plywood or heavy-duty plastic. (Siberians simply eat doghouses made of inferior materials.) One of plastic's advantages is that it doesn't hold odors the way wood sometimes does. If you paint the doghouse, use nontoxic paint. Despite all precautions, your Siberian will probably lunch on his doghouse from time to time, and you don't want him to be poisoned from toxic paint.

The best doghouses, homemade or store-bought, are equipped with an over-hang in front of the door. The house should also have a flap over the door, which keeps heat in and wind out. A doghouse with a hinged top makes for easy cleaning.

Other factors being equal, the doghouse door should be facing away from prevailing winds. (In most places, winds come from the northwest. So the door should be facing the southeast.) Put the house on blocks or a pallet to keep rainwater out. A well-constructed doghouse does not need to be heated.

The opening of your Husky house should be narrow, just wide enough to allow the dog to get into the house. A narrow passage helps conserve warmth. The doghouse itself shouldn't be too big either — you want it snug enough for your Husky's body heat to warm it easily. Smaller areas conserve warmth. Your dog should be able to stand up, stretch out, and turn around, and that's all. **Remember:** This isn't your dog's version of the Taj Mahal.

For insulation, you can't do better than clean, dry straw. It's warm, cheap, and easily replaceable. Blankets or discarded coats are all right (if your dog doesn't chew them up), but if they get wet, they tend to stay that way. Straw dries much more quickly, but it must be replaced every month or so. Don't use fiberglass insulation in the doghouse if your dog can get to it; fiberglass is extremely irritating to dogs' skin. Siberians really don't need insulation at all. I like to throw cedar chips on the floor of the dog house; they smell wonderful and repel fleas.

The roof of the doghouse should be flat. Siberians dearly love to sit on the roofs of their outdoor homes and observe the world from a higher vantage point. But don't put the Husky house too near a fence, or he'll jump over the fence and be gone before you know it.

Helping your Husky avoid heat stress

All dogs suffer the effects of extreme heat, but Siberians, because of their northern heritage and heavy coats, are particularly at risk. Because Siberians are working dogs with high energy levels, they are in danger of exercising or playing too hard in the hot weather. Old dogs, black dogs, and fat dogs are especially vulnerable to heat stress.

Save the trees!

Trees, of course, make wonderful shade. But many species of trees cannot tolerate dog urine day in and day out. So if you have decided to plant some trees inside your fenced yard for shade, choose a variety like poplar or green ash that can handle dog urine. Put a mesh wire around the tree while it is young, so your dog can't get to the tree while it is taking root and getting established.

If you have a prize plant or bush that cannot be easily moved to a dog-proof site, sprinkle it with mothball flakes. Do this every week or so until your dog becomes uninterested in the plant. You may have to put wire around the base of some young trees. One of our dogs chewed an ornamental crabapple nearly to death before we discovered what was happening.

If you leave your dogs in the yard for any length of time in the summer months, have plenty of water and shade available. We built a wooden *loafing shed* (a large doghouse with one side open) for our dogs, where they can lie in straw and cedar bedding, comfortably at ease in the shade. Dogs don't sweat, and direct sunlight can raise the temperature of a Siberian faster than you'd believe possible.

Provide water in a heavy, no-tip bowl. To be extra safe, use two of them. Toss some ice cubes into the dog dishes during the summer. It keeps the water cool, and the dogs like to play with the cubes. In very hot weather, use a whole block of ice.

An old tube cake pan makes a handy outdoor water dish. Just drive a wooden stake through the hollow center, and your rambunctious puppy can't tip it over!

Automatic dog waterers are a wonderful invention; they allow your dog to drink cool water whenever he wants. You can attach one right to your outdoor faucet or hose, eliminating worry about dog dishes tipping over, running out of water, or becoming foul.

Because plenty of fresh water is a necessity, try a wading pool, like the one shown in Figure 5-1. Your Siberian will probably lie in the pool during the hottest days of the summer. Remember, however, that mosquitoes lay eggs in standing water, so dump the contents of the pool into your garden every night and use fresh water the next morning.

If you have a puppy, do not leave him alone with a wading pool or even a deep bucket of water. Believe it or not, puppies have drowned in them.

Figure 5-1:
A child's wading pool is a great place for your Husky to cool off in the heat of the summer.

A product called Mist & Cool is great for outdoor dogs in the summer. It's a portable dog cooling kit with an adjustable nozzle which sprays a fine mist, lowering the ambient temperature about 25 degrees. If your Sibe likes the idea, it's a terrific way to ensure his comfort. Or you can get a cooling mat. One brand, The Polar Pad, is first soaked in water and then let dry on the outside. It will stay at 62 degrees for three days and doesn't need refrigeration.

While your dog is enjoying alfresco dining in the summertime, you may notice our little friends the ants sharing his dinner. You can avoid the situation by partly filling a big shallow pan with water and putting the pet dish like an island in the middle. (A commercial bowl on the market does the same thing.) The ants will drown trying to get to the food and your pet won't get his nose pinched. This won't work with those army ants you see in the horror movies, though. Those little suckers can make bridges out of their own bodies and get across that way. On the other hand, if you have hordes of army ants in your back yard, you have bigger worries than the pet dish. Call the Marines.

Giving Your Pup the Exercise and Discipline He Needs

Your pup's first few days home should be times of affection and love, not necessarily the most rambunctious times he'll have. But as he becomes more comfortable in your home, he'll need exercise and discipline. So in these sections, I give you the basics on these essentials of puppy-rearing.

Knowing when your Husky needs exercise

Siberians need lots of exercise, particularly at the following times:

- Before a bath
- Before grooming and nail clipping
- Before you leave him home alone
- Before taking him in the car for a ride
- Before company comes
- Before he goes to bed
- When he wakes up
- When he looks bored

In other words, most Siberians are desperately in need of exercise almost all the time. This is part of the fun of owning a Siberian!

Disciplining your puppy properly

Discipline is *not* a punishment. Proper discipline means a happier, more tractable pet; it makes your own life easier as well.

The first few days with your puppy are critical when it comes to discipline. Your new puppy is so cuddly that you may be tempted to let him do whatever he likes, thinking you can correct mistakes when he gets older. Why upset the sweet little thing when he's so new, right? But be forewarned. If you don't want your big dog to do something, don't let your puppy do it either. Failure to observe this simple rule is one reason why so many Huskies end up in animal shelters or with rescue organizations.

Your sweet little puppy has inherited the determined and obstinate nature of the persevering sled dog, and allowing him to run uncorrected will result in danger for him and heartache for you. Besides, your puppy actually *wants* to know what you expect of him. He is used to being nipped by his mother for improper behavior. He won't hold it against you when you keep him in line. A dark glare and a firm "no!" works perfectly well.

House-Training Your Husky

Believe it or not, your Husky *wants* to be house-trained. By nature, he is an extremely clean dog who does not want to mess up his living quarters. All he needs is for you to explain to him what you want. But remember, a puppy is a baby; you can't expect his bladder control to be perfect. Even though he may learn very early what he should do, sometimes it's just too hard for him to wait. Most dogs do not have sufficiently developed sphincter muscles to be completely house-trained until they are 4 or even 6 months old. Besides, their bladders are small. So having patience is important.

Train without pain. Never use physical punishment to house-train your puppy. Puppies between the ages of 8 and 10 weeks (the very time when they are learning house-training skills) are extremely sensitive to any painful experiences. If you use physical punishment at this stage, you may have a fearful dog forever. Some mistakes simply cannot be undone. This is the time to use petting, love, and positive reinforcement. Your puppy will then associate pleasant sensations with doing what you want. It's the most effective training device in the world.

Even if your Siberian spends most of his time outdoors, he still needs to be house-trained. He needs to learn that eliminating indoors is never appropriate. Training now will save you a lot of embarrassment later when you visit friends, pet sitters, the vet, and motels.

In this section, I give you all the information you need to house-train your Husky with ease.

Using crates to help house-train

For house-training, a crate is your best friend. Keep a favorite toy in the crate, and have your Husky sleep there with it. He will soon get accustomed to the idea of the crate as his bedroom. Because dogs hate soiling their sleeping quarters, you can take him outside as soon as he awakes from his naps and he won't have had time to have an accident. He will soon extend the idea to the whole house.

For a small puppy, you can even use a playpen, so that the pup can observe all the goings-on. Put down a shower curtain or plastic liner inside the playpen, under a mat.

During the day, don't keep a puppy in a crate for more than four hours. If you do, he will not be able to control his bowel functions, and then he'll lose any inhibitions he may have about messing in his crate.

How long can a puppy stay in a crate without needing to eliminate? The longest time a dog should be confined is eight hours (and that should be only on very rare occasions). Just consider your pup's age in months. Young dogs should be able to be crated for as many hours as they are months old. A 4-month-old puppy should be able to last four hours, a 5-month-old puppy for five hours, and so on.

Your dog will not get sufficient exercise if he is kept in a crate too long. He should have at least an hour, and preferably longer, between each crating session when he is allowed to run and play actively.

When your not-yet-house-trained dog is out of his crate, you may want to tie a leash to him and hook the other end to yourself. Then go about your daily activities. This way, you'll be sure that he won't sneak off to pee, and you can keep a close eye on him. This technique is especially useful in house-training an older dog. It also helps to bond you and your dog together — literally.

Pet store puppies are used to using their cages as a bathroom, because it's their only choice. So a puppy coming from this kind of environment will naturally have a more difficult time understanding that his crate is for sleeping only.

Dogs need to urinate more frequently in hot weather, when they are drinking more water. Remember to accommodate their increased need.

Getting the basics of house-training

When you have a puppy, you're responsible for taking him outside at all the appropriate times — in the morning and after naps, after a meal, and just before bedtime. Very young puppies may have to go in the middle of the night as well. **Remember:** The house-training process is trying, but extra effort now will save you a lot of aggravation later.

Set your alarm clock for about three hours after you go to bed, quickly take the puppy out, and do it again three hours later. Don't worry, he'll soon sleep through the night. In the morning, take him out before you do anything else.

Don't wait for your young puppy to inform you of his needs. He won't think of them himself until it's just about too late. And by the time he manages to get your attention, it's *really* too late.

Responding to accidents

If you actually see your puppy having an accident, yell, "Outside!" in an alarmed (not angry) voice, and race outside with him. (If you say "No!" he may think that eliminating is wrong, and that's not the message you want him to receive.) If he happens to use the bathroom again while outside, praise him mightily. Keep praising him excitedly every time he does what you want.

Timing is everything. You must go outside *with* your puppy when you see him start to make a mistake. If you just scold him and toss him outside, the message he's getting is, "Peeing is wrong," not "Peeing has its own special place — outside." If he thinks "Peeing is wrong" he will soon start to pee everywhere when your back is turned to avoid a scolding. (Obviously, he can't just stop peeing.)

If you don't actually see the mistake being made, just clean it up without comment. There's no point in telling him after the fact that he's made an error. Have the puppy out of sight when you clean up after him. If he sees you "playing with his pee" he may think he's pleased you. Also, because his mother cleaned up after him, he may think this is normal activity, so why should he change anything?

Do not drag your dog over to the mess and rub his nose in it. He won't have a clue why you're doing this. He may know you're upset with him, but he just can't make the connection. Besides, assuming that a dog's messes smell as bad to him as they do to you is wrong. He may even eat the stuff, thinking that's what you want. And of course, never strike your dog for making a mess — or for any other reason.

Use the same door every time you take your dog out until he is thoroughly house-trained and goes to that door every time. Use a particular area of the yard for your dog's bathroom duties. This approach will encourage the dog to think of this area as "his" for this particular purpose. Also, it will make yard cleanup that much easier. Go with your puppy. Do not leave him alone to wander around aimlessly. Praise him greatly when he does what's wanted!

At first, leave a little of your precious Siberian's poo in the area you want him to use. This will remind him of his duty the next time he goes out.

Sticking to a schedule

Eight-week-old puppies should go out every couple of hours. Puppies new to the household should go out even more frequently, because nervousness and excitement stimulates their bladders. Most adult dogs can be left alone for eight hours, but this is variable, just as it is with people.

When your Siberian knows that he can depend upon you to take him out at regular times (dogs have clocks in their heads), he'll be more inclined to wait for that moment. If he doesn't have a clue when or if you're going to take him out, he may feel as though he has nothing to wait for. So, as far as he's concerned, he may as well go now.

Keep a strict schedule with your dog's eating times as well, because the two events — eating and elimination — are connected. If you have to leave your dog alone all day, and he can't hold it, think about hiring a dog-walking or pet-sitting service. Or take some of that unused vacation time. Your Husky will appreciate the company, too.

If you cannot teach your Husky to bark when he wants in or out, you can buy a Doggie Doorbell designed to prevent scratching. A pad can be placed on either side of your door at dog-height. When the pet touches the pad, a built-in wireless transmitter activates a door chime! Or you can install a pet door. Some owners train their dogs to come and sit in front of them when they have to go out.

Figuring out what's behind the accidents your Husky has

One of the most thrilling things about canine urination is that it can mean so many things. For instance, it may translate into: "I'm very submissive — don't whack me." Or it can mean the opposite: "I'm a big tough dog. I'm leaving my mark." Or it can mean: "I'm not feeling well, and I wish my owner would be smart enough to figure out why I'm peeing all over the place." Or it can mean: "Oh boy, oh boy, oh boy! We're goin' for a walk! I can't control myself!" Or maybe the dog just needs to use the bathroom.

The marking of territory

Male dogs tend to mark areas they want to claim as their own. Unneutered male dogs, especially if they are new to an area, typically lift a leg against a chair, a wall, or a lamp. They are leaving something besides a wet spot: They're leaving important information for other dogs. This behavior usually begins between the ages of 4 and 9 months. Even dogs who don't do this in their homes may be tempted to mark indoors elsewhere. Neutering is one way to reduce or even eliminate this problem.

If there has been a recent change in household structure (typically if the dominant partner leaves), a male dog may attempt to elevate to a position at the top of the new pack. One of the ways he may try to assert his authority is by urinary marking in the home. When the proper dominance order has been reestablished, the marking should stop.

Illnesses

Diabetes is a disease that first declares itself by increased urination. If your dog exhibits unusual thirst, coupled with urinating in the house, suspect diabetes, and call the vet.

Cushings disease, certain medications like prednisone, and chronic kidney failure can also cause increased urination, as can urinary tract infections. Urinary tract infections are more common in females than in males; symptoms include unproductive straining and licking of the genitals. Bladder stones, tumors, and polyps may also be culprits in urinary incontinence. If straining accompanies the urination, suspect a urinary tract infection rather than Cushings, kidney failure, or diabetes.

Leaking

Older, spayed females may also have problems with "leaking," especially at night. In their case, the cause is loss of estrogen, which apparently results in weakening the urinary sphincter. Obviously, treating this condition is very important, because, in addition to the urine-soaked carpet and furniture, the prolonged contact with urine can cause skin ulcers in your dog. Luckily, there's a solution. Medications like phenylpropanolamine often work magic; they stimulate the secretion of norepinephrine, a hormone that increases the sphincter muscle tone.

Fear

Some dogs urinate whenever they are scolded. This response is rooted in fear. Do not punish your dog for urinating; that will only frighten and depress her more.

Often urination is a normal canine response to a dominant companion, and is called *submissive urination.* You are more likely to see submissive urination in puppies than in adult dogs.

The only way to cure submission urination is to let your dog know that she has nothing to be afraid of. Punishing her will merely confirm her fears. Praising her, on the other hand, will make her think peeing while scared is the correct move. Simply ignore the urination, clean it up, and otherwise just pretend it never happened. Gradually, she'll become more confident and lose her fear of you.

Excitement

Many dogs, particularly younger ones, don't have complete bladder control, especially when they are excited or overwrought. You need to reduce your Husky's excitement level by being calm yourself when exciting things happen. If your dog urinates when you come home, don't make a big deal over her when you walk in the door. Simply be blasé, and avoid eye contact for about ten minutes. If you don't make a big fuss, your dog will become less anxious and excited. Hug and cuddle her later, to make up for your apparent indifference to her when you first walked in the door.

Cleaning Up After Your Husky

Dogs are truly man's best friend — and Siberians are among the best friends you can find. But (isn't there always a but?) the downside is that dogs — all dogs — tend to find their way into messes. So in this section, I help you figure out how to quickly clean them up — whether inside or out — and get back to the joy of owning a dog.

Taking care of the yard

One of the joys of dog ownership is the challenge of trying to maintain a beautiful lawn while giving your dog room to do his business. In the following sections, I give you great strategies for doing exactly that.

Picking up after your pooch

In my house, we prefer the plastic bag method of picking up after our dogs. We just pick up the messes using plastic bags or rubber gloves we've designated for that purpose. If you're squeamish, you can opt for a variety of fancy pooper-scoopers that will save your back and nose. Most are a two-piece deal that operate on the rake-it-in-and-shovel-it-up plan. A few are actually designed to work in grass and gravel.

Pick up stools from around the yard twice a day if possible. They look bad, smell awful, make a mess if you step in them, and carry disease.

Getting rid of lawn spots

Those hideous yellow and brown spots you see all over your lawn are burns from urine and feces. They are just another reason for getting your Husky to use one corner of the yard for his bathroom responsibilities; at least you can reduce the damage that way.

Besides keeping your yard picked up regularly, you can add products like Grassaver or G-Whiz to your dog's diet. They act to neutralize your dog's urine and control odors. Other products like Spot Check and Green-Um, sprayed or sprinkled on the damaged area, will help reestablish grass. If you actually catch your dog in the act, rinse the grass immediately with 2 or 3 gallons of water.

A good chemical remedy is K-9 Turf, which is safe for both pets and kids. It's an all-natural product that doubles as a lawn fertilizer. Use it once a month and your problems with lawn spots should be over. Other good products include Spot Check and Dogonit. Dogonit gets rid of winter salt damage also.

If your dog is in the habit of urinating on and consequently destroying a bush, don't dig up the bush! He'll just urinate on another one. Leave the shrub there, while you attempt to discourage the dog from this habit. He may just continue to urinate only on the dead one.

Taking care of the grass

Although no normal yard can stand up to an exuberant Siberian, if you have the time and luxury, you can improve your lawn's appearance. Jessi Holcomb, a Siberian owner and professional greenskeeper, gave me a few hints on Husky lawn-keeping:

As impressive as a wolf, as friendly as a beagle, and as trustworthy as your best friend, the matchless Siberian Husky stands tall in any landscape.

These charming Siberian puppies play happily together and enjoy their own company, but they long for (and need) the human touch.

Winter/Churchill Photography

Winter/Churchill Photography

The enterprising Siberian can hunt down food in almost any arctic environment, but they do better when *you* choose the menu.

This blue-eyed beauty displays the famous pink *snow nose*. The pigment will darken again in the summer.

The Siberian Husky is one of the few breeds whose standard welcomes *bi-eyed* dogs. The intriguing combination of blue and brown eyes lends this dog the impish look characteristic of many Siberians.

The roving Siberian is best secured in a well-fenced yard or kennel run. This hardy dog gets all the outdoor shelter he needs in a sturdy barrel.

Winter/Churchill Photography

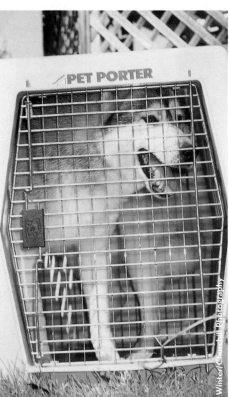

Winter/Churchill Photography

When travelling with your Siberian, keep him safe in a well-ventilated, portable kennel that allows him to stand and turn around.

The Siberian wanderlust is about to take over with this dog! Remember to keep your Siberian's doghouse away from the fence. Siberians are expert climbers.

Winter/Churchill Photography

Regular dental care does more than clean teeth; it gives you and your Siberian a chance to bond. This dog relishes his owner's attention.

Winter/Churchill Photography

A correctly trained dog keeps his eye on his owner's face. That way, he can read even the most subtle signals. This handsome Siberian is properly positioned at his owner's knee.

Face nuzzling is a classic way for dogs to get acquainted. Most Siberians socialize extremely well.

Siberians, when well socialized, can make reliable companions for your other pets—as long as they aren't too small. This Siberian is obviously fond of his Spaniel friend.

The Siberian Husky is a wonderful companion to children, because they are small enough to be nonthreatening and big enough to keep from being stepped on. This pair are friends for life.

Say what you will—this is what being a Husky is all about. Nothing makes a Siberian happier than pulling a sled through snow—and fast.

Winter/Churchill Photography

Winter/Churchill Photography

This pair of racing Siberians is grabbing a little shut-eye before the next leg of the race. A racing dog can learn to sleep anywhere, even in a harness.

The peerless Siberian brings a touch of the wild into the most humdrum life.
After they've lived with and loved a Siberian, most people can't live without them.

- ✔ **Try planting perennial rye grass for a lawn.** That's the stuff they use for football fields. You'll have to mow it twice a week, but it'll be sturdier and stand up to more wear and tear from your dog.

- ✔ **For a quick fix, add some annual rye grass.** This grass sprouts up green in a few days, although it dies back in the winter.

- ✔ **Fertilize the lawn when the dogs are in for an evening, and hose it down lightly to remove residual fertilizer before releasing the dogs into the yard.**

You can also try my personal method: Just mulch the whole yard and forget about the grass.

Getting rid of urine stains

When your puppy urinates on your rug, use one part vinegar to two parts non-ammonia cleaner and gently blot up the stain with a paper towel. Afterwards, apply a pleasant-smelling detergent, or use a specialized product like Urine Kleen, Natural d'Liminone (a citrus extract), or Odormute. There's also Nature's Miracle, an enzyme cleaner that helps devour smells.

Do not use ammonia for cleaning up urine. Ammonia smells like urine to a dog, and he'll be encouraged to repeat his error in the very same place.

If the urine goes through the carpet into the backing, you're in trouble. You may have to get the carpet professionally shampooed. If it has suffered quite a few accidents of this sort, you may have to remove it altogether.

If your dog urinates on a hardwood floor, you can't always get the odors out. But you *can* seal them in. Apply a coat or two of polyurethane to the floor. It does wonders and looks very nice as well.

Dealing with vomit

If your dog vomits on the carpet, the first and most obvious step is to pick up the vomit (that's always the worst part). Vomit, having just emerged from your dog's digestive system, is an acidic substance. The best cleanup (unless your dog has a house-training block) is a solution of 1 tablespoon of ammonia to ½ cup of water, unless you have a wool carpet. (Ammonia should never be used on wool!)

Cleaning up blood

If your Husky bleeds for any reason, your first consideration should always be to figure out what has caused the bleeding and get your dog the help he needs right away.

After you've gotten your Husky taken care of, you can follow these tips for cleaning up blood stains:

1. **Apply cold water to the stain.**

2. **Apply ammonia to the stain.**

3. **Add more cold water to the stain, and rinse fast.**

Make sure you use cold water so as not to set the stain. And if your dog has a house-training problem or if you have wool carpeting, don't use ammonia.

Chapter 6

Understanding What Your Husky Is Trying to Tell You

In This Chapter

▶ Listening to what your Husky has to say

▶ Noticing your dog's body language

▶ Making sense of your Husky's "strange" behavior

▶ Reading your dog's confidence level by observing the way he sleeps

*A*ll over the world, dogs speak the same language, and although that language isn't classical Greek, there's a lot more to dogtalk than a few grunts and sniffs. After all, dogs are not Neanderthals. Canine communication takes the form of auditory signals, facial expression, and body language. In this chapter, you'll figure out how to make sense of all of these.

Picking Up on What Your Dog Is Saying

Dogs partly communicate through *auditory* signals (signals that can be heard, like barks and growls). They use auditory signals to communicate over long distances among themselves. In their ancestral days, running wild in a pack, they needed to be able to communicate messages like, "Wait! It's this way!" or "You'd better leave Enid alone; she's promised to me!" Dogs haven't forgotten their roots; they still use auditory signals today.

Barking and howling are apparently no harder on a dog's vocal cords than talking is on ours. That's why they can howl or bark for so long, much to the irritation of some of us humans.

Barking

A bark is a juvenile noise, located acoustically somewhere between a snarl and a yelp.

Siberian Huskies, true to their heritage, bark less than many other breeds. When they *do* vocalize, they tend to woo, howl, sing, chirp, and chatter softly. The reason for the Husky's infrequent barking may be that barking is largely a territorial call, and Huskies, like wild dogs, are almost uniquely non-territorial. Huskies do occasionally bark to stake a claim on their territory, but not as often as other dogs.

Some Husky barking is an invitation to play, a juvenile trait.

Howling

Howling is a *primitive* trait in dogs, which means that breeds of ancient lineage are much more likely to howl than more modern breeds like the Irish Setter or Toy dogs, such as the Shih Tzu. Siberians, Malamutes, and hounds are howlers of high order.

The meaning of the howl is still mysterious. We do know that dogs sometimes howl when they're bored, but they are equally likely to howl amidst the company of other Siberians, in which case it may be a bonding strategy. The howl has another purpose, too: long-distance communication. The howl is a low-pitched sound with a long duration — the two qualities needed to carry it for miles. Each howl is individual, and wolves are known to recognize packmates by the unique sound of each member's howl. There is no reason to suspect it is otherwise in dogs.

The dog with the deepest howl or bark is usually the alpha dog.

Dogs belonging to breeds that don't howl often look curiously at dogs engaging in this peculiar behavior. They probably can't imagine what the fuss is all about. A non-howling Siberian can be taught to howl by his howling packmates or even by a human who is willing to crawl around on the floor like a dog and bay. (I have seen it done.)

There is no evidence to show that animals howl at the moon. There is a theory, however, that they howl more during a full moon, when they can see better and are consequently more active.

If you own more than one Siberian, you may find that they get up a community howl now and again, which is very pleasant indeed. Their eerie, wolf-like cry is haunting and evocative, sending a thrill down the back of the sensitive listener. Because the animals howl at different pitches and use different, modulating tones, which echo and bounce off walls, a pair of Siberians can easily sound like a dozen. Wolves use this trick too, and often fool their opponents into believing that the pack is much larger than it really is.

It usually takes more than one Siberian to get up a howl. You will find that one dog will nearly always initiate the howling; the others will follow. This is called a *chorus howl.*

Siberians also tend to howl along with fire engines or police sirens, as well as when the phone rings.

Wooing

The plaintive "wooing" sound is a Siberian trademark. It could mean anything, but it often says, "No, I don't want to," or "Please don't leave quite yet."

Whining

A whine is a care-soliciting noise. It's also a sign of submission. If your Husky is whining, you can bet he wants to come in, go out, or eat dinner. He may want to be petted as well.

Growling

Growling is best interpreted as a warning. It's commonly seen when Huskies are trying to protect their food from other dogs.

Yelping

When a Husky yelps, it's an unmistakable sign that he is in pain. He could yelp for something as minor as accidentally getting his toes stepped on. Or yelping could be a sign of greater pain. If your Husky is yelping, and you can't determine the cause, call your vet.

Soundless chattering

Sometimes an unneutered male Siberian snaps his teeth together very quickly, usually in the presence of a female. This behavior is a mark of sexual excitement and may be accompanied by trembling. Teeth chattering may also mean the dog wants to go for a ride or eat dinner. Of course, he may just be cold.

Interpreting Your Husky's Body Language

Even the vocal Siberian does not always speak in dog words; so interpreting his body language is very useful. Visual communication is more important in Siberians than it is among some breeds. Lop-eared dogs, curiously enough, are at a visual handicap, because they cannot lay back their ears to show aggression. Dogs with docked tails can't wag their tails completely. A Siberian, on the other hand, has full use of his ears and tail, so he can communicate very well. He may be saying something more than, or other than, you think. Pay attention — it's up to you to be the interpreter. A missed cue can be dangerous for both of you. Your dog may be trying to tell you that he is ill, or that he has delusions of grandeur, or that he really doesn't like your Maltese all that much.

Circling and sniffing

Circling and sniffing are the universal greeting among dogs. Greetings between dogs start nose-to-nose. If all goes well, the sniffing proceeds to the other end. (It seems rude, but it really isn't — at least when it's among dogs.) Your Husky will try to greet human guests in the same time-honored manner. Obviously, he needs to be discouraged from doing this, however.

Mounting behavior

Mounting another dog or attempting to mount a person is not usually an expression of sexuality. Females do it as well as males. It is, however, an indication of dominance. Your Husky is trying to tell you or his fellow dogs that he's the boss. If he mounts other dogs in his household, you'll have to let them sort it out among themselves. When the correct dominance order is established, the annoying behavior should stop. But if your Husky persists in mounting human beings, it's a signal that he is thinking of becoming leader of the pack. Disabuse him of this notion immediately.

Pawing

A dog who places his paw on the shoulder of another dog is trying to demonstrate his dominance over that dog. He may try the same thing with a person.

Bowing

A Siberian who crouches down in front, wagging his tail quickly, is performing play-soliciting behavior. He looks as though he were taking a bow. He may jump backwards and forwards, making weird little noises. He may put his head low to one side, and stare cockeyed at you. Have a good romp with him when you see him bowing. You'll both have a great time.

Nudging or punching

A Husky who nudges or punches with his nose is also designed to get you to play or pet him. It is a more dominant signal than bowing; in effect the dog is demanding, rather than asking, that you pay attention to him.

Hand-holding

Your Husky may gently take your hand in his mouth. This is a gesture of love and affection. He is also requesting your trust in him not to bite you. Allowing him to do so shows him that you have faith in him. This is a bonding strategy.

Mouth-licking

In puppies, mouth-licking is a care-soliciting behavior, in which the young-sters seek food from their mothers. This behavior often persists into adult-hood. Sometimes a dog just licks the mouth of the other dog; sometimes he actually pokes around in there, lifting the corners of the mouth and sniffing away. The dog may be looking to see what his friend has been dining on. Most of the time, it is the submissive dog who licks the mouth of the more dominant dog.

Constant licking or tail-chewing

In younger dogs, paw licking or chewing could be a simple nervous habit, indicating the need to eliminate. Chewing the base of the tail can mean fleas.

A dog who spends a few minutes or an hour licking everything in sight may be nauseated; he is about to throw up. Get him outside as soon as possible.

If licking behavior continues for weeks with no apparent organic cause, especially if carried to the point of raw or bleeding paws, suspect an obsessive-compulsive disorder. Like obsessive-compulsive disorder in human beings, this is *not* a psychological problem. It is not caused by loneliness, neurosis, or boredom. It is very seldom cured by getting another dog, or by giving your dog something else to do. So-called behavior modification doesn't work very well either. The only treatment that cures genuine obsessive-compulsive behavior is certain antidepressants. Only antidepressants that help control obsessive-compulsive disorder in human beings work with dogs; Anafranil and Prozac produce good results. Substantial improvement is seen in two out of three cases. (The National Institute of Mental Health performed the study.) Like obsessive-compulsive disorder in human beings, the precipitating cause may have been a raging infection, possibly not even diagnosed, that left an identifiable protein marker on the surface of certain cells. The protein marker responds to the antidepressant.

Figuring Out Your Dog's Facial Gestures

Although lacking the almost infinite variety of expression employed by humans beings, dogs can still say a lot with their faces:

- **Tongue flicking:** This serpent-like gesture may be a sign that your Siberian needs to eliminate. It's the canine equivalent of a child crossing her legs.

- **Head tilting:** When your dog tilts his head to one side, with a quizzical look, it means he is puzzled or curious about something.

- **Rubbing his face in the carpet:** Usually this behavior just means the dog has an itchy face, but constant face-rubbing may indicate an inhalant allergy.

Watching Your Husky's Tail

Siberians generally relax (and pull sleds) with their tails down. Excitement causes their tails to curl up. A dragging tail, on the other hand, means a tired dog.

When a dog wags his tail, he's giving the same message he does when he smiles. In other words, usually it's because he is happy, but sometimes because he is nervous. It all depends upon exactly how the tail is wagged.

Wagging a tail horizontally and fast means the dog is happy. Usually the whole rear end wags with the dog. Nervous dogs also wag their tails sometimes. It's not necessarily that they're happy to see the vet; they may just be nervous to be there.

A slower, incomplete wag from an erect tail may indicate dominant aggression, just like the smiling villain in those old westerns.

A tail held between the legs is a sign of complete submission or fear. Some low-status dogs eat with their tails between their legs, in the hopes that the dominant dog will take pity upon them and not steal their food.

Knowing the Difference between Dominant and Submissive Behavior

Being cognizant of the body language of dominance and submission in canines is very important, mostly because it can have a direct and negative impact on people. All dogs show dominance and submission, depending on the situation. Being able to read this behavior correctly can prevent a serious problem.

Dominance

Signs of aggression include rising of the *hackles* (shoulder hair) and rump hair. The dog's lips curl back, and sometimes his ears flatten. He may stand on tiptoe. In dominant aggression, the pupils will be contracted, and the dog will stare unblinkingly at his opponent. An aggressive dog may growl, of course, and his teeth may be bared.

Just because a dog bares his teeth doesn't mean he's mad. Some dogs grin. The difference isn't always easy for us to discern, although dogs don't seem to have any trouble with it. The snarl usually bares more teeth than the grin, usually going back to the incisors. If you're unsure, look at the context. (Like wagging, grinning bears a strong relation to the human smile. Usually, we smile when we're happy, but we also sometimes smile at the dentist, because we're afraid, or at our opponents, in order to intimidate them.)

A dominant Siberian has a curled tail and his ears are held upright. He stares pointedly at whatever or whomever he is trying to intimidate. A dominant dog may stand at right angles to a more submissive dog.

A dominant dog may also urinate frequently, defecate, or scratch the ground in the vicinity of the other dog. Dogs have scent glands in their feet; they want to spread their scent around as much as possible. This, combined with vigorously kicking up the dirt means, "I am king around this joint, and don't you forget it, mister."

If you are ever threatened by a strange dog, do *not* attempt to stare down the dog. Averting your eyes from the dog's may defuse the situation. Never try to outstare a strange dog. Do not run away, either; that elicits a chase response, and a dog is faster than you are. Look in another direction, and calmly move away.

To find out more about dominance, or aggression, and how to handle it, see Chapter 9.

Submission

If a less dominant dog wants to fight back, he pulls the corners of his mouth back until all the teeth are bared, but he often doesn't snarl. His ears go flat.

A more submissive dog stands very still, because running away elicits a chase response from the dominant dog. The submissive dog turns his head completely to one side. There is a myth that the dog is doing this to expose his jugular vein submissively to the dominant dog, but in reality he's just trying to avoid provoking a fight by standing still and avoiding eye contact.

Submissive dogs also assume a generally lower stance than the dominant dog. The submissive dog may crouch or cower; he will certainly try to look away. His pupils are enlarged. His ears may be lowered and his tail rigid.

If the submissive dog's fear is coupled with potential aggression, the dog assumes a classic approach-avoidance stance, alternately going close to and then backing away from the object of fear.

Just because a dog is submissive and afraid does not mean he won't bite. Fear-biting is a common response in a dog who feels he can't get away. Never corner a fearful dog or put a hand or head too close to him.

Frightened and submissive dogs put their ears back and carry their tails between their legs. They may turn sidewise to the dominant dog. In a final surrender, they may roll over to their side and urinate.

A frightened dog will lean away from the object of fear. If he raises his hackles or snarls at the same time, be careful. This is a potential fear-biting situation. Most fear-biting dogs have a space outside of which they will not bite. This personal space is usually about a foot or two.

If your dog has done something wrong, like tearing apart the trash can, he may look guilty when you catch him at it. As far as we know, guilt is purely a human emotion. What you're really seeing is submissive behavior; he is nervous about your anger and anticipates punishment. Even before you open your mouth, he knows you're mad. In dogdom, a very submissive stance often allows the miscreant to escape the wrath of the dominant dog; he's hoping it will work with you, too.

Making Sense of Weird Behavior

Sometimes dogs just don't act like people. They don't even live up to our idealized version of how *dogs* should behave. Still we should assume that dogs have reasons, however bizarre, for their behavior, even though we are not yet sure what those reasons may be.

Rolling in nasty stuff

Rolling in foul treasures like deer carcasses and cow manure may be a scent enhancement technique for dogs. Unlike cats, who depend on stealth to catch prey, dogs are uninterested in how they smell to their potential victims. In the wild, dogs rely primarily upon running their dinner down. Consequently, the smells they collect serve purpose within the pack, perhaps to help establish dominance.

Scooting

If your dog scrapes his rear end along the ground, he's scooting. Some people think dogs who scoot have worms, and they may, but more than likely, dogs who scoot are trying to empty their anal glands. Most dogs can accomplish this feat quite satisfactorily on their own, but in some cases you may need to see your veterinarian or your groomer. They will teach you how to express the anal glands yourself. It's not hard, but it *is* smelly. If you attempt this task, you'll probably need two assistants, one to hold the dog, and the other to hold your nose for you.

Eating grass

No one *really* knows why dogs eat grass. Some people think that dogs use grass to obtain roughage, which they may require in their diets, but grass is simply indigestible in dogs. Nonetheless, they persist in eating large quantities of the stuff and vomit it up everywhere. Actually, vomiting may be the idea behind the whole thing with grass acting as an *emetic* (something that causes vomiting). In any event, eating grass seems to cause them no harm, whatever the vomit may do to the furniture. If there's anything harder to remove than grass stains, it's grass stains mixed with dog stomach acid.

Eating manure

The formal term is for feces-eating is *coprophagia.* No one knows precisely why dogs sometimes engage in this disgusting behavior; it is probably programmed into their genes. A mother dog will eat the feces of her very young puppies, for example. This is normal behavior; it keeps the den clean.

But in most cases, feces-eating is really counterproductive. Manure is notoriously ill-supplied with vitamins or anything else useful. That's why it's excreted as waste. Still, dogs continue to engage in this behavior. They may eat their own waste, the waste of other dogs, or even those of other species (cat and horse manure are particular favorites). Coprophagia is not only disgusting, it's also dangerous for your dog.

Nearly all dogs will voraciously devour cat excrement. Cat excrement is especially dangerous, because it carries *Toxoplasma gondii,* which can cause all kinds of hideous things. The solution is to keep the litter box out of the dog's reach, and to clean up the yard frequently.

Coprophagia is more common in young dogs between the ages of 4 and 9 months, so it's possible your Husky may just grow out of it. On the other hand, he may learn to like the taste of poop and get worse.

Other than just-for-fun, and just-to-be-aggravating, some medical conditions seem to induce coprophagia, including:

- Exocrine pancreatic insufficiency
- Pancreatitis
- Overfeeding a high-fat, high-carbohydrate diet
- Intestinal infections
- Certain malabsorption conditions

Check with your veterinarian to rule out any of these disorders.

Another possibility is that your dog is merely bored. Dogs are notoriously maladaptive when it comes to entertaining themselves. They never want to collect stamps or do anything educational. So they turn to something that does interest them: feces.

Some people suggest sprinkling hot sauce on the feces in the hope that the dog will learn not to go near it, but I doubt this is effective. Dogs have an excellent sense of smell and will simply learn to not eat feces that smell like hot sauce.

Certain products are available that are designed to discourage coprophagia. You can start with something cheap, like meat tenderizer or monosodium glutamate (MSG) added to your Husky's food. Apparently the stuff makes dog waste taste bad even to dogs. If that doesn't work, you can try Deter, an over-the-counter pill you can give your dog every two weeks. There's also a veterinarian-prescribed product called Forbid that does the same thing.

Try changing your dog's diet to one lower in fat and higher in protein. You should expect results in a month or so.

Noticing Your Siberian's Sleeping Style

Dogs sleep a lot — over 14 hours a day (more than any other mammal)! And noticing the body position of your Husky as he sleeps tells you a lot about his comfort levels and his self-image.

In cold weather, the Siberian does what is known in the trade as the *Siberian swirl,* carefully tucking his tender nose under that furry tail for warmth.

A Husky curled snugly close beside you is probably not so much interested in keeping warm (he's hotter than you are) as he is keeping safe. If he's an alpha dog, however, you may notice that he keeps himself a little distant from you — maybe just a few inches. He wants to be secure, but at the same time he's letting you know that he is perfectly capable of handling anything that comes up. A dog farther down on the dominance scale may snuggle more closely.

If your Husky prefers to take his ease flat on his back, legs in the air, you may take comfort in knowing that you have a supremely confident, friendly dog without a care in the world. He is totally at ease. This is an extremely vulnerable posture, and only the most self-assured dog will assume it.

A dreaming dog exhibits the same rapid eye movement (REM) found in people. Do not disturb a dreaming dog. You may be walking right into his nightmare. The gentlest dog in the world has been known to snap if awakened at the wrong time.

A Siberian lying flat on his stomach, legs sprawling in every direction, is probably hot. He is trying to dissipate his body heat as efficiently as possible.

A yawning Husky does not necessarily mean a tired Husky. Yawns may also indicate anxiety or tension. You will often observe them, for instance, when getting your Husky ready for a walk or a ride.

Chapter 7

Socializing Your Siberian

In This Chapter

▶ Playing with your puppy from his first day home

▶ Getting your Husky used to other animals

▶ Helping your Husky and your children become the best of friends

Dogs are social animals, and among dogs, no breed is more social than the Siberian. Bred to live in groups and in close proximity with human beings, the Siberian Husky presents no particular problems in socialization — with the single possible exception of the family cat. Nevertheless, socializing your dog is an important part of his education. And in this chapter, I let you know how to go about making your dog a welcome and loving part of any family.

Interacting with Your Puppy

Your Husky puppy should be from 8 to 12 weeks old when he arrives. This critical period in the life of a dog is sometimes referred to as the *human socialization period* — the time when your Husky learns to adapt his behavior to the human environment. (The earlier period is the *canine socialization period,* when the puppy learns to associate with other dogs.) If a puppy is not sufficiently socialized with others of his kind, he could turn into a fighter. Luckily, Siberians rarely have this problem. They are among the most sociable of creatures, both with people and other dogs, although not always with other species.

Visiting with your Siberian

Restrict the number of visits with your Husky pup until he has had his second set of shots. That doesn't mean you shouldn't take him out at all, but you should limit his contacts with other dogs. Many contagious diseases are lurking around. Be particularly careful when going for a walk in the park, because many people do not clean up after their dogs and lots of viral diseases are carried in feces (another good reason to check your own shoes when returning from a walk — you may have stepped in something unpleasant yourself). And your curious puppy will want to investigate everything (and I mean everything!) he finds.

Socialization is essential for a young dog. He needs to be exposed to all different kinds of people — of different races, sexes, and ages. It's especially important for him to meet babies and children. He should meet some strangers once or twice a week, and in different environments. You need to take an active part in seeking out these places. All dog-human encounters should be pleasant experiences for your dog; it helps if the friendly stranger will feed or pet him.

When you do make your first visit, don't feed your puppy immediately before venturing out. The intense excitement of going on a trip may cause an upset stomach and subsequent upchuck. Not the best way to impress your friends with your new puppy. It's also a good idea to exercise your puppy before bringing him to a new place. The thrill of being in a new house may well make him wish to christen it — or worse.

Enrolling in puppy kindergarten

If possible, enroll your Husky in a puppy kindergarten class. You can usually enter your puppy at 3 months, with graduation at 5 months. These classes are valuable because they help your puppy develop socialization skills with people and other dogs. Siberians excel at this, so you may just have the class valedictorian on your hands. Your puppy will also learn some elementary tasks, and you'll pick up tips on basic obedience as well. Puppy kindergarten teachers can give you some good house-training advice as well.

Introducing Your Siberian to Children

Huskies and children were made for each other. With reasonable precautions, the introductions will go smoothly. Remember that the children and new dog will be curious about each other — maybe too much so. They may knock each other over, roll on each other, and steal each other's toys. So never allow young children and dogs to play unsupervised.

Clip your Husky's nails; more harm to children results from scratches than from bites.

Training the children to be pet-friendly

To begin with, children need firm instruction in how to be kind to animals; some of them are unaware of how annoying their teasing can be. They don't usually mean to be cruel; they just don't know any better. Sometimes children chase a small puppy relentlessly or scream in the pup's ears. This behavior is courting disaster. Even a gentle Husky may need to protect himself against this kind of abuse.

If children misbehave around animals, it is often the fault of their parents. I have seen adults sit around, seemingly oblivious, while their kids pummel, bite, scratch, or pull the hair or tail of a dog. Also, children copy their parents' behavior. If kids see their parents slap, annoy, or neglect a dog, they will do the same. Families like this are better off with pet rocks.

Although most children's abuse of pets is unintentional, sometimes it's deliberate. Maltreatment of animals is not only dangerous in itself, it's also a warning of future, escalating problems. If your child exhibits purposeful aggressive behavior toward animals, take him to a therapist and find a better home for your dog.

Most of the time, though, Huskies and children are born friends. Take advantage of their natural comradeship. Reward your children for responding appropriately to the dog. Most dominance problems occur because kids do not know how to be good leaders (not bullies but friendly people in charge).

Preparing your Husky for life with a baby

Unexpected problems may arise with the arrival of a new baby, especially a first baby. For one thing, the family structure has been altered. Things have changed. Some dogs may feel that the baby is an interloper, or at least a very junior pack member. Even dogs who have never shown any dominance tendencies need to be watched carefully in this situation.

What's more, the new person is very, very small. Because size matters in a dog's world, your Siberian is very likely to consider himself dominant over the new arrival. It is even possible that a Siberian could confuse your child with prey. This is not acceptable, of course, but don't expect the dog to automatically understand. He doesn't automatically comprehend that the new baby belongs to the family unless you teach him so.

The best way to cure this problem is to make sure it never occurs in the first place. Even before the arrival of the new family member, prepare your Husky.

✔ **Review all obedience commands.** "Sit," "stay," and of course "no!" are especially helpful.

✔ **Allow your Husky to meet new babies while he's on a short lead.** This way, the sight of one won't completely freak him out.

✔ **Carry big dolls around the house and practice changing diapers, and so forth.** Your Husky will get used to the sight of you attending to this new creature.

✔ **Make a recording of a crying baby; let your Siberian get used to the sound.** Don't exhibit any undue alarm when either the recorded baby or the real one starts to cry. Your Husky may misinterpret your reaction and regard the child as a threat to you. A baby's high-pitched cry can even sound like wounded prey to a dog. (It sounds like that to *me* sometimes.)

In the few cases where Huskies bite children, the incident is often triggered by some gesture of affection from the child, usually a hug or kiss. Dogs regard a person leaning over them as an expression of dominance, and while they may accept the gesture from an adult, some dogs apparently do not consider children in the same category and will unexpectedly attack. Have your child practice obedience commands with your dog.

Never allow any dog who has *ever* shown aggression against any person near a child. I have heard of cases where as many as four years passed between bite incidents. In one such case, the dog suddenly raced out from under a table and ran into the next room to attack a visiting 2-year-old who had not gone near the animal.

Helping your Husky welcome a baby into your family

Your Husky should not be present when the baby is brought home, for a number of reasons. For one thing, you will have your hands full with the baby, and you won't be able to give the dog all the attention he wants right away. Also, if the Siberian is brought in when the new child is already at home, he will be more likely to think of the baby as a new family member than as a guest. It's a territorial concept.

The greatest danger is not that your Siberian will attempt to bite the baby, but that he will try to jump up on you while you are holding the baby.

When he meets the new baby, give your Husky plenty of personal attention at the same time. It's nice if the mother pays attention to the dog, while the father or another family member holds the baby. Give the dog a new toy or a nutritious treat; he'll associate the appearance of the baby with something pleasant for himself. But keep a leash on him.

Allow him to sniff the baby's blanket; you can give him one to sleep with so that he becomes accustomed to the scent. He can sniff the baby too, while he's on a short leash, but he doesn't need to be right in the baby's face to do so.

Guard and secure the baby's dirty diapers, because your Husky may want to eat them. In the wild, animals devour the feces of their young to prevent the scent of vulnerable infants from wafting around the area.

Dealing with toddlers and your dog

Siberians are extremely family-oriented dogs, and few cases of aggressive biting in Huskies have ever occurred. However, it *can* happen and *does* happen, as with any other breed, so it doesn't hurt to be prepared.

Toddlers are in more danger from potentially aggressive dogs than are other family members. Not only may they pull a dog's hair or ears, but their low stature gives them direct eye contact with a Husky-sized dog. A potentially aggressive, dominant dog may perceive this as a threat. In addition, toddlers, unlike babies, are running unchecked all around the house, getting into everything. (You may have noticed this phenomenon yourself.)

Actually, young children are in considerably more danger of being knocked over by an exuberant Siberian, being scratched by overlong nails, or being playfully chewed on, than they are of being bitten. Toddlers often cannot distinguish this behavior from an aggressive attack, however, so this is another reason you should watch your child around all dogs.

Introducing Your Husky to Other Animals

Siberians are happiest when they can share their lives with other dogs. The Chukchis bred their Huskies to be social — it's one of their most endearing characteristics. Still, rivalries may pop up from time to time, and you must be prepared to deal with them.

Small dogs may excite a Siberian's prey drive. In some cases, Siberians make a distinction between large and small dogs, playing happily with dogs their own size or larger, but regarding tiny dogs as being on a level with rabbits and attempting to hunt them. Don't leave your Husky with a small dog until you are absolutely sure they are fast friends. Most of the time, it's best to crate one of the dogs, or separate them in some other way when you are gone.

Don't wait too long to introduce your new Husky to his animal housemates. They'll smell each other anyway. Do the introductions in a controlled setting, with potentially disorderly dogs on a leash.

Cats

Siberians are often poor housemates to the family cat. Sometimes they chase them, and they may even regard cats as prey animals. But if brought up carefully together, it *is* possible to avert this natural disaster. The dog and cat may even become the best of friends. This desired result is somewhat more likely if the cat is the prior occupant; however, you may be able to introduce a new cat to your Husky by carefully holding the cat close to you often. Let the dog clearly understand that the cat belongs to his family. But do not restrain the cat; let her run away if she's worried about the dog. If she does leave, don't follow her. Never let your dog see you chase the cat. He'll want to join in, and Fluffy will not appreciate it in the slightest.

If you are considering adopting an older Siberian, make sure he is safe with cats before you bring him home. Don't leave your cat and Husky alone together until you are *very* sure that they are friends. If they sleep together, it's a good sign. Still, always make sure your cat has a safe, Husky-proof area to which she can escape in case of trouble.

Having more than one Siberian makes the situation more difficult, because they may gang up on the cat. Like adolescents, Huskies seem to forget about polite upbringing when they are in a pack.

Even if your Husky gets used to the family cat, he may still chase or even kill *other* cats. Dogs are quite capable of distinguishing between family and strangers. Keep your Siberian restrained on a leash or safe in your yard at all times. He should be taught the "drop it" command in case he gets hold of a cat or rabbit.

When your Siberian gets used to your cats, you can *usually* have additional cats without problems. However, sometimes dogs accept the old cat but not newcomers.

Birds

Everyone knows that cats kill birds; fewer of us learn (until it's too late) that dogs kill birds, too.

We once had a pair of parakeets, one blue and one yellow, who, while deathly fearful of the cats, made it their life's work to torment the dogs by dive-bombing them. Unfortunately, they played the dogs too cheap, and our Basset Hound had her mouth open at exactly the serendipitous moment (for the dog, not the parakeet) that the parakeet flew into it. The parakeet did not fly out.

I have seen Siberian Huskies actually stalk and kill birds around a feeder.

Livestock

If you or your neighbors own sheep or cattle, you must absolutely keep your Siberian away from them. Huskies regard sheep as prey animals and sometimes injure or kill them. And they have been known to attack young calves, especially when the dogs are in groups. A pack of dogs is always more dangerous than a single one.

Chapter 8

Training Your Dog

In This Chapter

▶ Setting goals for your Husky's training

▶ Working together as a family when you train your Husky

▶ Being aware of which commands your dog should know and training him to follow them

▶ Working with a professional trainer

Siberians have an unfair reputation of being difficult to train. But anyone who has seen a well-matched team of Huskies pulling together, responding instantly to voice commands from a musher, turning left, turning right, slowing down, speeding up, or stopping on command, knows that Siberians, far from being stubborn, are almost infinitely trainable.

But the owner of Huskies must be trained to work with this amazing breed. It may be daunting at first; Siberians have such strong leadership qualities that they respond only to people who earn their respect. They are also highly intelligent and bored by routine.

To best work with your dog, you need to understand his natural character. Part of this character is species-specific (common to dogs in general), part is breed-specific, (common to all Siberians), and part will be his very own individual personality. Dogs vary in their temperaments, like people, and your best chance of success comes through understanding your particular dog's natural bent. Never assume that a technique that worked with your other dogs will work with this one, even if they are littermates. And if one technique doesn't work, try a different one. Every dog has his own learning style. Training a Husky requires creativity. You will need to work as hard as he does, but the rewards are immense — for both of you.

A Siberian will never be a slave, but he is a loyal friend and trustworthy companion you can be proud of.

The weak link

A Siberian is smart enough to discover the weak link in the family — the one person who will let him do anything: beg for food, charge the door, pull on the lead, and so on. This person can unwittingly undermine all the careful training done by the rest of the family. Of course, the weak link is usually a child. So train your children to be pet smart at the same time you train your dog to obey. This includes lessons in kindness, consistency, and healthy leadership behavior on the part of your child.

Training the Family Before You Train Your Dog

Before you can even think about training your Siberian, you must train the Siberian's family. Too many times, the family dog responds only to one person; but when that person is not at home, the dog is practically untrained. Training the dog needs to be a *family* project, even though it is best to have one person be the training leader. The training leader will do the actual teaching of new skills, and then practice them with the dog and the rest of the family. Everyone will then learn the same commands and be able to enforce them. A dog who will sit or come only for one member of the family is not trained. Furthermore, a family member who allows a dog to do as he pleases undermines the entire training project.

Consistency is the key to successful training. A dog has a difficult time learning when it's okay to be on the couch and when it isn't, or that it's fine to leap up on the teenagers but not on Great Aunt Rose, or that it is permissible to beg for food "once in a while." You will be much more successful in the long run if you never allow your Husky to do something that's usually prohibited. Siberians are so smart that teaching them right the first time pays off; you may not get a second chance.

Setting Your Training Goals

Every training session should have a specific goal. If you have no goal, you won't have any idea whether you've accomplished anything.

Keep a logbook of your training sessions, and write down what your goal is for each session. Then record how it went. If you do this faithfully, you'll have a valuable record that will be useful to you in the future. It will also help focus your mind and attention on the particular and specific aims of each training session. Don't try for too much at any one session.

Always wait until you are in a calm and relaxed mood to work with your dog. Siberians are psychic when it comes to picking up on moods, and your dog will respond to your mood. If you want your Husky to associate training with happiness, you have to, well, be happy.

Begin training your Siberian immediately, whether you have a new puppy or a recently adopted older dog. Siberians are strong-willed and independent, so you must establish yourself as *alpha* (the leader) right away. Do what it takes to earn your dog's respect — which is *not* the same thing as making him afraid of you.

Before you begin training, exercise your Siberian, just to take a little of the edge off. Your energetic, life-loving Siberian has a lot to occupy his mind. Start your practice in a quiet area where neither of you will be distracted. Train often but for short periods. I recommend about three times a day for 15 minutes each, but with a puppy, 5 minutes at a stretch is long enough. He has many things to think about!

Basic training requires only two items — a collar and a leash — both of which can be bought at your local pet supply store. And, although not absolutely necessary, a few small treats (like a little bit of carrot or a very thin sliver of cheese, not a whole dog biscuit) are always helpful.

To train without pain, begin by using a simple buckle collar. If it doesn't work, or the dog is a confirmed puller, you can ratchet up to a choke collar, or even, in extraordinary cases, to a prong collar, but there is absolutely no reason on earth not to begin as gently as possible. If you train correctly, a buckle collar may be all you ever need. Many people have the best luck of all with head-halter type collars, which let children walk even large dogs with ease.

If you do decide to use a choke collar with an older puppy or adult dog, put it on the dog correctly; otherwise it won't work or may even injure your dog. Make the collar into a "P," with the loop in your right hand, and the tail hanging straight down. Approach the dog from the front, and slip it on. The tail of the loop will now be on his right. Attach the lead, and keep the dog on your left.

Some Siberians have a problem with respect to their fur when wearing a choke collar; the guard hairs poke through and can be broken off. To prevent this from happening, you can make a cloth "collar wrapper" for the chain or you can buy a collar known as a Fur Saver, designed to protect against this problem.

If you are working with a young puppy, never use a choke collar; you can bruise or damage his windpipe, which in puppyhood is insufficiently protected by muscle.

Work on only one command at a time. If you get three correct responses from your puppy — three good "sits" or "downs" or "heels," for example — then it's time to call it a day. End all training sessions on a positive note. Go out and have fun together.

If your dog doesn't seem to be paying attention to your firm and repeated commands, try whispering. Your lower tone and distorted voice will tend to make your Husky look up, pay attention, and try to decipher what you're saying.

Agreeing on Commands

Keep your communication with your Husky simple. You'll never need to discuss Shakespeare with your Siberian. So make your commands short, clear, and consistent. For example, decide what the command for "come," will be. Don't say "come" one time and "here, boy" the next. Commands don't have to be one word each. Siberians are perfectly able to understand phrases and even to pick out important words within them. Just remember that, from your Husky's point of view, important words are more likely to be "ride" and "pizza" than "stay."

After your Husky understands what the command means, don't say the word more than once. This only teaches your dog that he doesn't have to sit or come the first time you give the command, and that's not the message you want him to get. Give the command once, and then wait. If he does not respond appropriately, quietly enforce the command the way you did when you were first teaching him. *Never* lose your temper with your dog.

As part of your own training, write down in your notebook every word you are using in your lessons, and what each word should mean to your dog. Put a star next to every command that your Husky reliably obeys. The point of the notebook is for you to keep track of how you are progressing in your lessons.

Commanding without words

You can also include whistles or gestures as part of your dog's vocabulary. Many people enjoy having their dogs respond to these cues in addition to verbal commands. You'll notice that your Husky will pick up some words, like *biscuit, ride,* or *bath* seemingly on his own, without any help from you, while other words, like *come,* seem to be beyond his capacity to understand.

Paying attention to your tone of voice

Try to cultivate two distinct tones when training your dog. First there's your bright tone: "Good girl!" and "Let's have a walk!" are all said in the bright tone. The dark tone, relying on the lower end of your vocal register, is reserved for "Bad boy!" and "Quit that!" Practice these assiduously. It's amazing how often people get them mixed up.

Using your dog's name

Never use your dog's name in connection with anything negative, like scolding or hauling him into the bathroom. Otherwise, he may not respond positively when you call him. He may not anyway, but there's no point in decreasing the odds.

Teaching Your Husky the Basics

Some things every dog must learn. So in the following sections, I fill you in on the most critical commands and how to teach them to your dog. Everything else is gravy.

I often add the word *please* to my commands. More for my own benefit than my dog's. Why? Because it reminds me to use a calm, pleasant tone of voice. This in turn calms and pleases the dog. When you're a team, attitudes are contagious. Saying "please" is not begging; it's only common courtesy.

"Come"

The most important command for any dog is "come." Unfortunately, it's also the hardest command for any dog to obey. Even the Siberian who will come instantly on command in the obedience ring may not do so outside if he has a decent chance of running fast and far in the other direction. And he doesn't need an excuse. Being free and unfettered is more than many a self-respecting Siberian can take.

If your Siberian does take off, it's not his fault. It's yours. Whack yourself on the head with a rolled up newspaper several times, and say, "I was told not to let him off the leash. I am bad. I am bad." Then go find your dog. Still, the command "come" can be taught so that your Siberian will be inclined to obey you even under trying circumstances. It is such a critical command that it should be the first one you teach. Your Siberian may escape from the house or slip his lead at any moment. You need at least a fighting chance of getting him back safely to you.

Many books tell how you can confidently train your dog to come to you every time without fail. These authors usually have Labrador Retrievers. Believe me, it is a rare Husky who will always obey. Don't take a chance on your dog's life. Keep him on a leash.

To increase your chance of success, you should always associate "come" with something *positive* for the dog. Reward him with a small treat or praise every time he approaches you. Don't call him to punish him, clip his nails, give him a bath, or anything else that he may regard as punishment, whether you mean it that way or not. Always praise your Siberian when he comes — even if you've been yelling at him to come for 15 minutes.

When calling your Husky, speak in a happy, cheerful voice, no matter how irritated you secretly are. If you punish your dog when he finally shows up, he thinks either, "Gosh, that must not have been the right response to that command after all," or, "Ha! Next time I'll know better. The next time she calls me, I'll just run away farther. She must think I'm stupid or something."

Begin training for "come" using a 10- or 12-foot lead attached to the dog. This way your Siberian will not even have the opportunity to disobey. If he moves in the wrong direction, pull gently on the lead to entice him to you. Then praise him.

Keep him on the lead until he responds eagerly every single time. If you have to pull to make him come, he is not ready for off-lead training. The single most common error people make is to overestimate their dog's obedience and take him off the lead too soon.

When you finally do begin off-lead training, make sure your dog is in a confined area (preferably the house) where you can easily retrieve him if he chooses to ignore your call or whistle. But don't punish him for an error. Reward him for correct behavior. Never praise or reward him until he comes all the way to you, right to your feet. Dogs are clever at knowing precisely how far your reach is.

You may want to use a whistle, clicker, or some other distinctive noise in addition to the "come" command. Dog whistles are useful aids. They have a far-carrying and distinctive sound. Of course, you may not be able to hear it yourself, so you won't know if it's working or not. It's one of those things you have to take on faith.

Positive reinforcement is a critical training tool, but it works best if you offer treats and effusive praise intermittently, even after the dog has learned the lesson. If you cease praising him after he's learned the behavior, he may revert to disobedient behavior in order to be rewarded, as in the old days.

"No!"

I never add the word *please* to *no,* because it sends the wrong signal. "No" means, "Immediately desist!" You may combine it with a reference to what he's doing wrong: "No chew!" means, "Stop eating that; it's my dress." Some people think that saying "no" is a severe punishment and should be used sparingly. But this isn't true; "no" is just a guide to correct behavior. Your dog will learn what it means and he won't hold it against you. If your dog is chewing something inappropriate, say, "No chew" and hand him something more acceptable. Then praise him. There's nothing to it, really. You will not confuse your dog or destroy his psyche.

Many pet owners have more trouble learning the meaning of "no" than their dogs do. When saying "no," don't betray your verbal command by your tone or body language. If you say "no!" but are really thinking, "Oh, that's so cute the way he ate my slippers," he'll know you don't really mean it. Next time he'll eat your hundred-dollar cross-trainers. If you say, "no beg," and then relent a minute later, he's not the one having trouble understanding what you're trying to communicate.

"No" is a mysterious word to dogs unless it is uttered immediately in conjunction with the forbidden behavior. You can't walk into a room five minutes after the doilies were devoured, shake one in his face, and shriek, "No! No!" He will probably think. "Gee, she's yelling 'No.' She should put that doily down."

"Sit"

"Sit" is the easiest of all commands to teach. Just push the Husky's rump to the ground while you say, "Sit, Icicle," in a firm encouraging way. If you want to use a treat, hold it up slightly above his eye level; this will encourage him to sit down. Praise him lavishly when he succeeds. Be careful to praise him as he sits *down,* and not as he starts to get up. When you want your Siberian to get up, give him a release command. I use the word *break.* Some trainers use *okay,* but because people use that word constantly in regular conversation, I think it's too easy for a dog to misunderstand it. You can even make up a secret word that will amaze all your friends.

But here's the problem with "sit": It's not a particularly useful command, unless you plan to do obedience, or for some reason you want the dog to take up less room. Most of the time, a quietly standing dog is just as good as a sitting one. People like to teach "sit" because it's easy, and they feel they have more control over a sitting dog than they do over a standing one.

Don't use "sit" to stop negative behavior, because that's not teaching a dog to halt the behavior. It's only reinforcing the "sit" command. Next time, he'll go right back to jumping up, or charging the door, or whatever, until you tell him to sit again. You can spend the rest of your dog's life doing that. "Sit" should just mean "sit" (for whatever reason) and not "quit it." When you want a dog to cease a behavior, teach him to cease that specific behavior. If you want him to stop doing something one time, say, "no."

"Stay"

Some trainers use a separate command for "stay," and others prefer to use "sit" for both actions. The philosophy behind "stay" is that the dog will antici-pate a longer wait period and not be so stressed. The theory behind using one command is that it's simpler for the dog, and teaches patience. I've seen both ideas put successfully into practice. You can also use "stay" with a standing dog. In any case, start small. It's unreasonable to expect your dog to stay for more than a few seconds at first.

Begin "stay" training by having your Husky stay in a corner. It reduces the number of major escape routes.

Gradually, you can increase the stay time. If he starts to get up, say "stay!" and shake the lead. Then put him back in position. Praise him as he responds correctly.

"Down"

Begin with the dog in a sit position. Say "down," and press against your Husky's withers. Or you can lure him down with a biscuit. If he tries to get up, lean against his shoulder until he resumes the down. Teaching "down" is a little easier when your dog is well exercised and perhaps even a little tired.

If your Husky resists lying down when you push his shoulders, you may have to pull his forelegs forward to get him into position. Praise him quietly after-wards. (Don't get too excited, or he'll get up.)

"Leave"

I use the "leave" command to remove my dogs from the kitchen, especially when we are cooking or dining. To teach "leave," take your dog's collar and remove him to the desired room. Then praise him. When he comes back, patiently say "Please leave," and repeat. Do this until he gets the message. You may use treats to explain what you mean.

Your Husky is perfectly capable of understanding the function of doorways. Soon he will leave any room when requested. My own dogs enjoy asserting their independence in this regard. They lie as close to the threshold as possible, usually placing one paw in the forbidden room and gazing in with a stricken look. But they stay out.

"Off"

"Off" means, "Get the heck off the couch, Blizzard!" You can also use "no," to make him get down, but "off" is more specific. It tells the dog exactly what you want him to do now. "Off" is a positive rather than a negative reinforcer. Besides, you can use "off" for other things, as a command for him to jump out of the back of the van and so forth.

"Give it" and "drop it"

These commands mean what they say, and they aren't identical. A well-trained dog knows both of them. After all, you may want him to give you the stick he has so unexpectedly retrieved for you, but you'd rather he would just drop the mouse he found. It's good practice for you to be able to remove anything your Siberian has in his mouth without a protest from him.

"Heel"

A correctly heeling dog is a pleasure to walk. The trouble involved in training him to move quietly at your side will be more than made up for later, when you are walking your Siberian with one hand and holding the baby/groceries/dog show trophy in the other. If you have a puppy, take heart. A puppy is much easier to teach to heel than an older dog is. A puppy naturally wants to come with you and has no bad habits to break — so far.

Use your 6-foot nylon or leather lead for training exercises. Nylon has a big advantage over leather; your Husky isn't quite so apt to chew it to pieces. On the other hand, if the Husky starts pulling on a nylon leash, you can get a serious rope burn. But then, your Siberian will never strain at the leash, because you will train him not do so.

Don't use a chain leash. They are too heavy and noisy.

If your dog works well on a regular collar, use that. The less control you need, the more pleasurable the exercise will be for both of you, and the better behaved you dog will ultimately be. You should be able to slip two fingers comfortably under the collar. If you must use a choke collar, adjust it correctly. Don't use a harness for training a dog to walk with you.

Don't wrap the leash around your hand. It's a less effective instrument that way. Besides, you could hurt your hand if the Siberian suddenly lunges at something.

Dogs traditionally are trained to heel at the left side of their owners, but there's no law about that. If you want your dog to heel on the right side, be my guest. Some left-handed people prefer walking their dogs on the right side. However, if you're planning on showing your dog in conformation or obedience, it's best to go with the flow and use the customary left side.

Begin by reaching out and touching your dog. He will probably look up at you expectantly, which is what you want. You must get him to pay attention to you, and keep his eye on you. Say, "Tundra, heel," and begin walking. Keep his chest in line with your knee. Do not allow him to lead with his nose.

The heeling exercise is not a potty break. Don't allow your Siberian to stop, lag, lunge ahead, or smell the roses while training. Every once in a while, after a successful heel, you can take a mini-break from training. Signify the break clearly by loosening the leash, while saying, "relax" or something similar. At these times, you can allow your dog to sniff about, but he should never be permitted to pull.

During a heeling exercise, stop at every curb. This is good practice for both of you. You do not want your Husky to get the idea that it's all right to run across the street.

When you are finished with the heeling exercise, loosen the lead completely, and say "break." This is the signal that your Husky may now sniff around and be dog-like.

Correcting forging in your Husky

Pulling at the lead is known as *forging*. It is a common trait among Siberians. Recall that the independent-minded Siberian is born to pull, and without your encouragement, he may not understand the difference between you and a sled.

Forging begins long before you have attached the lead to the collar. It begins when your Husky sees the lead. If you can't control him at this point, don't expect that the upcoming foray will be a walk in the park, even if it *is* a walk in the park. Have your Siberian sit or stand quietly while you attach the lead. Do not put the lead on while he's dancing around. Insist he remain calm. If he starts jumping around when the leash is on, take it off. Start again calmly. He will soon learn that the only way he's getting out the door is quietly. Otherwise, you will have a struggle on your hands before the walk even begins.

When your Husky starts to pull, turn the other way. Keep doing this. Don't use any pattern. This will focus his attention on you. Because no one likes to be pulled, he'll start paying attention to you, and trying to anticipate your moves. Say, "Heel," in a quiet firm voice as you turn.

Don't go around aimlessly turning, however, just in order to confuse the dog. Use those turns only in response to his pulling against you. Most of the time, Huskies can see the path and will walk along it of their own accord. This is true of sled dogs as well. They follow the trail they see.

You can also try walking backwards — this will make him stop to look at you. Do not allow your dog to pull you, ever. If you have to use an anti-pulling harness, do so, at least at first. The point is to break him from the habit of forging. (The opposite of forging is lagging. You will soon find that Huskies seldom lag.)

As your Husky's walking behavior improves, you can gradually loosen the lead so that you and he can take a pleasant stroll together without a struggle for leadership. When he is well-trained to heel, you can allow him to wander a bit on the lead, sniff about and so on. But when you say, "Heel, Snowbird," he should immediately resume correct heeling.

The leash is an extension of you. Never praise or treat your dog when the leash is taut. A taut lead indicates that your dog is resisting you and you don't want to reward that kind of behavior.

Sometimes, you may need a little mechanical help when you start training your dog to walk with you. This is especially true if you are working with an adult dog who has had no previous heel training, and you are not very strong.

The traditional choke collar may not work at all, because some dogs automatically throw themselves against it. This is called an *opposition reflex,* and yanking back has the opposite effect from what you want. Huskies are born to pull and their natural response is to pull back. Huskies are also amazingly adroit at snapping a choke chain.

A Siberian Husky can generate hundreds of pounds of force. If your Husky is a puller and you can't handle him, try one of the following as a supplementary training device:

✔ **No-pull harness.**

✔ **Halter.** Halters like Halti-collar, Gentle Leader, or Snoot Loop work well, attaching to the head of the dog. They work by steering the dog's head, and are both gentle and effective. They may be safely used in place of a regular collar. Many people prefer them, and they are especially useful when a child is walking the dog. Although it make take some time for your dog to get used to them, they are very effective and kind devices.

✔ **Self-correcting collar.** Another kind of collar, variously known as a *pinch, self-correcting, prong, spike,* or *German* collar, looks frightening, but really it isn't. Its action imitates the nipping a mother dog does to her puppies. *Remember:* The use of these collars is a signal that your dog is untrained and out of control. If you use one for more than a few days, you're doing something wrong.

Taking Advantage of Formal Obedience Training

You may decide that your Siberian is a little too much for you to handle by yourself, or perhaps you'd just like some more guidance. (This is fine — don't feel guilty or think that you've failed.) Maybe you're thinking of doing more advanced work someday, and want to get off on the right paw. All these reasons are good ones for working with a professional trainer.

Know what your goals are. Are you looking for a better pet, or do you plan to show your dog in obedience competitions? Find a trainer to suit your needs.

Finding a qualified trainer is not always easy. Unfortunately, no state requires licensing for dog trainers. Anyone who claims to be a dog trainer can be one, so far as the law is concerned. This means you have to do an extra thorough job of checking qualifications, experience, and recommendations. Ask whether your prospective trainer belongs to any trainers' organizations, and if so, which ones. Membership in one of these organizations is no guarantee, but it lets you know that your trainer is keeping up with the latest research.

Even the best general trainer may not be the perfect choice for your Siberian. Find a qualified trainer who is used to working with breeds other than obedience naturals like Border Collies and Labrador Retrievers. Your Siberian Husky needs special attention and responds to special training techniques (like treats) which are not used with standard obedience breeds.

Look for an instructor who will listen to you, and who uses positive rather than negative reinforcement techniques. Choose one who seems to like your dog, and vice versa. Training can be difficult enough without a personality conflict. Check with your veterinarian, breed club, or trusted friends who work with a trainer they like. Interview your trainer before committing to anything.

A good trainer will give you a price list and reasonable goals. She will give you and your dog homework to do. And she'll help you get results.

Chapter 9

Dealing with Dominance and Aggression

In This Chapter

▶ Knowing the purpose of dominance and aggression

▶ Recognizing common forms of aggression

▶ Preventing aggression in the first place

▶ Being prepared when encountering an aggressive dog

*I*n nature, dominance and aggression are not bad things. They're actually critical tools for the success of any predator, or indeed any animal, who lives in a social group. Within such a group, dominance and aggression play a useful part in sorting out domestic problems and deciding who will make important decisions for the pack. Today, professional dog trainers use a dog's natural dominant and aggressive tendencies to train guard and herding dogs.

Understanding Canine Dominance and Aggression

Aggression is normal. It's how dogs solve (or eliminate) conflicts. After all, dogs are not masters of witty repartee. Subtle revenge is beyond them. They have only a few ways of responding when someone asks them to do something they don't want to do. They can growl, snap, bite, run away, balk, or finally, submit.

In the human world, as opposed to the natural one, most kinds of aggression are distinctly undesirable. We don't want our dogs attacking each other, the family cat, or least of all — us. Nightmare visions of trips to the emergency room (or, even worse, to the courtroom) haunt us. Nor do we want our dogs to run away or turn stubborn. Instead, we want our dogs to submit to our requests. All this is just another way of saying that dogs must be trained to behave appropriately.

As humans in the human-dog partnership, our job is to encourage non-aggressive, non-dominant behavior in our dogs. We need to teach them to respond even to unwelcome attentions in an appropriate way — for us. Our beloved dogs have to conform to human expectations. This means never biting, snapping, or running away.

But the truth is that any dog may bite, given the wrong kind of stimulus, such as cruel or abusive treatment, pain, or even relentless teasing. If you never allow your dog to be subjected to this kind of treatment, he will have no incentive to resort to an extreme response.

But what about the dog who is never teased yet still seems headed for a life of aggression? Many aggressive dogs have never had a sharp word spoken to them in their lives, which may be the very source of the problem.

A dog is not a doll or an automaton; he is a complex living being. A single inappropriate behavior, like snapping, may have many different causes. Each cause needs to be carefully analyzed in order to figure out how to deal with it.

In the following sections, I guide you through some of the main types of dominance and aggression, so you can identify them in your own Husky and respond appropriately.

Relative dominance

All dogs are not born equal. And as much it may appall our egalitarian principles, one dog will be the *alpha* dog in your home — if you own more than one. The alpha dog is the one who will demand to be greeted first, eat first, go out the door first, and so on.

This *relative dominance* first develops in littermates at the age of about 4 weeks. Usually it is a self-limiting behavior. In other words, when you bring a new dog home, there may be squabbling among the housemates to discover who will be top dog. Usually the first dog in the home ends up becoming the alpha, but sometimes, if the new dog is used to being dominant and has a strong personality, you may have to prepare for a longer battle. Dominance squabbling most often occurs between dogs of the same sex.

Allow your Huskies to set up their own dominance order. You may find that older females will turn out to be the dominant dogs. Reinforce whatever hierarchy the dogs select (as long as you and all other human beings are first). Feed, greet, and pet the dominant dog first. This may seem unfair, but you'll be surprised how well it works. When a new dog joins the pack, everything will have to be sorted out all over again.

Dogs instinctively seek to know their place in the pack. If you upset the apple cart by trying to bring democracy to your household, you'll only confuse your dogs and promote continual infighting. The more submissive dog may think he now has a chance at dominance and try to assert himself. The dominant dog will merely try that much harder to remain the boss and attack the submissive dog. Let the dogs sort things out amongst themselves.

To help reduce canine household stress, make sure all dogs have equal access to food. (They will share water with no problem.) This means separate food dishes for each dog.

Rarely, relative dominance escalates into peer aggression, where one dog will continually attack other dogs. This type of aggression is fairly rare in Huskies, and when it does occur, it's usually limited to chasing or attacking smaller dogs (see the next section,"Predatory aggression"). Peer aggression is usually confined to intra-gender conflict — males attacking males, or females attacking females. You can intervene in peer aggression if a fight has not actually broken out. A dog fight is usually preceded by scuffling, noise, and even boxing behavior. If you can distract the dogs at this point by offering a walk or a treat, you may avert an actual fight. Don't yell; that only serves to excite the potential combatants.

If a dog fight breaks out, do not step in between the dogs, even if you think you won't be bitten. Your dogs are not in a normal state of mind when they're fighting. In most cases, no serious damage is being done, despite the shrieks and howls.

Throwing cold water on the fighting pair works with many breeds, but fighting Siberians respond better to a chair or some solid object thrust between them. You can also throw something at them or smack the instigator on the backside, just to get his attention. Speak loudly and sharply to the dogs, calling them by name, so they may recognize it is their master talking and they had better quit fighting. As a last resort, squirting the combatants in the eyes with vinegar or lemon juice works well.

Do not separate the dogs after the fight, especially if they are housemates. They must learn to get along, and crating one or both dogs will accomplish nothing. Instead, work with them together. Of course, when you have to leave them home alone, you must separate feuding dogs until you know they can get along.

You will have the best luck working with spayed or neutered dogs, especially in the case of males. Neutered males not only have a lower level of fighting hormones to make them more aggressive, but they also smell less male; hence they are less threatening to other males.

Sometimes neighboring dogs fight across a chain-link fence. If possible, conceal the dogs from each other by erecting a solid barrier. Better, introduce them to each other (unleashed) in a large area. Eventually they will probably become friends.

If you are walking your dog and come across another dog, the two dogs may exchange some threatening eye contact. Just keep your dog looking in a different direction and move along. If this behavior becomes a habit with your Husky, or if he's difficult to distract, use a Halticollar to keep him looking where you want him to.

Predatory aggression

Predatory aggression, evidenced by stalking behavior, is directed at instinctive prey animals, including chickens, cats, and smaller dogs. Predatory aggression is very common in Huskies, which is one reason why a Siberian must never be allowed to run loose. If your Husky happens to catch something, don't allow him to keep it. That only reinforces his hunting instinct. Remove the prey without comment (if you can pry it out of his jaws).

If you have both a cat and a Siberian, you must take strong precautions. Some Siberians are wonderful with cats, but most are not. At first, keep a short leash on the Husky so that you can restrain him if anything bad happens. The prey drive is a deep-seated instinctual behavior, which cannot reliably be trained out of Huskies, no matter what you do. Keep a Husky and a cat apart, unless they are under your direct supervision. Even Siberians who get along fine with the family cats will probably chase and try to kill strange cats.

If your Husky begins to show a little too much interest in the cat's movements, toss a small pillow, slipper, or some light, nearby object at him. Try to actually hit him, but not too hard, of course. Say, "No kill!" in a displeased voice, and give him something else to do. You may want to take the cat on your lap and pet him. Let your dog see that the cat is part of the family.

Closely related to predatory aggression is the *chase response.* In a simple chase response, pursuit is not carried out to its logical conclusion, which is to capture and kill the prey animal. The dog may only mouth or play with the captured prey. Cats and other small animals instinctively run when being chased, thus exciting the Husky further and encouraging his chase-response instinct.

Aggression toward people

Without doubt, aggression toward human beings is the most serious problem a dog owner can face. It's also a really serious and frightening event for the target of the aggression.

Animal aggression is a growing problem all over the country. Presently, reported dog bites are increasing at the rate of 2 percent annually. According to the American Veterinary Medical Association, almost 4.5 million dog bites occur in the U.S. every year, and 334,000 of them are serious enough to warrant emergency-room treatment. About 2 million children are bitten annually, half of them under the age of 12. In fact, half of all children 12 and younger have been bitten by dogs. Sixteen to twenty people (mostly children) are killed every year by "pet" dogs. In adults, most victims of dog bites are men (often postmen or deliverymen), and most biting dogs are owned by men as well.

Siberians are not usually aggressive. On the contrary, they are renowned for their friendliness. However, instances of Siberians who bite seem to be on the rise, and one recent survey listed them fifth among breeds in numbers of serious bites to humans. This is a disturbing trend, but the problem is not that Siberians as a breed have suddenly turned dangerous. More likely causes are the following:

- **Misidentification.** Many of these biting dogs were probably Malamutes, German Shepherds, or crossbreed dogs (including wolf-Husky hybrids), and not Siberians at all. Most people are notoriously bad at telling one breed from another, and Huskies sometimes get blamed for bites they had nothing to do with.

- **The phenomenal rise of popularity of the Siberian Husky.** From only a handful of registered Siberians in the 1940s and 1950s, the Siberian Husky now ranks 18th in number of AKC registrations. Naturally, there is a direct relationship between number of dogs and number of bites.

  The increased demand for Siberians makes it more likely that many will be coming from unscrupulous breeders who do not consider temperament when choosing breeding stock. It's also likely that the growing popularity of the breed has induced unsuitable people to acquire the Siberian as a pet. Dogs tend to behave like their owners. Aggressive, mean people tend to have aggressive, mean dogs. Because the Siberian looks "wolflike," some ignorant people think he should behave that way. If they abuse the dog, he can become mean.

- **Lack of socialization.** Many dog bites come from dogs who are tied up, left outside, and ignored by their owners. They get so little human contact that, when they do get it, they don't know how to respond. Siberian Huskies crave human companionship. When they have it, they are among the most loving of all breeds. When they don't, they tend to revert to more primitive behavior patterns.

Not all bites against human beings come from aggression, however. Factors like fear, pain, and overstimulated play-nipping may also play a part. Indeed, a combination of forces may be at work. Understanding why your dog is acting in a particular way is critical. Then you can attempt to cure the problem. In some cases, your dog may need professional help.

One major insurance company will not issue homeowner's policies to Siberian owners. (It also won't insure owners of Alaskan Malamutes, Staffordshire Bull Terriers, Bullmastiffs, Chow Chows, Doberman Pinschers, German Shepherds, or Rottweilers.) Many companies won't insure your home if your dog has a bite record.

Dealing with Dominance

Dominance and aggression can be related, although they don't have to be. Many strongly dominant dogs never think of biting. It's much more common for a dominant Husky to try to assert his dominance by stubbornness or refusal to yield to commands that he understands perfectly well.

The proper dominance-submissive pattern is that all humans are dominant over all dogs.

Dangerous dominant aggression against humans may surface when something happens in the family structure to upset that pattern. Perhaps there has been a divorce, or someone is in the hospital, or a family member has gone away to school. Dogs feel alterations in family structure as acutely as children do. They may experience stress from the change and try to fill the gap that has opened in the domestic leadership structure. Some dogs take advantage of the situation by becoming dominant, or, in rare cases, even aggressive towards a lower-status family member, usually a child. Unneutered males between the ages of 2 and 3 are most likely to express this kind of aggression.

Never allow aggressive behavior to go unchecked. No biting or aggressive behavior should be tolerated for any reason. If you make excuses for your dog, the situation will only get worse.

If your dog does bite a person, for any reason, do not physically punish the dog. Doing so will only add fear to the complex of factors that induced the bite and will increase the odds that the dog will bite again, especially if he has drawn blood. Professional training is required.

If your dog is bossy toward specific members of the family (usually women or children), those persons should take over feeding and training the dog. They need to communicate clearly to the animal that they are dominant over him. Obedience training is also essential.

Reward all signs of submissive behavior in dominant dogs, either with a treat, a pat, or playtime. Withhold these rewards unless the dog is behaving submissively.

After training

Some people think that after training, the dog is permanently cured. This is probably not true. A dominant dog always wants to be dominant and he will continually test his limits. He may regard any easing up of restrictions as an act of weakness on your part. Then you're back to square one. It's really better to be consistent, and maintain your alpha behavior.

Certain kinds of aggressive behavior respond well to drug therapy — antidepressants, sedatives and tranquilizers, hormonal therapy, or antianxiety drugs. The most effective psychoactive drugs are the selective serotonin reuptake inhibitors (SSRIs), such as Prozac and Zoloft, carefully administered in correct canine dosages. As the terms may suggest, SSRIs enhance the serotonin level in the brain, which in turn has a strong anti-aggressive effect on the dog's behavior. Although undoubtedly useful, these drugs should be combined with behavior modification training. (Prozac costs about $1.50 per day for a dog the size of a Husky.)

Trainers have also been experimenting with holistic remedies for aggression. Herbs like Saint-John's-wort, valerian, and hops have a soothing effect on dogs, and certain flower essences (snapdragon, for instance) may be useful in conjunction with training. Dietary changes, such as switching to a low-protein dog food with no additives, are helpful in some cases.

Lots and lots of exercise is important, if only because the dog becomes too tired to pick a fight. It also channels his energy into more constructive paths.

Dogs with a bite record need to be taken to a behavioral therapist qualified to work with aggressive dogs. This is a specialty — not all obedience trainers are certified to do this kind of work.

Recognizing Common Behaviors

In the following sections, I cover typical biting and nipping patterns, as a general guide. The remedies suggested, however, are not to be used in place of real professional training if your dog has or is developing a serious biting problem.

Playful nipping

Puppies frequently engage in play biting. Playing rough with one another is one of the ways they learn their limits. One of the things they learn is how hard they are allowed to bite without getting someone really angry at them. This schooling period usually occurs between the age of 5 and 8 weeks, which is one of the reasons it's important for a puppy to remain with his lit-termates that long.

This behavior is not true aggression; you will see young dogs wagging their tails and bowing to one another. In a natural extension, puppies usually attempt to carry play biting over to their human friends. And sometimes they nip hard. It never occurs to them that's it's not all right, so it's up to you to discourage the behavior. Puppy teeth are much sharper than adult teeth, although their jaws are weaker, which is a good thing.

Even though your puppy is only playing, you must not allow unrestricted play biting to continue, because it can escalate over time to more serious biting. And even if the puppy is not hurting you, a small child may perceive it differently.

A young puppy will often take your hand in his mouth. This is fine, so long as he doesn't clamp down on you with those wicked little teeth. As long as the pressure is light, all is well. He is merely telling you he loves you; you are telling him you trust him. But when you feel the teeth get uncomfortable, squeal "Ow!" in a hurt tone. He should withdraw his mouth. If he doesn't, snarl and give him a sharp tap on the nose until he does. It's important that *he* pull his mouth away from your hand, not vice versa. You must emerge as the victor, even from this silly game.

To halt actual nipping, grab the puppy by the nose or nape of his neck. Shake it, and growl sharply. "No bite!" (This behavior imitates what his own mother does.) Then walk away. He'll understand. Don't allow your children to play tug-of-war with him, either.

Do not use this nose-shaking technique with a dominant-aggressive adult dog, especially a new one. It can be dangerous, unless you are absolutely sure that the dog is only playing.

Fear-induced aggression

As the name suggests, *fear-induced aggression* occurs when the animal is afraid — usually of something new. Most fear-biters have experienced abuse at some time in their past; fear-induced aggression is common in rescue dogs. Fearful dogs often have a critical area, which, if intruded upon, may elicit a bite response.

A human head or hand close to the dog's face is especially threatening to a fearful dog. You can often cure fearful aggression by slowly desensitizing the dog to the frightening situation. Fearfulness dissipates with time in a loving and understanding home. Overprotection is not the answer, however. Your Husky must learn to cope.

Never corner a fear-biting dog. Allow him to come to you, and praise him, or even better, treat him when he does so. If he refuses to come to you, allow him to walk away. Don't move, however. After a while, approach him with a treat. Don't make a big deal of it. This is part of the desensitizing process; he needs to learn he has nothing to fear from you.

Some dogs fear certain kinds of people: males, people in uniform, people of a race different from their owner's. (In the latter case, dogs are more likely picking up clues from their owners. So examine your own attitudes and change them, for your own sake, and for your dog's.) The cure for this behavior is to have these people feed and pet the dog, so the dog learns there is nothing to fear.

Fear-biting hurts as much as any other kind of biting, and unfortunately, dogs who begin as fear-biters and go uncorrected can progress to more dominant biting patterns.

Territorial aggression

Territorial aggression arises from a dog's natural tendency to protect his area. Interestingly, many dogs who are not territorial in an open area become so when a fence is erected around their property. Along the same lines, the bigger the dog's area, the less aggression you are likely to see. This kind of aggression is very rare in Siberians, but it may develop, especially if the dog senses you are proud of him for his guarding behavior.

Food or toy guarding

In some ways, guarding is a form of territorial aggression, but it's keyed to objects rather than to area. Guarding is more common in Siberians than territorial aggression is. Guarding of food or toys can be dangerous behavior. Your dog should surrender any toy or even his food to you if you ask him. He may not want to do this and may play keep-away with his toy, but any growling must not be tolerated.

If your dog starts to display this kind of behavior, you must reinforce your alpha position. Make your dog watch you while you pour the food into his dish. If he has shown dominant behavior, pretend to eat some yourself first. Have him sit or stand away from the bowl, and do not allow him to approach it until you give him the signal that it's okay.

Stand near him and pet him while he eats. Practice picking up his bowl while he is eating, and giving it back a few seconds later.

With both toys and food, you can also try trading with him. Take away his toy or food, but offer him a preferred treat instead. When he learns to accept the fact that he'll get something in return, he'll be more likely to give up what he has. After a time, you can time the rewards to be more sporadic. Don't reward him every time, but only every third or fifth time. Take your time about this. When you begin this swap-training, start with taking away objects in which he has little interest. Only gradually work up to the food bowl or favorite toy.

Food and toy guarding, if left uncorrected, can worsen over time, as the dog acquires a larger and larger conception of what constitutes food or toys. Sometimes a dog will allow the person he views as his master to take away toys, but no other member of the family. This attitude must be corrected. *All* human beings should be alpha over *all* family dogs.

Pain-induced aggression

An injured dog may think that he can eliminate the pain by attacking what he believes is the source of his discomfort. A bite in this situation is really done in self-defense.

I was bitten rather badly by a dog who had been struck by a car. It was necessary for me to remove him at once from the site of the accident, and in the process, the poor creature bit me. One could hardly blame him.

In a few instances, it appears that aggression can originate from tumors, painful skeletal misalignments, or other serious conditions.

A family dog who snaps suddenly while he is being moved or petted may be suffering an injury. Take him to the vet for a thorough checkup.

A dog's face, ears, and rectal area are very sensitive to pain. Take particular care around these areas.

Irritable aggression

Irritable aggression is the mark of an old, grouchy, tired, or generally grumpy dog. Sometimes it's related to pain. Children are often the victims of this form of aggression, because they sometimes don't know enough to leave the animal in peace. Irritable aggression is usually controlled by leaving the dog alone. However, if you have small children, or if the dog tolerates no interference at all — for example, not allowing children on the couch with her — you have a more serious problem. See your veterinarian for suggestions. Tranquilizers or finding an all-adult home may be an option.

Maternal protectiveness

Although, strictly speaking, maternal protectiveness may be regarded as a kind of aggression, it is a common, hormonally-based behavior. We all understand that the mother wishes to protect her young, but she should not be exhibiting serious aggression toward her human family. Similar behavior may be associated with a false pregnancy. If a female dog suddenly begins acting in a protective or aggressive manner, it may be because she thinks she has young to protect.

Bitches prone to false pregnancies should be spayed. They not only tend to have behavior problems but are also subject to *pyometra,* a severe uterine infection.

Genetically based aggression

A few dogs are just born aggressive. In Siberians, it could be a genetic anomaly caused by inbreeding. Genetic aggression manifests itself at an early age by deep belly growls and an uninhibited bite response — usually by the age of 4 months. This form of aggression cannot be trained out of a dog. Aggression is a dominant trait, which makes it common; however, this also means it can easily be bred out of a strain. Breed nonaggressive dogs to non-aggressive dogs, and bingo, the dominant gene disappears.

Aggressive tendencies can be passed along in the gene pool. A puppy whose parents have exhibited aggressive behavior is more likely to do so himself. This is another reason why you should know as much as possible about your dog's relatives.

Environmental aggression

Toxins in the environment are suspect in certain cases of aggression, and some dogs have an allergic response to vaccines that can lead to aggression. If you've ruled out other possible causes of a dog's aggression, consider environmental aggression as a possibility and discuss it with your vet.

Establishing Your Dominance

If your dog exhibits symptoms of dominant behavior but has *not* bitten anyone, you can attempt to correct the situation yourself. However, if you are at all doubtful about your abilities to handle the situation, find a good animal behaviorist to work with your dog. (If your dog has bitten anyone aggressively, you absolutely must get professional help for him.)

Dominance always escalates if not controlled, because the dog's bite threshold is lowered with each uncontrolled bite.

Keep a short leash on a dominant dog when you are home; let him drag it around with him. If he exhibits incorrect behavior, you'll have a safe handle to grab him by.

Begin corrective training early. The longer you allow your Husky to feel he's in charge, the more difficult it will be to teach him otherwise. You are not being cruel to your dog; you're doing him a favor. Dogs are hierarchical creatures, Huskies more so than most.

Here are some general tips to establish your dominance:

- Never let your puppy nip or bite at you, even while playing.
- If you feel challenged, stare coolly at your Husky. Don't look away before he does. It is the alpha's prerogative to initiate staring.
- Decide when games begin and end. Make sure *you* end up with the toys.
- Don't play tug-of-war. If it happens by accident, make sure you win.
- Keep the dog off the sofa and bed. Dogs equate being high up with being boss.
- Practice giving and taking food away from your Husky. He should accept your right to do so without complaint.
- Initiate petting on your own. Don't let yourself be nudged into it.
- Have your Husky obey a command like "sit" before you feed, pet, or play with him. To establish yourself as alpha, make sure he works for everything he gets.
- Reserve your praise for something done really well, on command. Don't lavish him with praise, however, because you want him to keep trying.
- Neuter your male dog. Unneutered male dogs are three times as apt to bite as altered ones.

TIP

You didn't hear it from me

There's another technique that sometimes helps establish dominance, but it will only work for men. If you have the energy, privacy, and, most importantly, shamelessness (and if you drink enough coffee or other liquids), you can arrange to have one of those little contests with your Husky where you follow him around your privately fenced yard and, whenever he urinates, well, so do you. The important thing is to be the last one peeing. That makes you the winner. If this sounds ridiculous, it probably is. But I have it on good authority that it really works. Under no circumstances allow anyone to see you, and don't tell anyone about it either.

With a dominant dog, continually reinforce the concept that you are alpha. If your Siberian is lying across your path, move him aside gently with your foot. Do not walk around him. If he is sitting in your favorite chair, move him out of it. Don't get a chair from the kitchen for yourself because your dog has taken your seat. Don't let him walk through a door before you do. Feed yourself before you feed him. Make sure he allows you to touch or remove his food.

Avoiding Dog Bites

Approach a strange dog slowly, even if he appears friendly. Your hand should be outstretched, your fingers curled into a fist (not to punch the dog, of course, just so your fingers won't get nipped). This approach allows the dog time to sniff the hand and acknowledge you.

If the dog does not appear friendly, keep your hands to your sides and do not approach. Move quietly to the side without turning your back on the animal. Do not attempt to make eye contact with the dog. If attacked by a dog, curl up into a tight ball and remain as still as possible. Do not run away — you will only excite the dog's chase instinct.

WARNING!

Do not disturb a sleeping dog; an unexpected embrace can trigger a snap before the dog is even awake. Let sleeping dogs lie.

The same holds true for dogs who are eating; they should not be bothered. It's one thing to work with your dog while he's eating; it's another to suddenly race up and snatch away the dog's dish. This kind of behavior is enough to make even a well-behaved dog peevish. Teach your children all these tips as well.

TIP

Be sure you carefully watch your children's friends with your Husky as well. Even if *your* child is perfect, your neighbor's kids probably aren't.

Chapter 10

Breaking Bad Habits in Your Husky

*M*any of the canine activities that we human beings term *behavior prob-lems* are either normal canine activities that we find inconvenient, a result of a dog being left alone too long with insufficient natural stimulation, or an organic disorder. In no case are they forms of revenge exercised by your dog to get back at you.

If your Siberian is doing something wrong, you need to discover why. Only when you know the cause can you properly address the problem and channel your dog into more socially acceptable behavior.

Correct training can help you redirect negative behaviors into harmless or even beneficial activities. But it takes work, and serious cases may require a professional dog behaviorist.

Chewing, running, howling, and digging are natural dog activities. They stem from the ancient, ancestral urge to get food and shelter. But in the lonely, bored, or overstressed Siberian, these habits, natural as they may be, can become intolerable for you or your neighbors. You can respond to an unwanted behavior pattern in one of six ways:

✔ Change your behavior.

✔ Change your dog's behavior.

✔ Build a higher fence, get earplugs, confine the dog, and so on.

✔ Medicate the dog.

✔ Medicate yourself.

✔ Get used to it.

One size does not fit all. The cure you choose depends on the target behavior, its cause, and your patience.

According to one recent survey, Siberian Huskies rank fifth among dog breeds in destructive behavior. They follow West Highland White Terriers, Irish Setters, Airedale Terriers, and German Shepherds. Like these breeds, Siberians are energetic and highly intelligent dogs; much of their destructive behavior stems from perfectly reasonable causes. They do not chew or destroy furniture to get back at you. Dogs simply do not think that way. They are not vengeful. The message they are sending is, "I am sad and lonely." Or, "I am bored out of my skull." Or, "I am ill." It's not, "I hate you." In some cases of destructive behavior, the message is often simply: "I want your attention."

In this chapter, I guide you through some of the more common behavior problems in Siberian Huskies (and dogs in general), and let you know your options for responding. Only you (with the help of your vet) can ultimately decide what is best for your dog. But with the information in this chapter, you'll be armed with the knowledge you need to make an informed decision.

Separation Anxiety

Fear and loneliness combine to create many destructive behavior patterns. Experts think that 20 to 40 percent of dog behavior problems can be directly linked to separation anxiety. Dogs are pack animals by nature, and among dogs, no breed is more pack-oriented than the Siberian. Huskies simply detest being alone.

If you think your dog suffers from separation anxiety, he's not alone; it's estimated that 7 million dogs in America are keeping him company. A dog with severe separation anxiety may begin to salivate in terror the minute he thinks you are leaving; he may cringe and whimper. I knew one who would slink along the wall in a crouched position, whining the entire time. Separation anxiety is especially common in dogs who have been rescued from shelters or who have been moved from home to home. Dogs who have noise phobias (thunder, vacuum cleaners, and the like) also seem disposed toward separation anxiety.

Sensitize yourself

In his native land, the Siberian spent every day, all day, working alongside his human companions, which is what he was bred for. Don't blame your dog if you couldn't get a job as a sled driver. Be more sensitive to his needs. The best thing you can do to help a dog suffering from separation anxiety is to provide your Siberian with more of what he likes best — your company, or failing that, the company of other dogs.

Get up a little earlier than you have to and spend some time with your dog. Play with him, run with him, brush his teeth. He deserves more than a "Nice boy, here's breakfast, see ya in ten hours."

If you can, let your dog sleep in your bedroom with you. He'll enjoy your company even while you're asleep.

Or try bringing your dog into work with you once in a while. I did this for years, under the pretext that the animal was having medical problems and needed frequent medical attention. Well, it was sort of true.

The American Animal Hospital Association conducted a survey and found that 24 percent of dog owners take their canines to work with them, at least once in a while. A well-behaved dog relieves stress on the job and reduces blood pressure all around. Of course, if the dog eats the contract for your next big deal or pees on the office palm tree, you may be out of a job.

Desensitize the dog

Start desensitizing your dog to being left alone. You can't take your dog with you to the opera, but being able to leave him alone for a few hours without returning to a war zone isn't an unreasonable expectation.

Don't make a big fuss about either departing or returning. Pay no attention to your dog for about 15 minutes or so before you leave. Avoid even looking at your dog, strange as that may sound.

Prepare to leave, but don't actually do so. Do this several times a day, and soon your Husky won't necessarily associate you getting out your purse with being left alone.

Gradually lengthen the time that he's left home alone. Get him used to the idea of you being away. At first, leave and come back within a minute or two. Give him a toy as you depart, and collect it upon your return. Soon, he'll understand that you'll always return, and he won't become destructive.

Most people make the mistake of not being gradual enough in their separation training. If your dog behaves well for one hour alone, do not assume he can be safely left for eight hours. Increase his periods alone by only 15 minutes a time.

Crating your dog helps create a sense of security for him, and even if it doesn't, while he's in the crate you know he won't be chewing the furniture. It's not safe to leave a Husky under 4 months alone free in the house; he simply does not have the psychological poise to keep from ripping things into shreds. Crate or kennel him. Don't leave him in the crate for more than four hours, however.

Medicate the dog when necessary

The U.S. Food and Drug Administration recently approved the first behavioral drug designed specifically to treat separation anxiety in dogs. It's called *Clomicalm* (clomipramine hydrochloride) and comes in pill form. Clomicalm is a godsend for those people whose dogs do not respond to conventional behavioral therapy alone. It is neither a sedative nor a tranquilizer, and it won't change your dog's personality. It *will* calm him down and enable him to learn positive behaviors more easily, all for about a dollar a day.

Clomicalm is designed to be used along with good training; it's not a replacement. Owners who have used Clomicalm have noticed an improvement in their dogs in about a month. Although a few dogs will have to remain on Clomicalm permanently, most can be weaned off the drug in three to six months.

Digging

Siberians are born diggers. Their arctic heritage tells them that digging a hole in the snow is a fine way to keep warm and that digging in the moist ground is a good way to keep cool. They have also apparently found out that digging in the sofa is a great way to be comfortable.

Indoor digging probably indicates that your dog is bored. Or that he's lonely and wants to be with you. In elderly dogs, digging in the carpet can be a sign that they are too hot or cold. Older dogs may try to use the carpet to help regulate their body temperature for this reason.

If your Husky is pawing at the floorboards, he may be trying to tell you that you have a rodent problem. Call an exterminator.

If your Siberian is digging outside, observe the digging pattern. It's possible, of course, that your Husky is just burying a bone, but probably not. Random holes dug all around the yard indicate your Husky is not getting sufficient exercise. Holes dug in the vicinity of a fence could indicate his desire to escape. Holes dug in moist garden soil suggest that your dog is too hot; he's merely looking for a place to cool off. Siberians may also be hunting for moles or mice. In their enthusiasm for this sport, more than one Siberian has dug up a yellow jacket nest.

To discourage your dog from re-digging an outdoor hole, put a few pieces of carefully selected dog feces in the hole. Siberians know that dog feces should remain covered.

Some people recommend filling a hole with water and shoving the dog's head in it to make him stop. This cruel practice will not work; in fact, it will only terrify him or make him defiant.

If your Siberian digs near the fence line, take the hint and bury the wire a few inches underground. And keep checking it to make sure he can't escape.

You can also confine your Husky to a safe area, but let him dig. Give in to the Siberian's desire to mine dirt. Get a sandbox, and put it in an area that gets lots of afternoon shade.

Interact with your dog in positive ways, grooming, playing Frisbee, going for a hike — any activity to work off his excess energy. If you need help, rent or borrow a neighborhood child. They're always eager to play with dogs!

Chewing

Siberians are chewers, especially when they are young. All puppies are oral, using their mouths to investigate new things. Your dog may go right to the new pillow you've just brought home and chew it to pieces, even though he's never bothered the old ones. So, let him become well-acquainted with the new item before you leave him alone with it.

Don't punish your dog for having chewed something inappropriate. It's a temptation to hit the roof when you come home to find your living room in shreds, but doing so will only make your Husky associate your return with something awful. He has no idea why you're angry with him. Dogs must be caught in the act to make the connection between inappropriate behavior and your displeasure. Sometimes you need to manufacture a situation where you can correct your Siberian immediately.

Understanding why dogs chew

Unfortunately, many dogs regard any attention as better than no attention. Not responding to negative behavior with negative attention will take some self-control on your part. But you must resist the urge. Remove the target item (or the dog) with the minimum amount of fuss. Give him plenty of loving attention when he is behaving himself, not when he's being a nuisance.

Your Siberian may be also be teething, and chewing helps relieve his discomfort. A few ice cubes are a good chew toy at teething time. In addition to giving the pup something to crunch, ice has a numbing effect on his sore gums. You can even freeze or chill any of your pup's regular toys, or use a cold, rolled-up washcloth. Siberians like the cold anyway; it may remind them of their roots.

If your older Husky suddenly begins chewing, he may have dental or upper gastrointestinal difficulties. This problem is definitely one that needs to be addressed, because the chewing can become habitual, even after the initial problem goes away.

If your dog is not on a regular feeding schedule, his instincts tell him to hunt for food wherever it may be. He may be eating the sofa because he's hungry. If your work prevents you from getting home at the same time every day and you have a couch-cruncher, consider getting a pet-sitter or using a self-feeder.

On the other hand, if your Husky starts devouring a large number of items that are not food, he may have a condition called *pica*. If you suspect this condition, check with your veterinarian.

Maybe your dog is plagued with existential angst or ennui. More so than almost any other breed, Siberians crave companionship, human and canine. A bored Siberian is a destructive Siberian.

I once got a letter from a dog who had this tale to tell: "I was forced to chew up three remote controls, two pairs of gloves, a valuable textbook, and a watch before my slovenly owner learned to put her things away properly. She was a slow learner, but eventually, with positive reinforcement (I would lick her face as she stooped to pick up the chewed articles), she got the message."

Curing chewing

Remember, it's normal and natural for dogs to chew. If you see your dog chewing something inappropriate, substitute something better, without fussing about it. When your puppy begins to chew the chair leg, offer him another favorite toy, and praise him when he accepts it. Young dogs are particularly prone to digging and chewing; a chewing frenzy often develops between the ages of 6 and 10 months. It may subside and then peak again at about 18 months. As dogs grow older, most become less apt to chew things.

Try to exercise your Husky before leaving him alone. If he's pleasantly tired, he'll be less likely to chew or dig.

I heard of one Siberian who destroyed all the linoleum in the laundry room when he was left alone for ten minutes. Locking dogs in small areas is almost bound to result in destructive behavior if your Husky is not crate-trained.

Confining your dog in a windowless area increases his destructive propensities. Dogs should be able to look out the window; they get endless amusement spying on the neighbors, just like we do. Provide toys in his confinement area as well.

Most of us have to be away from our dog for at least a few hours every day. To keep your Siberian company, try leaving the television or radio on. As far as music choice goes, it's up to you, but my experience has shown that elevator music has a stupefying effect on dogs — not a bad idea in the case of Huskies.

Preventing chair chomping

A variety of bitter-tasting sprays and foams (including the widely used Bitter Apple) are available to stop a dog's destructive chewing. Tabasco sauce also works nicely. So do deodorant, mouthwash, and cheap perfume. (Finally, a use for that cologne Cousin Mildred sent you last Christmas.) A product called Protex is designed to keep dogs from chewing fabric — or their own fur.

However, preventive products like Bitter Apple are at best temporary remedies. You can't expect to go around for the rest of your days spraying Bitter Apple on all your possessions. The only surefire cure to chewing is steady, consistent training, or separation of dog and valuables.

Some anxiety-reducing drugs, like Clomicalm, can help immensely in reducing your dog's anxious tension and the destructive behavior that accompanies it. I recommend these only as a last resort, but they have produced some excellent results. Like Bitter Apple, they should supplement, and not replace, training.

You can also stop a dog from jumping on the couch by covering the furniture with soda cans partially filled with marbles or coins. There's also a product called Snappy Trainer, which has the effect of mousetraps without the potential danger. You can even buy no-jump plastic strips that make a noise when your dog steps on them. A product called Scat creates static pulses (at various levels) to make your pet uncomfortable when he gets on the couch. Or you can always keep the Husky out of the room.

Counter-Cruising

In the dog trade, stealing food off the kitchen counters is referred to as *counter-cruising*. It's a habit that gets worse in the winter — probably a holdover from the Siberian's arctic past. The bitter weather triggers a "food-now-at-any-price" response.

Although some people have good success battling this behavior by placing noisy mousetraps and other anti-nosing-around items on the counter, most people rely on good old management techniques. Never leave anything juicy on the counter when you're not there to watch it.

Some Huskies can learn to open refrigerators. I know two people who have had to put chains and padlocks on their refrigerators to keep the contents inside.

Leslie Anderson of Oklahoma City reports that she and her husband discovered a perfectly good, frozen turkey, still wrapped, on the interstate. Never one to pass up a free meal, Leslie's husband snatched up the turkey and brought it home. The turkey was promptly dubbed "Skidmark" and left in the sink to defrost. Shadow, Leslie's heretofore completely well-behaved Siberian, somehow managed to amputate a leg, thigh, and breast from Skidmark, hoping no one would notice. Shadow was scolded and put out in disgrace. On her return, she devoured a pecan pie and a quiche left on the table. Skidmark was discarded. "Poor Skidmark," sighs Leslie. "Even in death it was a tough life."

Trash Dumping

Related to food-stealing is trash dumping. Because dogs are scavengers, a loaded trash can is hard for them to resist. If your dog is considering a career in Solid Waste Dispersal, get a trash container with a lid and foot pedal, or keep the trash can somewhere where he can't get to it. You can hide the trash basket under the sink, behind the cellar door, or in some other Husky-proof place.

If you feed your Siberian from the table or allow him to beg during meals, you are essentially inviting him to help himself. Don't blame him if he grabs something while you're not looking. You have taught him everything he knows.

If you actually catch your Siberian in the act of stealing food or trash dumping, you can try squirting him with a mixture of water and lemon juice or vinegar. Say, "No!" firmly at the same time, so he doesn't think you're just playing with him.

Running Off

Siberians are tremendous escape artists. They can slip collars, break chains, and dissolve into the mist. And once they escape, they tend to stay gone.

Siberian Huskies are also runners by nature. Running is bred into every bone in their bodies. They were born to run long and hard (and pull a sled while doing so). Siberians run in a very fast, straight line in the opposite direction from you. This doesn't mean he's running away. He's just running off.

JUST FOR FUN

Take it from a veteran

Lois Leonard, who describes herself as owner, trainer, handler, and friend of a Siberian named Lojan's Very Special Sula told me an interesting tale. Sula was more than the average obedience champion. In fact, in her nine years of competition, she earned 248 qualifying scores in AKC obedience. She won 18 area Specialty High in Trials, 2 National Specialty High in Trials, and 3 all-breed High in Trials. This achievement earned her the title of OTCH (Obedience Trials Champion), an honor won by only two Siberians in history.

Guess what? Obedience Trial Champion Lojan's Very Special Sula, Canadian C.D.X, Schutzhund A.D., took off from Lois when the dog was 15 years old and stone deaf. She darted across the road after another dog, while Lois screamed uselessly after her (after all the dog was deaf). Sula wasn't struck by a car, but she easily could have been. As Lois says, "You will never be able to trust a Siberian, *any* Siberian, off lead in an unfenced area. *Never.*" It's as simple as that.

A Siberian Husky can run so fast that he may be 20 miles away before he wonders what happened to his owner. By then it's too late. Although Siberians are truly excellent at running off, they are not nearly so good at finding their way home again.

To keep your Husky in, you must build a secure fence, preferably one 6 feet high. A few Siberians have been known to scale fences as high as 8 feet. You may have to deter a serious climber with a hot wire placed low to the ground.

The best fences are made of wood and wire. If you have a digger, bury the fence in the ground deeper than the Siberian can dig. Unfortunately, some of them can dig pretty deep. Most Siberians seem to dig more for the joy of digging than as an escape plan.

Although many people swear by the so-called invisible electronic fence, it is far from Husky-proof, particularly if you own more than one Husky. The call of the wild is very strong in Siberians. Some Huskies will charge through an invisible fence, shock or no shock. Furthermore, the radio-control collars often don't work well on the heavily-furred Siberian, so you may have to shave the dog's hair to use the collar effectively.

WARNING!

After your Husky has broken through the electronic fence, he will not be anxious to charge back in. And if there is a power failure or the battery goes dead, he'll soon be out of your yard. Invisible fencing doesn't keep predators (human or animal) out of the yard, so if you're relying on it to control your dog, you're inviting a dog fight. Huskies are a highly prized, frequently stolen breed, partially because they are so friendly, and innocent of the intentions of dog-nappers. Be forewarned.

 Electronic fences may be suitable for large areas if you are outside playing with your Husky. They are also useful for containing small areas inside your yard. If you keep him busy, he will probably not challenge the fence.

Having a yard, however, is no guarantee that your Husky will actually use it to exercise in. More than likely, he'll spend quite a bit of time sitting at the back door waiting to be let in. Regular walks or supervised play are very important for all dogs, and the exercise will make your Siberian less bored and more tired — hence more anxious to escape.

In short, you cannot train a Siberian to stay at home. He is not a guard dog or a Retriever. Nor can you train a Siberian to stay reliably by your side as you walk along; you must keep your Husky on a leash at all times.

Hunting Other Animals

Siberians have a strong hunting instinct. Given a chance, they may kill chickens, strange cats, rabbits, and groundhogs. Some have even been known to kill lambs or calves.

Because hunting is instinctive in Siberians, it cannot be trained out of them, at least not completely. Although some Huskies are totally uninterested in hunting anything, many more are passionate about it. It is your responsibility to keep your Siberian away from livestock and neighbors' pets. Do not expect your neighbors to take extraordinary precautions to keep your dog away from their livestock. That's your job.

Charging the Door

You're just ready for work. You are loaded down with your briefcase, lunch bag, and a plant for one of your coworkers. You struggle cautiously with the door, fearing the worst. And then *pow!* Before you know it, the Siberian has crashed by, knocking the plant, the contract, and the egg salad sandwich to the floor in a smashed mess. He's also ripped your nylons and slammed your face against the wall on his way out.

Obviously, you must put a stop to this behavior. But if charging the door is an already established pattern, it may take some time to correct. You will also need to enlist the help of everyone in the family, especially the children. Children are the most likely culprits in the behavior getting started in the first place. They are also the chief victims of it.

Never attempt to open a door or gate while your dog is crowding you. Stop short, and whirl around, facing your Siberian. Speak in your firmest voice, and hold your hand right in front of his face, nose-level. Use your leg or whole body if necessary to prevent his getting by you. Say, "Wait!" or "Stay!" Begin to open the door, *very* slowly. If your Siberian makes a move toward the door, slam the door shut, shake the dog's collar firmly, and repeat your command. You and your family need to practice this routine several times a day at every door in the house to put a halt to this undesirable and dangerous behavior.

Never allow your Siberian to go out the door before you do. Alphas go first. And you are the alpha.

Jumping Up

The Siberian's friendliness may evidence itself in a great, not always appreciated, Siberian hug. He is leaping up on you. And why? For one reason: to get your attention.

To cure this behavior, you need to enlist the help of friends and family alike. Never allow your friends to say, "Oh, it's okay, I don't mind if he jumps." They may not mind, but your 87-year-old great-aunt may be less appreciative. A strong dog like a Husky can seriously injure an older person or a child just by expressing his love too exuberantly.

Do not greet your Husky until he is sitting or standing quietly. Keep your greetings low-key and he will imitate your behavior.

The simplest method to stopping your dog from jumping up is to ignore the dog. Fold your arms, look away, and say, "No." Greet your dog only when he is quiet and sits down. The theory is that, because your dog is trying to get attention, he will cease the unwanted behavior when attention is withdrawn.

If the dog jumps up, grab his front paws and hold them up. Keep him up. Do not let him down. This is uncomfortable for the dog, and he'll soon try desperately to get away. Hang on to him a few minutes, neither praising nor scolding him. Then relent and let him down. The theory is that he will soon desist jumping, because of the negative consequences. Be careful not to step on the dog's toes or you could inflict serious injury.

You can also try getting down and letting your Husky see your face without his having to jump up to reach it. It is natural for him to want to lick your face; it's the way his mother taught him when he was a puppy. So even if you don't let your dog kiss you, allow him to get close. Just remember that this technique may not prevent his leaping up on guests.

Some people recommend kneeing the dog in the chest. But not only have I not found this to be successful, it can also hurt your dog if you're not careful.

Don't allow your Husky to jump up on you when you have old clothes on and then expect him to stay down when you're dressed up. A dog really can't tell the difference between your around-the-house clothes and your Sunday best.

Whatever technique you use, save your praise until all four of the dog's feet are on the ground. This takes some critical timing, but it's absolutely essential.

Part IV
Keeping Your Husky Healthy

In this part . . .

Part of owning a dog is knowing how to take care of him. After all, your Husky is completely dependent upon you for his well-being. So in the chapters in this part, I fill you in on all you need to know about your Husky's health. You'll get tips on everything from feeding and grooming, to finding a good vet and responding to health problems if and when they arise. Illness and accident aren't things any of us like to think about, but in this part you'll figure out how you can help your Siberian make it through even the most dire of situations with quick thinking and the appropriate response.

Chapter 11

Feeding Your Husky

More ink has probably flowed over the issue of nutrition than any other single canine topic. Commercial dog foods versus homemade; raw versus cooked; people food versus dog-only food; bones versus no bones; chicken wings versus no chicken wings; supplements versus no supplements — all have stirred dog fanciers to varying degrees of frenzy. The good news is, you can *relax*. Dogs are scavengers by nature and can survive and thrive on a remarkable variety of foods. A good commercial dog food will probably satisfy your Husky's nutritional needs. And just being aware of what's out there and talking with your vet about your options is really all you need to do.

Knowing Your Husky's Nutritional Needs

One big controversy concerning canine nutrition is over whether your dog should remain on one dog food or whether he should consume a variety of different foods. Some nutritionists claim that the canine system does better when it stays on one complete food and that switching around could be upsetting to the digestive tract. They compare a dog to a finely-tuned car, saying that when you find the right brand of gas with the right octane, there's no point in changing. Some people also maintain that switching dog foods can make a dog finicky.

Others, citing the fact that dogs are natural scavengers, believe that dogs enjoy variety and even thrive on it. They argue that, because we don't yet know everything about canine dietary requirements, changing a dog's diet occasionally is actually safer, because it increases the chances that he's getting what he needs. These proponents of the "variety is the spice of life" school think dogs are a lot closer to humans than they are to cars. And I agree.

My own seven dogs eat a little dry food, a little canned food, and a lot of people food. And I have never had a dog with cancer, bloat, hip dysplasia, or hypothyroidism. Now, this *could* be coincidence. But I believe that dogs like and need a variety of different foods, both for their spiritual and their physical well-being.

Original dietary requirements for dogs were developed in the 1940s by the National Research Council of the National Academy of Science. Since then, the responsibility for setting canine dietary requirements has shifted to the Association of American Feed Control Officials (AAFCO).

This is what we know about canine nutrition: Like human beings, your dog needs the following components in his diet: protein, fat, minerals, water, and carbohydrates. I cover each of these in the following sections.

Protein

Proteins contain the important amino acids that mammals need to grow and keep in good repair. Dogs need more protein than people do. Although no optimum level has been established, even 30 percent of the total calories in their diet is not too much protein.

Siberians do not do well on soybean-derived protein; it can cause colic and diarrhea. Meat protein is usually considered best; a dog's diet should be about 75 percent meat and the rest vegetables (not grain).

Fat

Fat is not bad for Working Dogs; on the contrary, it's an important energy source. Omega-3 and omega-6 fatty acids, which are oils, are essential to a healthy coat and may confer other health benefits as well. Once in a while, you'll see omega-9 fatty acid on a label. But this is mostly an attempt to capitalize on the word *omega*. Omega-9 (or oleic) acid is the main ingredient in olive oil and is usually simply referred to as monounsaturated fat. Too much fat, however, especially when given all at once (as tends to happen at the holidays, when people feed their dogs fatty leftovers), can result in pancreatic problems.

Most commercial dry dog foods contain between 5 and 10 percent fat, which is sufficient for sedentary dogs. *Working* Siberians require at least twice as much.

What about fiber?

Currently, there is disagreement about whether fiber is necessary in a dog's diet, and if so, how much. Most veterinarians agree that diabetic dogs, especially overweight ones, can benefit from eating fiber, because it slows the absorption of glucose in the intestine, which in turn helps control blood sugar. However, fiber may also decrease the absorption of certain critical minerals.

Dog food labels don't adequately reveal how much fiber is contained in the product. The guaranteed analysis may list "crude fiber" as an ingredient, but that term refers to what's left over from the food manufacturing process. The dietary fiber contained in the product can be several times higher.

You don't need to worry about fiber content in your dog's food unless he shows signs of diabetes, diarrhea, constipation, or other health problems. Then consult your vet.

Racing Siberians need 50 percent of their calories to come from fat! To achieve this level, mushers supplement their dogs' meals with beef fat. They also often feed their dogs raw meat.

Minerals

Just like humans, dogs need the following minerals in their diets: calcium, phosphorus, potassium, salt, magnesium, iron, copper, manganese, zinc, iodine, and selenium.

All AAFCO-approved dog foods provide the minimum amount of minerals your dog needs.

Water

Providing your Siberian with plenty of fresh, clean water to drink is essential to his health. Dogs need between ½ and ¾ fluid ounces of water per pound of body weight per day. That's about 2 pints per day for a 50-pound dog.

This estimate of the water requirements for dogs includes the water taken in through food. Just keep plenty of fresh water available all the time. Healthy dogs won't drink too much. Excessive water consumption can be a sign of diabetes, so be sure to keep an eye on how much your Siberian drinks, and if his water intake changes drastically, consult your vet.

Carbohydrates

You may wonder why I haven't mentioned carbohydrates in your dog's diet. There's a good reason for that. The carbohydrate requirement for your Siberian Husky is 0. That's right, 0 percent. (There is some research that indicates that pregnant bitches need carbohydrates, but the evidence is tenuous.) Despite this fact, commercial dog foods usually contain about 40 percent carbohydrates, because they're a cheap source of energy. And dogs can indeed use the energy carbohydrates provide. They just don't need to. Because avoiding carbohydrates in commercial foods is impossible, look for brands that contain rice rather than corn, wheat, or soy. Rice is easier for dogs to digest.

Reading the Labels

Although most dog owners feed their pets commercial foods, few of them know how to read the label. You may be surprised to hear that as far as federal regulations go, very little is actually required of pet food manufacturers. Companies are required to accurately identify the product, provide the net quantity, give their address, and correctly list ingredients. They are *not* required to list the ingredients in any particular order. Some security is found by looking for the Association of American Feed Control Officials (AAFCO) label. The AAFCO provides model regulations that pet foods must follow in order to carry the AAFCO label.

AAFCO-labeled foods provide a guaranteed analysis of the food, calorie statements, and a nutritional adequacy statement. The AAFCO label also lists ingredients in order of their weight in the food, starting with the greatest and descending to the smallest. (Inherent water content is included in this calculation.) But the AAFCO label doesn't necessarily guarantee that the product is any good or that it's right for your dog. It just means that the food is properly labeled.

Part of the problem with dog food labeling stems from the fact that most members of AAFCO work for pet food companies. Their primary allegiance may be with their employer rather than for the consumer. Critics claim that the testing that AAFCO performs is not particularly stringent and is in no way tantamount to a controlled scientific study.

However, the good news is that the highly competitive dog food market is improving the quality of commercial foods. Today, owners have more choices than ever before; however, they also need to educate themselves on how to know what they're buying.

Check out the following list for keywords that pop up on dog food packaging. Here you'll find out what those terms really mean:

- ✔ **Beef, chicken, fish, or lamb:** If an AAFCO-labeled product has the words *beef, chicken, fish,* or *lamb* in its product name, it must be 95 percent beef, chicken, fish, or lamb, exclusive of the water needed for processing. Even counting the water, the food must be 70 percent beef, chicken, fish, or lamb. These foods are all canned foods, by the way. No dry food is 95 percent beef, chicken, fish, or lamb.

- ✔ **Dinner:** If the word *dinner,* or a similar word like *platter* or *entree* is used in the product name, each featured ingredient must comprise between 25 and 94 percent of the total. So, a product with a name like "Diane's Chicken Dinner for Dogs" must contain at least 25 percent chicken.

- ✔ **With:** If the word *with* is used, the named ingredient must be at least 3 percent of the total. So "Diane's Chicken Dinner for Dogs with Liver" must contain 3 percent liver, as well as at least 25 percent chicken. "Diane's Chicken Dinner for Dogs with Liver and Sirloin" must contain 3 percent liver and 3 percent sirloin, as well as at least 25 percent chicken.

- ✔ **Flavor:** If the label reads *beef flavor,* rather than *beef,* it need only contain enough beef to be taste-detectable. Because you're probably not going to be taking a big bite of the food to see whether you can taste the beef, you'll just have to trust the label at its word. The word *flavor* must appear in letters as large as those of the named ingredient, however, which ensures that you won't mistakenly buy a product you think contains at least 25 percent beef, when really the food contains far less than 25 percent beef and only *tastes* like beef.

- ✔ **Premium, Lite, Gourmet, Natural, Organic, Performance, and so on:** These labels mean nothing. Not even AAFCO has so far devised regulations that products using these terms must meet. Read the content label carefully and compare.

 You may see the words *crude fat* or *crude protein* on the label. These terms refer to the method of testing of the product. It doesn't mean that the protein or fat contained is any cruder than any other kind of protein or fat. You may notice that levels of crude protein are lower in canned foods than in dry foods. This is because of the large amount of water in canned food.

Taking a Look at the Main Types of Dog Food

When it comes to dog food, your choice is practically unlimited: dry food, canned food, semi-moist, people food, or any mixture thereof. There isn't just one kind of food that's right for you and your dog. Many factors come into play — convenience, expense, nutritional value, taste, availability, and allergies, just to name a few. What's right for one dog is not right for all.

The most important guideline to keep in mind is that you shouldn't feed your Husky something he dislikes. Mealtimes should be a pleasurable experience for everyone, so why not shop around until you find something nutritious that your dog really *does* enjoy? If he seems to like something for a while, but then gets bored with it, change his food. It's not hard to do, and you'll be improving your dog's overall happiness. Seems like a small price to pay, when you think about it.

Dry food

Dry dog food, sometimes referred to as *kibble,* was introduced to the world during World War II. It was a convenience for feeding military dogs. And that's what it remains — a convenient, nutritionally adequate food for dogs. Dry food helps reduce tartar buildup on the back teeth (but not as much as brushing the teeth does).

Don't be seduced by fancy colors and shapes when it comes to dry food. Shape doesn't matter, and the colors come from vegetable dye, not food nutrients.

In comparison with other food choices, dry food is the least expensive, largely because of its high grain content, which is cheaper than meat. Dry food tends to be low in fat, which can be dangerous if your Siberian is a working dog.

Don't store dry food too long (no more than 2 weeks); it can lose some of its vitamin content over time.

Canned food

Canned food is much more expensive than dry, and it's usually about 75 percent water. In AAFCO-labeled products, the maximum amount of water in canned foods is 78 percent, unless the food is labeled as *gravy, sauce,* or *stew.* In that case, water content can be even higher than 78 percent! Canned foods are also high in fat. They can be useful for mixing with dry food, however, because most dogs find them highly palatable.

Some canned dog food contains grain products, and others have only meat. Whether grain products are good for dogs is controversial. (Foods containing corn, for example, tend to give dogs gas.) Dogs do need a vegetable element in their diet, so if you feed a pure meat dinner, you should supplement it with dog biscuits or fresh vegetables. Fresh meat is sometimes deficient in calcium.

Semi-moist food

Semi-moist food is about 25 percent water and can be just as high in sugar, in the form of corn syrup, beet pulp, sucrose, and caramel. This food promotes obesity and tooth decay, and of the available food options, it's the least desirable.

People food

It's perfectly okay to spice up your dog's diet with some well-chosen people food. Dogs enjoy variety as much as we do. Many times, the same things that are good for us are good for them: fresh vegetables and even fruit, lean meat, and yogurt are fine. Avoid sweets, chocolate, high-fat dairy foods, and processed meat. Don't give them to your dog either.

I don't recommend giving many dairy products to dogs; after weaning they are usually not able to digest them well. Yogurt is an exception, however. Most dogs benefit from a teaspoon of plain yogurt in their food, especially if they need extra calcium. Dogs like milk, too, but milk gives most adult dogs diarrhea.

Never give raw eggs to dogs. Raw eggs contain *avidin,* a protein which can destroy the B vitamin biotin.

If you do feed your dog people food, you should serve it at room temperature if possible, not directly from the refrigerator or a hot oven. Very cold food eaten rapidly can make a dog vomit. On the other hand, some food seems more palatable to dogs if slightly warmed. Even the Chukchis fed their dogs at room temperature. Of course, they had rather cold rooms to begin with.

Considering Supplements

A high-quality commercial dog food *should* be complete, although there is plenty of controversy about whether any commercial dog food really is. Some people believe that if you're feeding a good commercial dog food, you don't need to supply anything else. Other experts claim that we still don't know enough about nutritional requirements to be sure of anything in this department. My advice is to start with a high-quality dog food and keep a careful watch on your Husky's coat, energy level, weight, and general health. Add or subtract ingredients as you find necessary.

Vitamin A and beta-carotene seem to enhance immune functions and may help to prevent some kinds of cancer. Be careful not to over-supplement, however. Large of amounts of vitamin A, for example, are poisonous. A couple of carrots a day will be just fine.

Although dogs can manufacture their own vitamin C, unlike humans, a vitamin C supplement appears to lower cancer risk, and many holistic veterinarians suggest its use in managing the care of a dog diagnosed with cancer. Vitamin C also seems to reduce the side effects of some anticancer drugs.

I give my own dogs vitamin E (for skin and coat) along with other antioxidants, like vitamin C. Some people further supplement their dog's diet with selenium, but be careful not to give too much.

Never give a Siberian puppy a calcium supplement; it can contribute to hip dysplasia, *osteochondritis dissecans* (a form of arthritis), and enlarged joints. It also binds zinc, resulting in zinc deficiency and a poor coat. And Siberians are prone to zinc deficiency. (Wheat germ is loaded with zinc; it makes a good addition to many dogs' diets.)

Figuring Out How Much to Feed Your Dog

Research at the Ralston Purina Pet Care Center indicates that an inactive 50-pound dog requires 1,450 calories a day in the summer. The same dog requires 1,800 calories during moderate work or training, and 2,160 during heavy work. Now, get out your calculator! In the winter, for every 10-degree drop in temperature, add 7.5 percent more calories.

These calorie requirements are for dogs in general, not for Siberians in particular. Siberians do need fewer calories than other breeds their size, but requirements vary greatly between different breeds and even between individual dogs within any breed. Consequently, it is not possible to predict accurately how many calories a particular dog will actually require. Use these estimates as a general guide and keep an eye on his weight; then adjust his diet as needed.

For a quick check on your dog's condition, look at him from above. A working dog of the proper weight will have an hourglass figure. If your dog looks like a rectangle from an aerial view, he is overweight. You can also view your dog from the side; his belly should tuck up neatly.

Pet Huskies often carry more weight than their working counterparts. How much is too much? Run your thumbs firmly along your Husky's ribcage. If your dog isn't too fat, you'll be able to feel each rib distinctly.

If your Siberian lives and works outside in the winter, he may need twice as many calories as he does in the summer. You will also need to feed him more on working days.

Looking at Performance, Maintenance, and Low-Calorie Foods

Most high-quality dog foods come in performance and maintenance levels; however, the standards for these labels are not set by law or even by the AAFCO model regulations. Read the label carefully to determine how many calories and nutrients the food really provides. The difference largely depends upon how much exercise your Siberian is getting. A dog who just trots around the block or goes for a lazy stroll along the river bank with his owner will not need performance-level dog food. Pregnant or nursing bitches, of course, require higher levels of nutrients.

Performance foods often contain higher levels of protein. Extra protein, however, is not stored in the body but simply metabolized and excreted in the urine.

If your dog is overweight, he's not alone. Recent studies show that 80 percent of household pets are overweight. The American Animal Hospital Association rates obesity as the top nutrition-related health problem in dogs. Don't put your overweight Husky on a crash diet, however. You can buy commercial dog food in reduced-calorie varieties. Or you could simply cut out the cupcakes, lower his food and fat intake, and exercise him more. Your Siberian will love that.

Feeding your puppy

Although a Siberian does not reach maturity until about 18 months of age, I don't recommend that he stay on puppy food for that length of time. Some Siberians show adverse reactions to the dairy products often added to puppy food. The most common problem associated with dairy products is loose stools — certainly not a pleasant thing to deal with when you are house-training your puppy! In addition, research has found a link between hip dysplasia and the higher levels of calcium found in many puppy foods; so gradually switch your dog to an adult food at around 6 months or so.

If you decide that you need to make a major alteration in your Husky's diet, do so gradually. An abrupt change can cause digestive upset. Replace part of the old diet with part of the new, gradually increasing the amount of new food over a period of about a week. It may take 6 weeks to 3 months to notice an improvement in coat or other conditions you're trying to correct.

Feeding your senior dog

Dogs are old for a lot longer than they are puppies, and proper nutrition is, if anything, even more critical for the older dog than for a pup. Studies show that older dogs need about 80 percent of the calories that 1-year-old dogs do, and recent research indicates that senior dogs need about 50 percent more protein than do young adults. That's right: 50 percent *more* protein. The experts used to think that lower protein would prevent certain kidney problems common in older dogs, but they have since found this not to be the case. Between 20 and 30 percent of all calories your older dog consumes should come from protein. Lower protein intake slows wound healing and lessens immune function.

Increasing B-complex vitamins, vitamin E, and ester-C (a form of vitamin C), for older dogs is also a good idea. Add extra zinc, selenium, the omegas, and coenzyme Q10 as well. Always check with your vet before you give your dog any supplements.

Chapter 12

Grooming Your Dog

Maintaining your Siberian in top condition is essential for his health and happiness; it's not merely a cosmetic makeover. Too many people, however, view grooming as some dreaded chore, like cleaning the oven or defrosting the fridge. But it really isn't. Grooming is your opportunity to spend quality time with your dog. And with today's new grooming technology, it's easier than ever.

In this chapter, you find all the information you need on grooming — everything from brushing and bathing your dog to trimming his nails and brushing his teeth. And I also give you tips for finding a good professional groomer, who can be a great supplement to your own grooming.

Brushing and Combing

The Siberian Husky has a double coat of hair. Underneath is a woolly or downy undercoat, protected by a harsh outercoat (which actually grows through the undercoat). The rainproof outercoat protects the Siberian from brambles and thorns, and the undercoat serves as insulation.

Very little dirt can penetrate this excellent protective device. This fact, combined with the Husky's meticulous grooming habits, makes the Siberian an essentially self-cleaning machine. It's not the dirt that causes the grooming challenge, however; it's the hair.

The key to happy grooming is to teach your Siberian to accept being brushed by standing quietly while it's done. Wild dogs perform grooming sessions on each other frequently; it promotes social cohesion and reaffirms the hierarchy. It is a natural activity. When your Husky learns that he's getting a lot of loving attention from you during the grooming session, he'll look forward to it. It's also a good time to check him for parasites, cuts, suspicious lumps, or other anomalies.

Regular grooming (at least twice a week) helps remove loose hair and allows the dog's skin to breathe. It removes dead, scaly skin and encourages the sebaceous glands to produce healthy oils.

Some people tend to forget about grooming as the weather turns cold. This is a mistake. A well-groomed, unmatted coat is essential for keeping your Siberian snug when he's outside during the colder months. Mats destroy the insulating properties of even the thickest coat.

Your grooming routine should include flea inspection. Use a fine-toothed metal flea comb, and be prepared to leap into action if you see one! Keep a glass of hot water nearby and dip the flea-bearing comb in it; the fleas will drown.

It's best to use a grooming table, but if you don't have one, the kitchen table will work fine. Put a non-slip mat on it for traction. You can also use a different table, perhaps in the basement or on the porch, if you'd rather not have your dog on your kitchen table. You may decide to groom your Siberian outdoors in pleasant weather. Let the neighbors wonder where all those unusual tufts of hair are coming from.

Start off by misting your Husky lightly all around. This makes grooming easier, and helps keep the guard hairs from breaking off.

Begin the actual grooming process with a wide-toothed comb, preferably one with rounded teeth. This will help break up mats, although you can buy a special de-matting tool for this purpose. Then proceed to brush the coat vigorously, following the natural *hair stream* (the way the hair grows). Do a small section of the coat at a time.

If you encounter tangles, start at the outside of the tangle and gradually approach the hair closest to the skin. Don't begin at the root end and start pulling. That's not the best way to teach either of you to enjoy the grooming hour. Besides, you'd end up with a bald Siberian.

Do not shave, strip, or clip your Husky close. It's not necessary, and may even be detrimental. The undercoat insulates against the bitter cold, and the topcoat provides protection from harmful UV sunrays. And never clip your dog's whiskers. They are sensory devices that your dog needs. Besides, whiskers add to a dog's character.

Technically, whiskers are known as *vibrissae* — because they vibrate as a warning when they come in contact with something solid.

You may trim the extra hair from between the toes if it gets unsightly, a common occurrence with the heavily-furred Siberian.

When you are through combing, you can finish the job by using a long-bristled brush. The bristles must be quite long, otherwise they won't reach through the dense coat of the Siberian. If mats go unattended, they not only get bigger but tend to tighten up next to the skin, where they cause all kinds of trouble. So don't skip this important step.

Some people have good luck removing loose hair by using a pin brush. Be careful, though. Some kinds are too scratchy — rub the brush against your own arm first to test.

For most of the coat, brush vigorously forward, then brush back, especially along the flanks. This back brushing is necessary to de-mat the thick under-coat. Be especially attentive to the armpits and rump of the dog, where mats often hide. Most of the time, you'll need to brush *with* the direction of the coat at the rear end; it just works better. Then comb the dog again; you'll be surprised at how much hair you rake up.

Be sure to groom the whole Husky — including the belly and underneath the tail!

If your dog is tremendously matted, you may decide to take him to a professional groomer. When he's properly de-matted and clean, you can take over further grooming sessions yourself. Be sure you exercise and let your Siberian out before going to the groomer, and don't feed him immediately beforehand. Don't bathe the dog right before he goes to the groomer, either; that will just make his mats worse.

A poor coat is often the first sign of illness or other problems. If you know you're doing a good grooming job, your dog's poor coat could be an indication of a nutritional deficiency, heartworm, roundworm, hookworms, underactive thyroid, kidney problems, or even cancer. Check with your veterinarian.

Cleaning up is an important part of the entire grooming process. If you're grooming inside, vacuum up the loose Husky hair immediately afterwards; otherwise you'll have the stuff all over the house. Use a disinfectant (preferably with bleach) to clean the grooming implements.

Bathing

Siberians are fastidiously clean dogs. They do not actually need a bath more than three or four times a year, unless they get into something horrible.

Still, if you're like me, you may want to bathe your dog more frequently, just on principle. I use a mild, unmedicated shampoo. Most of the time, I use an inexpensive kind made for people, but there are some very nice texturizing shampoos in the pet market designed particularly for double-coated dogs. These texturizing shampoos keep the coat clean but don't allow it to get too soft.

Some people say that because the pH value of canine and human skin differs (our skin being a little on the acidic side and dog skin on the basic side), you should not use a human shampoo on dogs. But this is simply not true. For one thing, canine skin has a wide range of pH values; for another, no one has shown that using a human shampoo based on average human pH values does any harm to a dog.

Shampooing improves both the coat and skin, and helps keep parasites and hot spots at bay without resorting to chemical treatments. An aloe shampoo is especially soothing.

A good shampoo does not strip the oils from a dog's coat any more than a good shampoo strips the oils from people's hair. If you're worried about a dry coat, add a conditioner.

There are even no-tear and hypoallergenic shampoos designed especially for dogs. A drop of mineral oil in the eyes and some petroleum jelly around the eyes helps keep soap out, too.

When you bathe your dog, the most important step is to rinse, rinse, rinse. You should spend at least twice as long rinsing as washing. Soap residue can cause hotspots on the dog's skin.

In a pinch, you can use a dry shampoo for dogs. Dry shampoos are powder-like substances that help remove excess oils from the coat. They don't work as well as the regular kind, but hey, your dog isn't going to tell anybody.

Most dogs hate getting a bath. Even those who will joyfully run into the iciest pond or stream, cower or go rigid at the very sight of a tub. Still, nearly all dogs can be trained to put up with it. You can bathe your Husky outdoors in the summer if you like, but I use a bathtub during all seasons of the year. You can get special long, flexible attachments to make showering your pet easier. A raised dog-bathing tub is also nice.

Make sure the water is a warm, at a comfortable temperature. When you apply the shampoo, begin in the neck area. This way you're making a natural flea barrier, so the little stinkers don't climb up on the dog's head.

If your dog refuses to stand up during bathing, and you can't get human assistance, various devices are on the market that loop around the dog's body to prevent his sitting down.

Provide a rubber bathmat for your dog to help prevent his slipping in the tub. Even the feel of a slick tub can make him nervous.

The first thing your Siberian will do upon emerging from the tub is to shake. To save yourself and your house from getting drenched, grab the dog firmly by the head and hang on. A dog shake begins at the front, and if you can stop it there, he'll quit — at least long enough for you to throw a towel over him.

Dry your dog thoroughly, especially if it's cold outside. You can use a hand-held dryer (set on low), or a special dog dryer manufactured just for that purpose. All this will take some time. Give yourself an hour to bathe, rinse, and dry your Siberian. If the weather is not cold or wet, you may want to send your dog outdoors to dry.

Dealing with Shedding

"Wait a minute! I thought Huskies didn't shed!" I can hear you saying it. I know, that's what they told me, too. And they don't. At least not in Siberia, which is cold and dry. They merely "blow their coats" twice a year. But if you don't live in Siberia, you may be in for a little shock. In most of the United States, with its rapid climate changes, the Husky may shed his coat all year long — by the bushel. Just think, all that stuff that looks like a mixture of dandelion seeds and tumbleweed used to be on your Siberian.

Shedding is a natural phenomenon. Hair growth progresses through a three-phase cycle. During the first phase, the *anagen* phase, the hair grow actively. When it has reached its genetically predetermined length, it stops growing. This is the second, or *catagen,* phase. In the third, or *telegen,* phase, the new hair grows in, and the old hair falls out. Dogs perspire only through their paw pads; so getting rid of that extra hair in the spring is an absolute necessity to prevent heat stress.

If you live in the north and keep your Husky outside most of the time, he will probably revert to his ancestral pattern and shed only twice a year, in spring and fall. This whole-coat shedding is called *blowing the coat* and may take from three to six weeks, from start to finish. The hair comes out in clumps — sometimes big clumps. And it seems to get worse in periods of dry heat.

Besides the normal seasonal shed, Siberians may lose hair due to other factors, like stress, illness, or whelping. Dogs who have a change in lifestyle may likewise shed. Some people think that central heating and artificial lighting also play a role in shedding. Keep a close watch on your Husky to determine whether the shed is normal or a sign of something possibly more serious.

Even in a climate where the male sheds only once, the female will shed twice, owing to *estrus* (the female's time of heat). The female shed will usually occur in the spring and fall.

Huskies also go through something awful known as the *big shed*. The big shed occurs when your cute little puppy is maturing. Over the period of a few weeks all the fine puppy hair is shed and replaced by the coarser hair of the adult dog. Expect this happy event to occur between 10 and 14 months. And brace yourself.

Because shedding is natural, you can't do much to stop it. Make sure your pet is receiving sufficient quantities of B vitamins, as well as unsaturated fatty acids. These can reduce shed due to stress or whelping.

A product called Mrs. Allen's Shed-Stop, a natural liquid dietary supplement with sunflower oil, vitamins, antioxidants and all sorts of trendy stuff, may also help.

Paying Attention to Your Husky's Entire Body

One of the reasons that regular grooming is so important is that it gives you the opportunity to check out every aspect of your Husky's body. You can give him a once-over to be sure that everything's in order. And if there *is* a problem, you're more likely to detect it sooner if you groom your dog regularly.

Feet

Check the pads of your dog's feet frequently for mats between the toes, gravel, and sores. Lawn chemicals and snow-melting chemicals can both cause burns on your Husky's feet. A dog's pads can also be the target of a fungal infection similar to athlete's foot. Weed seeds can penetrate the tender skin between the pads. Any excessive licking of paws could be sign of trouble.

Nails

Trim your Husky's nails at least once every other week. If you wait too long, the nails and the quick (depicted in Figure 12-1) will both overgrow. You'll have to trim off a little bit of nail each day, and the quick will gradually recede.

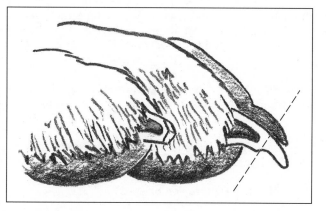

Figure 12-1: When you trim your Husky's nails, avoid the quick.

Overgrown nails can lead to serious foot problems. Yet the nails should not be so short as to be scarcely visible. Dogs need their nails to gain traction on the ground when they run. Nails of the correct the length should not quite touch the floor when the dog is standing.

If your Husky gets lots of exercise on pavement, he may keep his nails short naturally. Otherwise, the task falls upon you. After all, the dog isn't going to volunteer. If you can hear your Husky's nails clicking on the floor, it's time to trim. If you're in doubt about your nail-trimming skills, ask your groomer or veterinarian to show you how to do it correctly.

My favorite tool for nail trimming is not a set of clippers but a variable-speed Dremel tool. When your dog becomes desensitized to the noise, you can do a quicker, cleaner, neater job with almost no chance of getting the quick. All my dogs love it. Even if you happen to hit the quick, the Dremel tool cauterizes it automatically.

Don't forget to trim the dewclaws, if your Siberian has them.

If you prefer to use hand clippers, get the guillotine kind with replaceable blades. Clip from the back and bottom, at a slight angle, and be careful not to cut the quick. Squeeze the clipper quickly so as not to risk splitting the nail. If you do cut into the quick by mistake, use styptic powder, flour, or cornstarch to stanch the bleeding.

Teeth

Dental care is a must for dogs. Because they have 42 teeth, cleaning them can be an imposing job. Regular cleaning of teeth and gums will help your Husky avoid tartar buildup. Feeding your dog hard kibble and bones specially made for teeth-cleaning are helpful, but these products can't remove plaque from your Husky's teeth by themselves. Plaque buildup in dogs can result in periodontal disease, just as it can in humans. And periodontal disease not only leads to tooth loss but can release dangerous bacteria into the bloodstream. Some of these bacteria can lodge in the heart. The message is clear: Brush your dog's teeth!

Use a toothpaste designed for canines, preferably every day, but at least once a week. Dog toothpaste comes in a variety of flavors, commonly beef and chicken.

Even though young puppies are usually problem-free tooth-wise, puppyhood is a good time to get them used to the procedure. For a toothbrush, you may use:

- A baby's toothbrush (with nylon bristles)
- A specially designed canine toothbrush that fits over your finger
- A regular looking toothbrush from the grooming supply store (see Figure 12-2)
- A washcloth
- A piece of cotton gauze wrapped around the finger
- Your bare finger

Start with your finger, because your dog will probably accept it fairly readily. When he gets used to the idea, you can advance to a toothbrush, the bristles of which will get into the groove along the gum line where plaque can build up.

Aim the toothbrush at about a 45 degree angle, and brush in a circular motion. Scrub the tooth from crown to gum. Most of the plaque buildup occurs on the outside of the tooth, which is a good thing, because the insides are a lot harder to reach. Brush both the upper and lower teeth, especially the big canines and *carnassials* (shearing teeth) toward the back of the mouth.

To help reduce the tartar buildup, feed your dog some dry dog food every day, and give him lots of hard chew toys. Be careful, though. Some toys are actually too hard and can result in broken teeth.

Halitosis (bad breath) can be a sign of dental trouble. So are receding or red, inflamed gums. Halitosis can be caused by stomach disorders, as well as decayed or abscessed teeth.

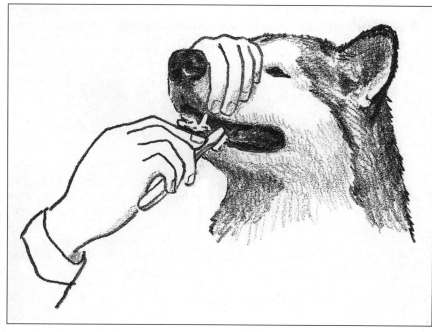

Figure 12-2:
Make brushing your Husky's teeth part of your daily routine.

Even with the greatest brushing care, you will still need to take your Husky to the veterinarian for a thorough tooth-cleaning job every year, especially after the dog reaches the age of 6 years or so. Your vet will clean and scale the teeth using ultrasound. This treatment removes plaque below the gum line, which you can't reach through brushing alone.

Eyes

Clean any ocular discharge every day with a clean, damp cloth. Don't use cotton balls; they contain fibers that can get in your dog's eyes and irritate them. If your Siberian has particularly sensitive eyes, you can get a cream to use in them while bathing your dog.

Ears

Because Siberians have erect ears, they are less prone to ear problems than lop-eared dogs. No Siberian should have foul-smelling ears, red ears, or ears that exude junk. Normal ear wax is clear or very pale yellow. Black or brown discharge probably means your dog has ear mites or a yeast infestation. A yellow, pussy discharge indicates an infection. Any time you notice a lot of ear scratching or head shaking from your pet, suspect mites or an infection. A mite infestation requires a special preparation, which you can obtain from your veterinarian.

For routine ear cleaning, swab the ear gently with a cotton ball or wipe using a liquid ear-cleaning product, or with an alcohol-vinegar solution. Don't cram anything in the dog's ears; you can rupture one of his eardrums.

Anal sacs

Emptying your dog's anal sacs is one of the worst chores involved in dog ownership. Most of the time, the dog handles this job himself, but every once in a while, you may need to help a little. If you notice your dog scooting along the ground, it's probably because those sacs need to be *expressed,* or emptied. Gently press your thumb and forefinger on the outside of each sac, at the 10 and 2 o'clock positions under the tail. Use a tissue and stand to one side (the stuff really smells).

If you don't like doing this yourself, your vet or groomer can do it for you.

Don't fix what's not broken! There is evidence that routine expression of the anal sacs contributes to future impaction. Only do it if it's needed.

In some cases, the anal sacs can become impacted and even may need to be surgically removed. Because Siberians don't really need them, it's no big deal.

Finding a Professional Groomer

For various reasons, you may decide to take your Husky to a professional groomer — at least once in a while. You can ask your veterinarian for recommendations, or check with breeders, boarding kennels, or friends with Siberians who are pleased with their groomers.

Call the prospective groomer, and check on prices, products, and procedures. You don't want a nasty surprise. Ask whether the groomer requires proof of bordetella (kennel cough) vaccination; even if she doesn't, make sure that your dog is vaccinated against it, because there may be other dogs there who have it.

Although a professional groomer can make your Siberian look slick, only you can do the regular ear, eye, foot, and tooth care that's necessary. Your groomer should be an enhancement to your total dog care, not a replacement of it.

Take time to watch the groomer with your dog. Any groomer who is rough should not have the care of your precious Siberian. Siberians can be particularly trying for groomers; they often simply will not do what is asked of them. So find a groomer experienced with the breed. In very rare cases, your Husky may require a mild tranquilizer before grooming; your veterinarian (not the groomer) should provide it. If you do use a tranquilizer, make certain the groomer knows how to administer the medication — or do it yourself.

Inform the groomer if your Husky is fearful of being groomed, or if he doesn't like being left. If he has ever growled or snapped during the grooming process, the groomer needs to know this as well. Likewise, inform the groomer if the dog has arthritis, a heart problem, epilepsy, or any other condition that could be aggravated by the grooming procedure.

Watching Out for Fleas and Ticks

Not only do we become attached to our dogs, dogs sometimes become attached themselves. And what's attached to them can make us shudder, itch, and get sick. But knowledge is power, and armed with the right arsenal, you can rid both your dog and your home of the pests that plague them.

Fighting fleas

Among the canine set, flea season lasts from April through November. The high flea season is from June through September. Wet summers make for even more fleas. They prefer to lay their eggs in temperatures of 70 to 85 degrees, with humidity around 70 percent. If you own a carpet, however, or even a bed, it's always flea season. Cedar chips and pine needles repel fleas, but not all people want to cover their floor with cedar chips. It's good for pet bedding, though. Frequent vacuuming helps, too.

After it's on your dog, the flea bites down and gets a good long drink of blood. She then lays her eggs, preferably on your dog. The eggs are smooth, however, and often fall to the carpet, sofa, or grass.

In the worst-case scenarios, fleas carry deadly typhus and bubonic plague. They carry tularemia, too, and have been implicated in the spread of Lyme disease. Fleas are also intermediate hosts for tapeworm. They feed voraciously, and dogs can lose a substantial amount of blood from a severe infestation. Puppies have actually been known to die from fleas.

If your dog has fleas, he will probably do the obvious: scratch. The itch from a flea bite lasts from 3 to 7 days. If you see your dog scratching, investigate further. Fleas like to stay very close to the skin (they abhor sunlight), so you may need to take a fine-tooth flea comb to your Siberian. Fleas tend to be worse on the head and neck, which are areas hard for the dog to tend himself.

You also know your pet has fleas when you see those hideous black and white specks in his fur. These are flea feces, I'm sorry to say. Flea feces are composed of partially digested blood. You can test this yourself by dropping a bit of water on them. If they're flea feces, they will turn red. (You can turn this into a science fair project for your child, if you like.)

Lots of dogs are allergic to flea bites. It's the protein in the flea saliva which is the culprit. A flea bite can turn into a so-called *hot spot,* a raw, perhaps oozing area on the dog's skin.

Preventing fleas

Disgusting as they may be, fleas *are* a curable problem. But you have to rid both your home and your dog of them at the same time. Otherwise, you will get a reinfestation. To completely rid your dog and your home of fleas, follow these suggestions:

- ✔ **If you have the money, get rid of the carpets in your house altogether.** Your soft, warm carpets make a wonderful flea nursery. Put down vinyl, wood, or linoleum instead.

- ✔ **If you must have carpets, avoid the deep-pile kind.** They attract fleas. If possible, replace heavy carpeting with cotton, washable rugs, at least during flea season.

- ✔ **Apply traditional flea-ridders, like dips, powders, and sprays.** Many of these contain pyrethrins, which kill adult fleas. Their effects are short-lived, however. A genetically altered form of pyrethrin, called permethrin, lasts longer, about ten days.

- ✔ **Use indoor foggers, but only as a last-ditch measure.** They leave an oily film over everything. Plus, they're toxic. Read all directions before use.

   Move all portable pets and cover the aquarium if you must fog your house! Turn off the pilot lights on your stove. Some of these pesticide foggers contain flammable repellents.

- ✔ **Vacuum frequently with a flea powder/carpet freshener combination.** Use mothballs inside the vacuum bag to kill the fleas. And be sure to hit all those little cracks and crevices where fleas love to hide. Wash your dog's bedding the same day that you vacuum, and while you're at it, vacuum the drapes.

- ✔ **Use cedar chips in your dog's bedding to repel fleas.**

✔ **Try flea-control products available from your veterinarian.** These include Program, Advantage, and Frontline. Program is one of the few anti-flea products that works to get rid of both flea eggs and larvae (a so-called *insect growth regulator*), so it can help stop the problem at the source. It prevents the fleas from laying eggs, but it does not kill adult fleas. If your dog is allergic to flea bites, try one of the other products, which are applied to the skin. Frontline and Advantage are not absorbed into the dog's bloodstream. My preference is Frontline. It lasts for three months and is the only one of the three products that works on ticks, too. Unlike Advantage, it does not need reapplication after swimming or bathing. Some topical anti-flea products are available over the counter.

Many anti-flea products cannot be used on puppies. Read the directions carefully, or check with your veterinarian. Use these flea poisons with caution if your Husky is a fanatical self-groomer, because he'll be ingesting much of the product.

✔ **Sprinkle some diatomaceous earth (available in hardware stores and pool-supply places) in dark, flea-friendly crevices.** This stuff is really a collection of fossilized sea shells and similar microscopic creatures. It's all natural and kills fleas by piercing their little body parts and drying them to death.

✔ **Have your home professionally exterminated.**

Knowing what doesn't work in getting rid of fleas

Flea collars are not only ineffective against fleas in heavy-coated breeds like Siberians, but they also contain *neurotoxins* (the substance that a cobra delivers in his bite), which are not good for your pet. Besides, dogs may develop a contact dermatitis from a flea collar.

The same holds true for those electronic or ultrasonic devices that are supposed to rid your house of fleas, including ultrasonic flea collars. Forget it. They don't work.

Paying attention to what may work

Some people swear by natural flea inhibitors like brewer's yeast, which may contain vitamin B1 and garlic as additives. They are supposed to make the pet's blood taste bad to the fleas. The verdict is still out on this, but it certainly won't hurt to try.

You can also try insect repellents. The most effective ones contain DEET (benzyl benzoate, diethyltoluamide). There are some safety concerns about these products, but they unquestionably do repel fleas. Natural flea repellents like pennyroyal, rosemary, wormwood, eucalyptus, and citronella *may* work also.

To help rid your yard of fleas the safe organic way, buy *nematodes* (creatures that feed on flea larvae) at your garden center. A beer-size can of them contains about 100 million microscopic nematodes, enough for any lawn.

Tackling ticks

Although hundreds of tick species exist, dog owners need to watch for just a few. Among these are the Brown Dog Tick, the American Dog Tick, the Northern Deer Tick, the Rocky Mountain Tick, the Black-Legged Tick, and the Lone Star Tick. That seems to be plenty for starters.

During tick season (primarily in early spring to mid-summer), check your dog for ticks daily, especially if he has been playing in the woods or tall grass. The ears, toes, neck, and head are the major tick sites. Ticks are slow feeders, so it takes about 24 hours for actual disease transmission to start.

Ticks become active any time the temperature rises into the 40s — even if it's January.

Keep the grass in your yard short to reduce the number of ticks.

If you find a tick on your dog, remove it as soon as possible, using tweezers and wearing gloves to protect your hands. Lint rollers will help remove unattached ticks. Never touch a tick with your bare hands! The dangerous Lyme disease spirochete can penetrate directly into your skin. Grasp the tick as close to its head as possible and pull. The sooner you remove the tick, the more likely it is that no disease has been transmitted.

Make sure you grab the tick by its head. If you squeeze the body while it's still attached to your dog, you may eject the tick's disgusting contents (including all disease-carrying material) right into your dog.

Don't worry about losing the head of the tick in the dog's skin. You won't. After you pull it out, throw the tick in the toilet and flush. Wash both the affected spot and your hands thoroughly. The area where the tick was attached may look nasty, but it's probably not infected, even though it may scab over or swell for a week or so.

Never use lighters, gasoline, or matches to "burn" the tick. It's too dangerous. Smothering the tick with Vaseline or nail polish is also a bad idea, because it takes too long to kill the tick. The longer the tick is attached, the more likely it is to transmit a disease.

Chapter 13

Establishing a Good Relationship with Your Vet

In This Chapter

▶ Finding a vet you like and respect

▶ Going for routine checkups

▶ Taking care of your dog at home

*Y*ou, your Siberian, and your veterinarian will form a three-way partnership — a partnership for life. So it only makes sense that you need to find a vet you trust, like, and respect. In this chapter, I help you know what to look for in a good veterinarian, and I guide you through your first visit to the vet's office. Here you also get some useful information on ways you can help your vet, by giving your dog medication at home or checking his temperature, for example.

Choosing a Vet

Choosing a vet isn't a decision to be taken lightly. The life of your Husky may depend on your making the right decision. You can ask your dog's breeder, knowledgeable friends, or the local kennel club for recommendations, but you should also do some research on your own. Here are some major factors to consider:

✔ **Location:** The closer you are to your vet's office, the better. Location is not merely a convenience; it may save your dog's life someday. The outcome of accidents, poisoning, bloat, and other emergencies often bear a direct relationship to the amount of time it takes you to get him to the vet.

✔ **Practice orientation:** Some vets prefer to work with cats, birds, horses, or other pets. So when you're considering a vet, ask what percentage of the vet's patients are dogs.

✔ **Breed familiarity:** Your vet should be familiar with the Siberian Husky's special health concerns, particularly eye problems. The more accustomed your vet is to doing eye examinations, the better. This does not mean your vet needs to be a veterinary ophthalmologist, but she should be able to get you in contact with a good specialist, if necessary.

✔ **The facility:** The veterinary clinic should be clean, well-lit, and free of clutter or unpleasant odors. Pay attention to how the staff interacts with other clients and their animals. Are people and pets treated with courtesy? Does the vet schedule appointments so that each client has time to talk to her? How long do you usually have to wait? Do you feel rushed? Ask to see the place where animals are kenneled if they need to stay overnight, and check to make sure the kennels are clean and offer enough room.

Many veterinarians operate a boarding facility. Although they may not offer all the amenities of some private boarding facilities, particularly in the all-important area of exercise, your Husky is sure to have veterinary attention within minutes if he needs it.

✔ **Office hours:** If you work long hours, you may need to find a vet who is open on weekends or evenings. Find out what the regular office hours are, and who covers the practice when the vet is not available. Is there 24-hour coverage on site, and if not, how often does someone come by to check on the animals?

✔ **Expense:** Although cost shouldn't be a deciding factor, there's no reason why you can't take it into consideration. You have a perfect right to call around and get prices for routine procedures like spaying and neutering, office visits, and shots. Care and quality being equal, there's no reason not to choose the less expensive option.

Most vets nowadays take credits cards or have payment plans, at least for expensive treatments.

✔ **Philosophy:** More important than cost or location is the quality of care the vet provides. You want to find a vet whose philosophy about vaccines, acupuncture, herbal medications, and diets agrees with your own. Ask your vet in advance how he would treat common conditions like cataracts, hip dysplasia, and other ailments.

✔ **House calls:** Many vets make emergency or compassionate house calls; this is especially true when the time comes that you need to have your dog euthanized. It is much less traumatic for a dog to spend his final hours in his own home. Find out whether your vet will do this, and for what cost.

✔ **Behavior with animals:** How your vet handles animals is one of the most important items for consideration. Any vet who is rough or seems to dislike animals (and sadly, there are some) should not be your vet. Take note of how your puppy responds to the vet.

> ✔ **References:** Check around with friends, owners of other Siberians, and your local Siberian Husky breed club to see whether they've heard anything about the vet you're considering.
>
> ✔ **What procedures the vet performs:** All veterinarians perform regular care, but some can do more. Find out what your vet can do. Is your vet certified in a specialty? If not, is she willing and able to recommend a specialist if such care is needed?

Knowing What to Expect on the First Checkup

Your dog's first checkup should include the following: heart and respiration, tooth condition, ears, eyes, and overall condition. Choose your vet early, because you will want to bring your new friend in for a checkup within two or three days after you get him. Write down any questions you may have; that way you won't forget them.

Teeth

Your puppy has 28 sharp little teeth, which will eventually fall out to make room for 42 big teeth. Although puppies aren't prone to getting cavities, puppy teeth sometimes fail to fall out. This can cause all kinds of problems with the permanent teeth as they start to erupt. Your vet may need to remove the impacted baby teeth under anesthesia.

Fecal check

Most vets also want to perform a fecal check. It's really best to have fecal checks done twice a year, although heartworm medication automatically gets rid of most kinds of worms.

Vaccines

In his native Siberia, the Husky was exposed to few diseases and could do without vaccinations. (This is a good thing, because the Chukchis didn't have any vaccines to give them.) Today, however, an army of infections lurk nearby, ready to pounce on any unprotected dog, especially unvaccinated puppies.

Distemper, parvo, hepatitis, and rabies are just a few of the dangerous diseases your dog, or any dog, is susceptible to. Because your dog will inevitably come into contact with at least some of these diseases, most vets believe that your best defense against illness is a well-planned vaccination program begun when your puppy is just a few weeks old.

Vaccines are weakened forms of a disease. When the vaccines are introduced into the body, the immune system reacts just as if it were invaded by the real disease. It learns how to produce the same defenses it would against the real, full-strength disease. Then, when the real disease comes along, the body is ready to quickly repel it, and the dog doesn't get sick. Unfortunately, the vaccines don't last forever, so your dog will need occasional booster shots to keep his defenses in a state of readiness.

Each disease requires its own vaccine, although sometimes several vaccines can be mixed and administered at the same time. (This is called a *multi-valent vaccine.*) In some cases, more than one vaccine is available for a single disease. Currently, there are three general types of vaccines on the market, each classified according to how the vaccine is made:

- **Killed virus vaccines:** As the name implies, these vaccines are prepared from a dead virus. The immune response results from exposure to the viral protein in the vaccine. Killed virus vaccines are safe and easy to handle, and they will not cause suppression of the immune system, although some dogs develop reactions to them. They do, however, require more frequent vaccinations, and they're somewhat less effective than the other types. Unlike the modified live-virus vaccines, they are safe for pregnant bitches.

- **Modified live virus vaccines:** These are made from a weakened, but still living, form of the virus, or sometimes from a related organism that causes the same reaction in the immune system. Modified live virus vaccines provide better and longer-lasting immunity than killed virus vaccines. It is possible, however, for the organism in this kind of vaccine to revert to disease-causing form, especially in dogs with weakened immune systems. Autoimmune problems also crop up occasionally. Puppies, with their immature immune systems, are more susceptible to the dangers of this type of vaccine.

- **Recombinant vaccines:** These vaccines do not use live or killed virus or bacteria in any form. Unlike the killed virus and modified live virus vaccines, the whole virus is never introduced into the body so there is no possibility of getting sick. The vaccines are made from bits of DNA coding for the protein that actually causes the immune response.

> There are two kinds of recombinant vaccines. In the first kind of vaccine, the viral gene is grown in bacteria, yeast, or other cells to produce large amounts of the viral protein. The viral protein is then purified and administered as a vaccine. In the second kind, the viral gene is attached to a harmless virus and introduced into the body of the animal or human to be protected. The virus "infects" the cells and the viral proteins are produced right in the dog or human.

Vaccines for a particular disease may be available in more than one of these forms. Some of the vaccines are administered combined with *adjuvants,* substances added to make the vaccine work better.

Because your puppy will need to be vaccinated, bring his previous shot record when you go to the vet for his first visit. Controversy rages about when and how often to vaccinate (see the nearby sidebar for more information), so don't be surprised if your vet wants to change the scheduling a bit or use a different type of vaccine.

If you have many dogs, get your puppy a bordetella intranasal spray. Bordetella is the scientific name for kennel cough, which, although not very serious in older dogs, can be very bad in puppies. It is extremely contagious and many kennels, groomers, and obedience classes require this shot before they will work with your dog.

All dogs are required to be vaccinated against rabies. The first rabies shot is usually given at 16 weeks, the booster shot a year later. Most rabies shots are good for three years, although some places require yearly vaccinations. Check with your vet to see what the laws are in your area.

Mild fever or lethargy is not uncommon for a day or two following a vaccination. A small bump and hair loss may develop at the vaccination site, although this is unlikely with Siberians. These effects usually resolve without further treatment. More serious, and fortunately rare, is *anaphylaxis,* a severe allergic reaction to the foreign protein in the vaccine. (This is the same kind of reaction seen in people and dogs allergic to bee stings.) Wait in the vet's office for ten minutes after your dog is vaccinated in case vomiting and collapse (indications of anaphylaxis) should unexpectedly occur.

Spaying and neutering

On your first visit to the vet, you also want to talk about spaying or neutering your Husky. Unless you have a show-quality Siberian, you should have your puppy spayed or neutered.

The other end of the needle

Not all veterinarians are in agreement about the frequency of booster shots, or even about the need for vaccines at all. A few vets practicing *naturopathic* medicine believe that vaccines are poison and present a greater risk to canine health than the diseases they protect against. Other vets are worried about the very real risk of over-vaccination and recommend checking the dog's *vaccine titer* (a measure of the dog's readiness to fight a particular disease) before administering a booster shot.

The final research on these questions has not been completed. In the meantime, I follow my vet's recommendations and let her follow the latest research findings about vaccination schedules.

Neutered dogs have a lower rate of testicular cancer, fistulas, and perianal tumors. Spayed bitches are far less subject to ovarian and mammary cancers. They will also never get *pyometra,* a potentially deadly infection of the uterus. Neutered animals are also easier to keep and less apt to cause dominance problems. Neutered dogs are easier to house-train, as well. They are also less likely to wander far away if they get loose.

Any male who has only one testicle that has "dropped" should be neutered. The retained testicle is at a high risk for cancer.

Dogs can be neutered as early as 8 weeks old, according to the American Veterinary Medical Association. Many vets, however, prefer to wait until the puppy is 4 to 6 months old, fully vaccinated, and strong enough to safely undergo anesthesia. Your dog will bounce back to normal within a day or so. In males, the testicles are removed; the scrotum itself is left. It will eventually atrophy and disappear.

Recognizing How You Can Help Your Vet

If you learn to perform some simple procedures yourself, you can help your vet immensely. Practice these skills when your dog is well; it's important for you and your vet to know what's normal in your dog.

Giving your dog pills

Know how to give a pill. Most dogs will readily swallow a pill coated in peanut butter or cheese. If for some reason, your Husky seems reluctant to take a pill, you can help him. Tilt his head slighty back, and insert the pill down his throat. (See Figure 13-1 for an illustration.)

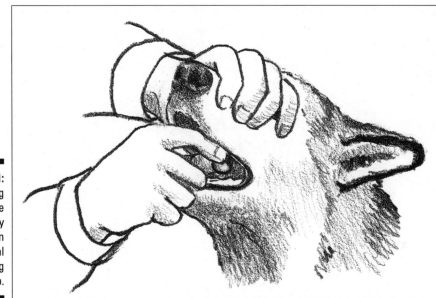

Figure 13-1:
Knowing
how to give
your Husky
a pill is an
essential
part of dog
ownership.

Don't tilt his head all the way back, however. You may end up cramming the pill down his windpipe rather than his gullet, which will cause him to choke.

Administering liquid medications

To give your dog liquid medication, use an oral syringe and gently insert it in the side of the dog's mouth. Gently hold his jaws closed around it and squirt the medication toward the side, not straight down the dog's throat (which could cause him to choke).

Taking your dog's temperature

To take a dog's temperature, it's best to have an assistant. The assistant stands at the head of the dog, while you insert the thermometer from the rear. Lubricate the end of the thermometer with oil or Vaseline and, lifting the dog's tail slightly, insert the instrument to between ½ and 1 inch. Leave it in place for about 30 seconds, holding the dog so he doesn't sit down or run away. Disinfect the thermometer after each use.

A healthy dog's temperature reads 100 to 102 degrees. An excited dog may have a slightly higher temperature.

Special canine thermometers are available; check with your vet for the best type.

Checking your Husky's pulse and breathing rate

Your dog's pulse can be found on the inside of the thigh. You'll feel a groove at the right spot. You can also place your hand on the left side of the chest, just below the elbow. A normal resting pulse rate is between 70 and 120 beats per minute.

Normal breathing rate is 12 to 32 breaths a minute.

Paying attention to gum color

A Husky's gums should be pink (except where there is naturally dark pigmentation). Pale gums can indicate anemia; dark red gums can indicate fever or poison; and yellow gums may signal liver dysfunction.

Measuring your dog's capillary refill time

Capillary refill time (CRT) is the length of time it takes for blood to reach the capillaries. Measure this by pressing your thumb near the canine tooth. Remove your thumb and notice how long it takes for the white mark to refill. This refill time should be no longer than 2 seconds.

Chapter 14

Preventing and Responding to Health Problems

In This Chapter

▶ Recognizing some common canine illnesses

▶ Helping an older dog age gracefully

Siberians are among the healthiest and longest-lived of all breeds, many remaining spunky right into their teen years. I have known Siberians to reach the age of 20. Still, everyone feels under the weather sometimes, and it's necessary to keep a watchful eye on your best friend to make sure you can help him when he does. In this chapter, I provide some information on common ailments that affect dogs in general and Huskies in particular. And I let you know how to prevent them from affecting your dog, as well as how to respond to them if they already have.

Viruses

All dog owners need to beware of viral diseases; no breed is immune or even has any special resistance to them. Some of the worst diseases known to dogs are viral: rabies, distemper, parainfluenza, infectious hepatitis, parvovirus, and coronavirus. To make more of their evil kind, viruses must invade the living cells of their hosts. Antibiotics are of little use against a virus, because viruses hide out inside cells.

One class of drugs (the *antivirals*) can stop viruses from reproducing. Unfortunately, the prohibitively high cost of such medications currently makes their widespread use for canines off limits. In addition, most of these drugs are pretty toxic to the dog.

Until your puppy is fully immunized against the following diseases, he is in danger of contracting them. See Chapter 17 for the lowdown on vaccines.

Canine parvovirus

Canine parvovirus (CPV) is a comparatively new disease, first reported worldwide in 1978. It is apparently a mutation of a parvovirus previously affecting only cats, which somehow changed its genetic structure slightly and leaked across the species barrier. CPV affects the stomach and intestines of dogs and is transmitted by dog feces. From there, it can be carried on dog hair and humans' shoes. It is resistant to most disinfectants other than bleach. Parvo causes a diarrhea so severe that a dog can literally waste away from it. It's most commonly seen in puppies between the ages of 6 weeks and 6 months. Susceptibility is increased by keeping puppies outdoors, where parvo can stay in the soil for up to two years. Puppies should be completely immunized against CPV between 16 and 18 weeks of age. Human beings are immune to CPV.

Parvovirus is not curable, but a promising new treatment is being developed. It involves injections of lyophilized canine immunoglobulin (Ig)G, extracted from the serum of dogs who have recovered from parvo.

Canine distemper

Distemper is still the main killer of dogs worldwide; it is airborne and extremely contagious, killing 50 percent of unvaccinated adult dogs infected with it. In puppies, the percentage is even higher — almost 80 percent. Canine distemper or *hardpad,* affects the dog's nervous system. In the early stages, it is accompanied by a dry cough, fever, and yellowish discharge from the eyes. Even dogs who survive distemper can be permanently affected. Human beings are immune to canine distemper, although the disease is similar to human measles. Puppies should be completely immunized between 12 and 14 weeks of age.

Infectious canine hepatitis

Canine hepatitis affects the liver. It looks a lot like distemper and is passed through the urine of infected dogs. It is especially dangerous, because even after a dog recovers from the disease, he can pass it along to other animals for a period up to six months. Human beings are immune to canine hepatitis. Puppies should be immunized at 12 weeks.

Rabies

Rabies affects the central nervous system. It is transmitted via the saliva, usually through bites. A person or animal bitten by a rabid animal has about a 75 percent chance of contracting the illness. All warm-blooded animals, including human beings, are susceptible to it. If a dog develops rabies symptoms, he will die. Puppies should be immunized against this disease between 16 and 24 weeks of age.

Canine coronavirus

This disease, related to the human cold, was first identified in 1971. It is passed through food that has been contaminated by the feces of an infected dog. It is very contagious and produces vomiting, diarrhea, and depression. It is most serious in puppies.

A vaccine is available, but many vets regard the vaccine as more dangerous than the disease and recommend against its use. A new modified live vaccine which has rapid antibody development, cell-mediated immunity, mucosal immunity, and minimal risk or allergic or adjuvant reactions has been developed.

Lyme disease

Although not so devastating an illness as it is in people, dogs can contract Lyme disease, which is transmitted by a bacterium found in ticks. Dogs inhabiting tick-infested areas should be vaccinated against Lyme disease. However, because the vaccine can cause reactions, it may not be advisable to administer it unless your dog spends a great deal of time in wooded areas.

Leptospirosis

Leptospirosis is a bacterial disease that affects the liver and kidneys. Recently, the disease has returned in a new and virulent strain, one that was previously seen in horses and cows. Dogs contract it through direct contact with the urine of infected animals, but not all dogs who encounter it will be become sick. They may turn into carriers themselves, shedding the virus in their urine and infecting other animals in turn.

In its most dangerous form, leptospirosis can affect and shut down the kidneys. Treatment includes antibiotics and, in cases of kidney failure, dialysis. A vaccine is available for some forms of leptospirosis; however, many vets do not recommend its use, especially for young puppies. The older forms of leptospirosis are seldom seen nowadays, and the vaccine can cause reactions in some dogs. A vaccine against the new lepto strain is being tested.

Kennel Cough

Kennel cough is an acute respiratory disorder, often found where dogs share close quarters, like kennels, shelters, boarding facilities, and veterinary hospitals. Kennel cough is a complex of symptoms, rather than a specific disease. It can be caused by a host of agents, including viruses *and* bacteria, so it shouldn't be considered a single disease. In adult dogs, kennel cough is sort of like a bad cold; the dog often shows no symptoms of ill-health other than a runny nose and a cough. Some have fever or lack of appetite. For puppies, the condition can be more serious. You can immunize your dog against *Bordetella bronchiseptica,* the most common agent for kennel cough. Puppies should be immunized at 16 weeks.

Canine Hip Dysplasia

Canine hip dysplasia (CHD) is an abnormality that occurs when the head of the *femur* (thighbone) does not fit correctly into the pelvic socket (see Figure 14-1 for an illustration). Eventually the joint becomes malformed, sometimes to the extent that it is unusable. A dog may have dysplasia in one or both hips. The earlier the disease manifests itself, the more serious it is. Unfor-tunately, even though the disease is painful, your stoic Husky may give little indication that he's hurting.

The origin of CHD is at least partially genetic. Geneticists consider it to be a *polygenic condition,* meaning that several genes play a part in passing it on. No one has yet identified all the genes responsible. And not all dogs who have a genetic predisposition to get hip dysplasia actually develop it.

The Orthopedic Foundation for Animals (OFA), a non-profit organization affiliated with the School of Veterinary Medicine at the University of Missouri will, for a small fee, inspect the radiographs of dogs 2 years or older desired for breeding purposes. They will then issue a report to the dog's owner, good for the lifetime of the dog, evaluating the dog's hip joint conformation. A reputable Siberian Husky breeder will not breed an animal without a favorable rating from the OFA, and prospective buyers should ask to see the OFA report on both parents before committing to buy a puppy.

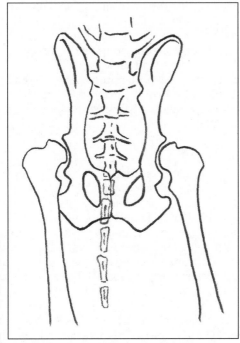

Figure 14-1:
Canine hip
dysplasia is
a painful
abnormality.

Although hip dysplasia is not noticeable at birth, the condition is progressive and causes pain, inflammation, and eventually arthritis, which can be severe. Rigorous exercise makes the problem worse. Dogs with only slight hip dysplasia are frequently overlooked or misdiagnosed. The only way to know for sure if a dog has dysplasia is to have him x-rayed by a competent veterinarian. The diagnosis should be confirmed by a veterinary radiologist. This condition is sometimes extremely difficult to detect, and unless the dog is properly positioned for the x-ray, a misdiagnosis could result.

The most important factor for developing hip dysplasia is probably rapid growth rate. The more rapidly your puppy grows, the more at risk he is for developing hip dysplasia, and other orthopedic problems. Carefully monitor your young dog's diet, especially between the ages of 3 and 8 months, the peak growth period. If your puppy seems to be growing faster than other Huskies in his age group (ask your vet to be sure), you must be especially vigilant and lower his caloric intake.

You can ask your veterinarian to perform an OFA or Penn Hip style x-ray when your dog is being spayed or neutered. (**Note:** Hip x-rays are not completely accurate, unless they are done after the age of 2 years, but an earlier x-ray can still provide useful information.) This will give you a baseline reading, and if your Husky develops hip problems later, you and your vet will be able to check the new x-rays against the early ones. Treatment for dysplasia includes diet therapy (usually involving weight loss), enforced rest, exercise and stretching exercises (swimming is good), drug therapy (ascriptin, Naproxen, Adequan, and Cosequin), acupuncture, and surgery.

In addition to genetic predisposition, breeders recognize that environmental factors may also play a significant role in the disease. Rapid weight gain, improper nutrition (including too much calcium), too-rapid growth rate, and other factors can all contribute.

Arthritis

Dogs suffer from arthritis as frequently as human beings do. Arthritic dogs may limp or have problems getting up or climbing stairs. They may cry when touched. Symptoms are usually worse in the morning, because the joints are likely to be stiff from lack of movement during the night. There are two basic types of arthritis: degenerative arthritis (osteoarthritis) and inflammatory arthritis (joint disease).

In degenerative arthritis, the cartilage that protects bones around the joint is damaged, usually by stress. Active, sporty dogs are particularly susceptible. This kind of arthritis can be acquired from too much jumping, or it can result from a tear. Sometimes, years will go by before the disease actually manifests itself. Hip dysplasia, a malformation of the hip socket, is a common form of degenerative arthritis.

Older dogs, overweight dogs, and genetically predisposed dogs are particularly at risk for degenerative arthritis.

Inflammatory arthritis is result of an illness or infection. Tick-borne diseases like Rocky Mountain spotted fever are common sources. It can also be hereditary.

Eye Problems

Serious eye problems should be treated by a veterinary ophthalmologist, preferably one certified by the American College of Veterinary Ophthalmologists (ACVO). In addition, the Siberian Husky Club of America has encouraged its local member clubs to sponsor annual eye clinics at a reasonable cost. The procedure is painless.

Only dogs who are free from genetic eye defects should be used for breeding purposes. Siberians can be screened by the Siberian Husky Ophthalmologic Registry (SHOR). If a dog of 1 year or older has been found to be free of eye defects by a diplomate of ACVO, SHOR will issue a certificate (good for one year) to the animal. A reputable breeder should offer proof to any purchaser that the sire and dam of the litter in question have been registered by SHOR.

Recognizing common eye problems

Siberian Huskies are susceptible to three genetically passed eye defects: progressive retinal atrophy (PRA), bilateral cataracts (and other corneal disorders such as crystalline corneal opacities), and glaucoma. These disorders can affect animals of either sex or of any eye color. All can cause blindness.

In the following sections, I cover these three genetically passed eye defects, in addition to some other common eye problems your Husky may encounter.

Progressive retinal atrophy

In progressive retinal atrophy (PRA), the retina, which forms the light image, loses first its night vision capacity, then its day vision capacity. The disease develops if the light-sensitive cells in the retina receive an inadequate supply of blood; if this happens, they wither away. Both eyes are always affected, but the disease progresses slowly; its presence can be detected by ophthalmoscopic examination. PRA is caused by a recessive gene, so parents should be screened. There is no cure or treatment for the disease.

A disease related to PRA is Central Progressive Retinal Atrophy (CPRA). In CPRA the animal has better night vision than day vision, and although he may bump into stationary objects, he can usually see moving objects with varying degrees of acuity.

Cataracts

Cataracts are a major source of blindness, usually seen in older dogs. They can result from diabetes, poor nutrition, inflammation, or trauma. In this condition, the lens of the eye becomes cloudy or opaque. Cataracts are classified by the dog's age at onset, physical appearance, state of development, and cause. Cataracts usually begin as tiny dots, then progress to a haze, pearly sheen, streakiness, or a totally white lens. Not all cataracts will progress to the point of causing blindness, however.

According to some estimates, the incidence of cataracts in Huskies may be as high as 18 percent.

Bilateral, developmental, or juvenile cataracts is, as one of its names suggests, characteristic of young dogs. The primary cause is genetic transmission. Only five breeds of dogs inherit this condition; unfortunately, the Siberian Husky is one of them.

The disease shows up as a cloudiness in the lens, and develops rather slowly, usually first in one eye, then in the other. Inherited canine cataracts in Huskies is caused by an autosomal recessive trait that appears between 4 and 18 months of age. Some cases do not show themselves until the dog is between 4 and 6 years old; this is particularly unfortunate because most dogs are bred before that age. Severe cases of juvenile cataracts cause blindness; in some cases, there is considerable discomfort as well.

There is no treatment that will prevent or slow the development of cataracts. Surgery to remove the opacity is the only treatment. One new treatment is called *phacoemulsification,* an ultrasound technique that actually shatters the bad lens, and removes the pieces!

The AKC Canine Health Foundation, a nonprofit organization, has begun funding research to identify the DNA marker that causes juvenile cataracts in purebred dogs, specifically in Siberian Huskies, Alaskan Malamutes, and Samoyeds.

Glaucoma

In glaucoma, the internal pressure of the eye's aqueous fluid increases to the point where it damages the retina or optic nerve. Glaucoma usually has a genetic component (primary glaucoma), but can also be acquired from trauma or an infection (secondary glaucoma). Glaucoma is prevalent in certain lines of Siberians, particularly in some racing lines.

Although blue eyes are regarded as defective in many breeds, there seems to be no evidence that blue eyes are related to increased incidence of cataracts or other eye problems in Siberians.

Early stages of glaucoma are characterized by pupil dilation and a slightly enlarged eye, symptoms that are very easy to miss. Later, the eye will be red, swollen, streamy, and obviously painful. There may be a green or yellow discharge. This is an extremely dangerous condition, requiring emergency, aggressive medical treatment from your veterinarian. Laser surgery is used to relieve pressure within the eye by decreasing the eye's ability to produce fluid. Permanent blindness can occur within hours.

To test for glaucoma, your vet will use a *tonometer,* an instrument that calculates how far the cornea of the eye is indented when pressure is applied to the surface of the eye.

Drug therapy, laser surgery, and a freezing procedure called *cyclocryothermy* are partially successful if the glaucoma is caught very early, but the ultimate prognosis is poor. Most dogs with this condition eventually lose their sight.

Nuclear or lenticular sclerosis

Nuclear or lenticular sclerosis is a common condition in older dogs, starting at around 8 or 9 years of age.

You may notice a greenish or bluish haze on the eye, which is caused by a hardening of the lens. It's part of the natural aging process, and although it may impair your dog's close-up vision, it's not a serious disability. Note the difference between this condition and cataracts; in cataracts, the haze is white.

Crystalline corneal opacities

Crystalline corneal opacities (CCO) affects the *cornea* of the eye. The cornea is the outer, transparent portion of the eye's outer coat. The lens is farther inside the eye and focuses light rays so they form an image on the retina, which is the light-sensitive inner layer of the eye. With this condition, the cornea sometimes takes on a hazy appearance; at other times, it looks as if crystal needles have invaded the eye.

Both eyes are affected, but not always to the same extent. Research, using the Siberian as a test model, is currently being done on this problem.

Conjunctivitis

Conjunctivitis is an inflammation of the membrane that lines the eyelid. The white (or *sclera*) of the eye looks red. It is caused by a variety of things, such as infection, inadequate lubrication, and injury. It can also be a by-product of another disease.

Knowing what to do if your Husky goes blind

Blindness is not the tragedy to dogs that it is to human beings. And because humans can lead a rich and interesting life although blind, think how little blindness may affect your Siberian, who has his keen ears, sensitive nose, and loyal heart to guide him through life. Besides, Siberians have little interest in reading books, going to the movies, or even admiring a glorious sunset.

The biggest problem for a blind dog is his owner, who is convinced that his dog's life has been irretrievably ruined. The dog may notice his owner's change toward him, and become worried and fretful. *This* bothers a dog more than sight loss does.

Testing your Husky's sight

Sometimes it's not easy to tell if your dog is going blind. Blindness usually happens very slowly, and your dog is so good at using his other senses to maneuver around the house that you may not even notice until it is too late. Here are a few safe, simple tests you can perform at home to check your dog's vision. These are not recommended as alternatives to regular veterinary checkups, of course, but are useful for between visits.

- ✔ **Wave your hand or another object quickly before your dog's eyes.** He should blink.

- ✔ **Move an object slowly in front of your dog's eyes.** He should follow the object visually.

- ✔ **Shine a flashlight in one eye.** Both eyes should blink in response. The pupils of both eyes should contract.

- ✔ **Pick up your Siberian (if you can) and carry him to a table.** If he sees it, he'll stretch out his forelegs in an attempt to reach it.

- ✔ **Throw a ball.** He should see where it goes.

- ✔ **Design an obstacle course between you and your dog.** See if he can negotiate his way through it.

Epilepsy

Epilepsy is a frighteningly common inherited disorder among Siberian Huskies, usually manifesting itself when the dog is about 2 to 4 years or older. Epilepsy is an uncontrolled electrical activity in the brain. It results in seizures that can last from a few seconds to over half an hour. The dog may go stiff and jerk, his eyes may roll back in his head, he may blink or pace.

Treatment includes use of anticonvulsant drugs like Dilantin, Phenobarbitol, Primidone, and Valium.

An epileptic dog can live a happy life, and if his family members can get over their fear of the seizures, the disease can be fairly easily managed.

Diabetes

Like human beings, dogs can get diabetes. Diabetes is caused by a deficiency of insulin, a hormone produced in the pancreas, but no one is sure how this happens. There are two types of diabetes: type I (insulin dependent) and type II (non–insulin dependent). The first type is common in older dogs; the second is associated with obesity.

The body needs insulin to absorb blood sugar. If not enough insulin is produced, the sugar stays in the bloodstream and eventually passes into the urine. Overweight animals, older dogs (between 7 and 9 years), and females are most at risk. In fact, females are twice as likely to contract diabetes as males. Your vet can check for diabetes using a blood test.

Most experts think that type II diabetes can be prevented by keeping your Husky lean. Some studies have also suggested that the addition of chromium to a canine diet may help prevent the onset of the disease. (Chromium can be found in brewer's yeast.)

Danger signs include increased hunger, thirst, and urination.

The medical treatment for diabetes is usually dietary changes and administration of insulin, often by injection once or twice a day. If your dog is diabetic, you also have to learn how to monitor your dog's blood glucose level. Regular exercise and a special diet are also important. Companies like Eukanuba, Hill's, Ralston Purina, and Waltham's have developed special commercial feeds for diabetic dogs.

Although experts aren't sure yet whether healthy dogs need fiber, you can help manage your dog's diabetes by including fiber supplements in his diet. Feeding high-fiber foods reduces the amount of insulin your diabetic Husky requires. As an additional benefit, we know that high-fiber foods help in weight reduction, a common problem accompanying diabetes.

Dogs with diabetes should have about 40 percent of their calories come from complex carbohydrates, 20 percent from fat, and the rest from high-quality protein.

Hypothyroidism

The thyroid gland consists of two lobes, located in your dog's neck. This gland produces hormones that regulate your Siberian's metabolism. If the thyroid fails to function at its proper level, the condition is called *hypothyroidism*. Many dogs seem to lose thyroid function as they grow older.

Hypothyroidism (underactive thyroid) is a serious, inheritable disorder that is becoming increasingly common in dogs. More females than males are affected, and it usually doesn't show up until the dog is at least 2 years old.

Some people believe hypothyroidism is reaching epidemic proportions among many medium to large breeds, including the Siberian Husky.

Hypothyroidism has a multitude of symptoms, including lethargy, lack of coordination, increased weight, inability to tolerate cold or exercise, seizures, aggression, compulsive- or anxiety-related disorders, diarrhea or constipation, loss of hair, a rat tail (a tail without hair), skin problems, and eye problems. Many of these symptoms develop very gradually.

A simple blood test can detect an underactive thyroid. Treatment consists of an inexpensive hormone supplement (Soloxine or Synthroid) in pill form administered twice a day for the rest of the dog's life. In a very few weeks, your Siberian should show signs of improvement.

Some controversy is stirring about whether or not to medicate dogs whose thyroid reading is low but not yet abnormal. One problem is that veterinarians do not yet know if every breed should have the same level of thyroid activity to be considered "normal." We do know that the normal level changes throughout the life of the dog. Explore this issue carefully with your veterinarian, keeping in mind that the target organ of the disease may not always be the easily noticed skin and hair, but the liver. Many dogs have lost their lives to undiagnosed hypothyroidism. It may be advisable to use a hormone supplement if you have concerns over your Husky's test results.

The Orthopedic Foundation for Animals (OFA) offers a new registry to identify dogs who have normal thyroid function. A dog must be 1 year old to be eligible for the test and should be retested every year or so. Hypothyroidism usually manifests itself between ages 2 and 5. Properly screened parent dogs must pass three tests, the Free T4 by dialysis test (FT4D), the Canine Thyroid Stimulating Hormone test (cTSH), and the Thyroglobulin Autoantibodies test (TgAA). Dogs who pass these tests can be issued an OFA certification number.

The OFA program is a useful addition to breeding programs; eventually, it may help to drastically reduce the number of dogs born with a propensity towards hypothyroidism. When purchasing a Siberian puppy, ask the breeder if she has submitted the parents of the litter for a thyroid test.

Cancer

Cancer is one of the most common dog ailments, especially for the aging canine. The most common type is skin cancer (of which there are many varieties). Most skin tumors found in dogs are benign, but for cancerous ones, early detection is critical. Owners find most cancerous growths themselves, so during your grooming routine, look for any unusual lumps. Fast-growing lumps and hard lumps that seem to be attached to bone or muscle are especially suspicious.

Other common types of cancer include lymphoma, brain tumors, *osteosarcomas* (bone tumors), testicular tumors, and oral tumors. Treatment options include surgery, diet therapy, chemotherapy, and radiation. Plus, it's not always successful.

Zinc Malabsorption Disorder

Zinc malabsorption disorder is a genetic condition that Huskies share with Samoyeds and Alaskan Malamutes. In this disease, the intestine does not absorb zinc properly. A dog with zinc deficiency will develop noninflammatory lesions on the skin and may lose his hair. He will need a zinc supplement. Follow the dosage recommended by your veterinarian.

Allergies

Like people, dogs can be allergic to any number of things, the most common being fleas, foods, and inhalants. I knew one dog who was allergic to fescue grass, pine, and maple. I knew another one who was allergic to the family cat. It's also possible for dogs to be allergic to human beings.

Where humans react to many allergies by sneezing, dogs tend to react by exhibiting various skin disorders. These include redness, itchiness, and rawness around the feet, ears, armpits, face, or groin area. In very serious cases, maggots can infest the oozing sores of allergic dogs. Most allergies, especially food allergies, tend to show up when the dog is about 2 years old.

Allergies cannot be cured; they can only be controlled, and usually with difficulty.

For temporary relief from allergies, bathe your dog frequently, using a gentle shampoo. If possible, avoid using tap water, which may contain chemicals that irritate your dog's skin further. Rinse thoroughly with cool water, to which you may add some soothing like witch hazel or peppermint tea. Then apply an herbal deterrent or antibiotic or cortisone spray to help heal the sore spot to prevent your Husky from licking it.

Corticosteroids are another option. They relieve itching but have innumerable side effects. Usually, your vet will prescribe high dosages for a few days, with the amount gradually being reduced over time.

Immunotherapy, which relies on a series of injections to identify allergens and then desensitize the dog to them, is slow-acting and can be expensive. Neither is it always successful.

The best way to control the allergy is to remove the allergic agent from the dog, but this is not always possible. Fleas can be hunted down and destroyed, but if your dog is allergic to grass, mold, or pollen, you're in for a difficult time.

Because allergies can be inherited, an allergic dog is not a good choice to be a parent. Make sure when you buy your puppy that the parents of the dog have no allergies.

Food allergies

Food allergies account for between 5 and 10 percent of canine allergies. Like other allergies in dogs, they usually manifest themselves as itchy skin, although they have also been implicated in canine inflammatory bowel disease. Head-shaking is another possible symptom of food allergies.

Just because your dog has been on the same diet all his life does not mean he hasn't suddenly developed an allergy to one of the ingredients. These things happen. Eliminate the suspect foods from your dog's diet for as long as 16 weeks. Substitute some kind of meat that your dog hasn't eaten before.

Food allergies are notoriously difficult to pin down. Lamb used to be the meat of choice for this purpose, but unfortunately lamb is now a common component of dog foods, so it can no longer be used to test for allergies. People are now using rabbit or venison. If you have a puppy, don't feed him any product containing lamb; that way if he does end up with an allergy later on, you can still use lamb as a high-protein elimination diet.

Many of the fillers commonly found in commercial foods are allergens. The key is to find an elimination diet that contains none of the common foods your dog has been consuming. This includes treats like dog biscuits and rawhide bones. Because food allergies are both fairly uncommon and hard to detect, other sources of allergies should be eliminated first.

There is no cure for food allergies; your dog must simply avoid the suspect foods. Always talk with your vet if you suspect your dog may be allergic to certain foods.

Inhalant allergies

In a dog who is allergic to inhalants, the culprits are often the same ones that affect human beings — dust, mold, and pollen. An allergic Husky will react by scratching, chewing, and licking. He may develop an ear infection, and his skin may become greasy with an uncharacteristically strong odor. These allergies can be identified the same way they are in human beings — by injecting a small amount of the suspect stuff in a shaved patch on the dog.

Flea allergies

The flea itself is probably not causing an allergy in your dog, but the proteins present in flea saliva are. If your dog has fleas, the usual scratching symptoms are present. The best cure is prevention — keep the fleas off your dog by using Frontline or another effective flea-repellant product.

Dental Problems

A dog's mouth is a perfect quagmire of microbial lifeforms. In fact, over 450 species of bacteria have been found there. Lots of them can cause dental disease, one of the most common afflictions of older dogs. Left unattended, bad teeth can abscess and lead to *septicemia* (blood poisoning) and even serious heart problems. Brush your dog's teeth regularly (see Chapter 12), and make sure he gets regular dental checkups.

 Many veterinarians use broad-based antibiotics, in addition to professionally cleaning the teeth, to treat periodontal problems. To save a sick tooth, veterinarians can apply an enamel matrix that actually helps regenerate jaw and gum attachments.

Bloat

Bloat is a disease that is most common in large breeds with deep chests, but it can and does occur in Huskies. When it hits, it can be deadly, killing a dog within two hours. Its cause is unknown, but predisposing factors seem to include gulping food and air, and drinking a lot of water or exercising right after eating. There may be a hereditary link also.

In bloat, the dog's stomach becomes distended with gas or fluid (or both). The stomach can then twist, trapping the gas. Not only is the stomach affected, but pressure is put on the large blood vessels of the abdomen, leading to organ failure. Dogs with bloat will vomit (or try to), whine, groan, pace, and salivate. Their stomach may become visibly swollen and sound hollow when tapped.

Treatment for bloat is both expensive and of uncertain success.

Often surgery is the only option; it must begin as soon as possible if the stomach has started to twist. Sometimes the veterinarian will perform a procedure called *gastropexy*, in which the stomach is attached to the body cavity in an effort to prevent further twisting.

The best treatment for bloat is prevention. Feed smaller meals at more frequent intervals, and encourage your dog to eat more slowly by scattering the food over a larger area. Do not exercise your Husky immediately before or after eating.

Aging

When does a Siberian reach retirement age? Well, if the human retirement age is 67.5 years, your 10-year-old Husky meets the criterion.

Dogs reach retirement age at various rates. Although it is true that giant breeds like Great Danes and Saint Bernards age more quickly than smaller ones, a great variation exists. Shih Tzus, for instance, age more quickly than Old English Sheepdogs.

In the United States, 14 percent of all canine companions are 11 years old or older. This is a tribute to better veterinary care and to keeping dogs in fenced yards. But aging brings its own difficulties. As dogs grow older, you can expect certain medical problems to occur with more frequency. Among the more common are eye problems, dental disease, hearing loss, Cushings disease, cancer, arthritis, obesity, and kidney and liver problems.

Take your older Husky for regular veterinary maintenance checkups, so he can be monitored for the development of any of these diseases. When your Siberian reaches the age of 8 or 9, you should begin geriatric screening.

This is the time to pamper your older dog; a bed raised a little off the floor, for example, is easier for him to get in and out of.

Regular exercise is as important for the old dog as for the young one, even though the exercise will not be so vigorous. An 11-year-old may be past his sled-pulling days, but he won't object to frolicking with you or his canine pals in the backyard.

As far as diet goes, recent research has indicated (somewhat surprisingly) that the older dog requires about 50 percent more protein than a young adult dog! The greater amount of dietary protein is needed to make up for a decreased ability to synthesize protein.

Canine cognitive dysfunction syndrome (CDS) is a form of senility just recently recognized as a specific disease. If your older dog (10 years or older) suddenly seems confused, withdrawn, sleepless at night, or begins to regress in the house-training department, suspect CDS. The drug Anipryl (L-deprenyl) has been approved for use in treating CDS. Its active ingredient is selegiline, the same medication used for Parkinson's disease in humans. Dogs with CDS need to take Anipryl for the rest of their lives, but 69 percent of afflicted dogs improve dramatically with treatment. The medication costs between $1.50 and $2.00 a day.

Chapter 15

Responding to Emergencies

· ·

In This Chapter

▶ Assembling a first aid kit

▶ Knowing when to call the vet

▶ Dealing with life-threatening situations calmly and wisely

· ·

Recognizing an emergency is a necessary skill in dog ownership. Quite simply, it can make the difference between life and death. Dog sicknesses can be serious precisely because dogs are stoic creatures; by the time the dog is actually showing distress, the illness may be far along. Besides, dogs can't tell you when they are sick — they can only show it through their symptoms.

This is why you need to pay attention to small signs, such as lack of appetite, increased thirst, or lethargy. These are often the first symptoms of something seriously wrong. I am conservative with my dogs; at the first sign of something unusual, I rush them to the vet.

Sometimes, however, you may need to undertake certain measures to help your dog before you can get him to the vet. This chapter is designed to recognize emergency situations and give you a first-line defense.

The following symptoms are serious enough to warrant a call to the vet:

- ✔ Blood in feces, urine, or vomit
- ✔ Pale gums
- ✔ Persistent coughing
- ✔ Seizure or shaking
- ✔ Prolonged lethargy
- ✔ Unexplained weight loss
- ✔ Refusal to eat (for 48 hours) or drink (for 12 hours)

The Complete Pet First Aid Kit

Be prepared for any emergency by assembling a first aid kit for your pet. You can use an old fishing tackle box or lightweight tool box for this purpose. On the inside of the box, write down the correct dosage for medication for your each of your pets. And remember to keep your first aid medications up to date.

Here is a complete list of what to put in your first aid kit:

- ✔ Ace bandage
- ✔ Activated charcoal
- ✔ Adhesive tape and gauze
- ✔ Alcohol prep pads
- ✔ Antibiotic ointment
- ✔ Benadryl antihistamine (1 to 2 milligrams per pound, every 8 hours)
- ✔ Buffered aspirin (5 milligrams per pound every 12 hours)
- ✔ Cold pack
- ✔ Cotton balls
- ✔ Ear and oral syringe
- ✔ Epsom salts
- ✔ Eye wash
- ✔ Gauze sponges
- ✔ Hydrogen peroxide (1 to 3 teaspoons every 10 minutes until the dog vomits)
- ✔ Imodium A-D (1 milligram per 15 pounds, once or twice daily)
- ✔ Kaopectate (1 milliliter per 1 pound every 2 hours)
- ✔ Magnifying glass
- ✔ Milk of magnesia, antacid and laxative
- ✔ Mineral oil, laxative (5 to 30 milliliters per day)
- ✔ Pepto Bismol, anti-diarrheal (1 teaspoon per 5 pounds, every six hours) or tablets
- ✔ Providone-iodine ointment
- ✔ Rectal thermometer (specifically made for canine use)

✔ Rubbing alcohol

✔ Safety pins

✔ Soft cloth muzzle

✔ Scissors (small blunt-end type)

✔ Splints

✔ Tweezers or hemostat

✔ Vaseline

Accidents

In case of an accident, you may need to restrain your dog either by muzzling him or binding his feet. If you have no muzzle handy, you can make one from a strip of cloth or nylons crossed over his nose and tied behind his neck (see Figure 15-1). Loosen the muzzle periodically to allow him to pant or vomit. In severe cases, you may need to throw a blanket over him.

Figure 15-1: How to make an emergency muzzle.

Avoid moving an injured dog unless you have to do so.

If your dog has been struck by a car, assume the worst. Even if he trots away apparently unaffected, he may have internal injuries. Take him to a vet just to be safe.

Serious symptoms include bleeding from the nose, mouth, and ears, although some internal injuries are slower in making themselves noticed. More subtle warning signs include pale gums, weakness, or general listlessness. By the time you notice these, it may be too late.

Bites

The curious Siberian is forever poking his nose where it doesn't belong. Many times he will be rewarded with a sharp and sometime poisonous reprisal.

Snakebite

Dogs are curious by nature, and a number of them get popped in the nose or leg every year by snakes. Most snakebites are nonvenomous, but even a non-venomous bite can lead to infection.

The wrong kind of snakebite can be deadly. Snake venom is a complicated mess of enzymes, peptides, and proteins. It can affect the nervous, muscular, and urinary systems. To make things worse, snakebites hurt. Treatment includes intravenous fluids, antivenin, steroids, and antibiotics.

Do not try to cut the wound and suck the poison out! It's probably too late for that anyway, and you'll only end up making yourself sick.

In as many as one out of every three cases, even a bite from a venomous snake is not poisonous, because the snake has complete control of his venom sacs. He may wish to save his good stuff for real prey and just bite to frighten your dog.

Spider bites

There may be 100,000 different species of spiders in the world, and sooner or later, one of them will probably bite your dog. Almost every species of spider is venomous, but the venom of most is very weak — good enough to paralyze a fly, but just a minor irritation to people and dogs. In the United States, we have two kinds of dangerously poisonous spiders: the black widow and the brown recluse. The bite of the brown recluse is especially nasty, because it not only makes a dog sick, but results in ulcerated flesh around the bite. Often the skin necroses and falls away from the wound.

 If possible, capture the offending spider, and bring it with you to the veterinarian. Unfortunately, of course, it is unlikely you will be present or notice the bite. If you just suspect a spider bite, get your Husky to the vet as soon as possible.

Bleeding

Apply direct pressure with a clean cloth. Minor bleeding should stop in five minutes. For major wounds, keep applying pressure until you get your Husky to a vet. Use an ice pack if necessary.

Rectal bleeding can be a symptom of parvovirus, whereas bleeding from the vulva can indicate *pyometra* (a serious disease of unspayed females) or other internal infections.

Bloat

A hard, swollen abdomen is a sign of bloat. Get to the vet immediately; there is no time to lose. (For more information on bloat, turn to Chapter 14.)

Breathing Difficulties

If your Husky is having trouble breathing, it is a major emergency. Labored respiration, gasping, and a blue tongue are danger signals.

Broken Bones

If your Husky has an injured leg, tie the leg to a temporary splint made of a board or something similar. Place the leg in as natural a position as possible, but don't try to set it yourself.

If the back, pelvis, or ribs seem broken, stabilize the dog as quickly as possible without repositioning him, and get him to a vet.

Coughing

Coughing can be a symptom of anything from heartworm to secondhand smoke. Pay attention to the elements of the cough. Is it hacking or wheezing? Gagging? How often does your dog cough? This information is important for your vet to know.

Diarrhea and Vomiting

Diarrhea may result from a simple digestive upset, although it could also be a sign of something more serious. If the bout of vomiting or diarrhea doesn't last more than a day or so, it probably isn't anything to worry about. But a continued or frequently recurring digestive upset should be checked by a vet.

Dogs have the ability to throw up with ease, and almost anything can cause it: trash eating, diet change, poison, allergy, infection, and so on.

Bloody feces, bloody urine, or straining are all indications of trouble.

To help your dog over a round of vomiting or diarrhea, a little Pepto Bismol works wonders. Fifty-pound dogs require a little over a tablespoon. The liquid kind seems to work better than the pills but is harder to administer. Have your dog skip a meal or two afterwards, and follow with a bland, low-fat diet.

The best way to get the liquid in your dog is with a syringe (minus the needle, of course), available from your vet or drugstore. In a pinch, you'd be surprised how well a turkey baster works.

If the vomiting or diarrhea continues, take your dog to the vet, and bring a stool sample with you. The more you can tell your vet about the vomiting or diarrhea episodes (timing, frequency, severity, and so on), the more help you can be in making the diagnosis.

Heat Stress

Signs of heat stress include staggering, loud panting, vomiting, bright red gums, and a red, bleary look in the eyes. The body temperature may rise above 104 degrees. If your Siberian exhibits these symptoms, quickly provide water, submerse the dog in a tub of cool water, or apply cold wet towels. Then call your veterinarian.

Heat can also increase the chances of your dog getting a fungal infection.

There's an old saying that a cold, wet nose means a healthy nose. This is not necessarily true. However, a hot, dry nose *may* indicate the first stages of dehydration; see if your dog would like some water. If his nose stays hot and dry, and if there are other symptoms, consult your veterinarian.

Poison

For most poisonings, other than caustics like Drano, making the dog vomit is a good first step.

To induce vomiting, force down a solution of one of the following:

- Half water and half peroxide (1 to 3 teaspoons of each)
- Lukewarm salt water (2 or 3 tablespoons of salt per cup)
- 1 tablespoon of dry mustard in 1 cup of water

If the dog does not vomit soon afterward, repeat the dosage while waiting for veterinary care.

After the dog has vomited (or if you can't get him to vomit), give him 4 table-spoons of activated charcoal to absorb the remaining poison.

Antifreeze poisoning

Antifreeze depresses the central nervous system and enters the cerebrospinal fluid. Symptoms include vomiting, diarrhea, and a staggering gait, which may lead you to wonder if the animal is drunk. Unfortunately, these symptoms may not appear for 8 to 12 hours, after irreparable damage has been done to your pet. If you suspect your dog has ingested antifreeze, get him to your veterinarian immediately. Do not wait to see if the dog appears sick. Treatment is most effective if given within four hours after your dog drinks the fluid. The best antidote for dogs now on the market is 4-methylpyrazole, sold under the brand name Antizol.

Chocolate poisoning

Dogs love chocolate, but it contains a substance called *theobromine,* which is toxic to canines. Theobromine is also present in tea and cola.

Symptoms of chocolate poisoning include vomiting, diarrhea, frantic running around (even worse than usual), and frequent urination. If you're able to take your dog's pulse, you'll also notice a faster, more irregular heartbeat.

Hydrogen peroxide can be used to make the dog vomit, if the dog has eaten the chocolate within the previous two hours. In any case, call your veterinarian immediately.

Onion and garlic poisoning

Onions can destroy canine red blood cells by oxidizing the hemoglobin inside them, reducing their ability to transport oxygen to the rest of the body. An onion-poisoned dog may become anemic. A quarter cup of onions can do a job on a medium-sized dog. It makes no difference whether the onions are cooked or not. The condition is not permanent, but dogs poisoned with onions have been known to need a blood transfusion.

Large amounts of garlic can have the same effect as onions.

Rat poison

Keep rat poison away from pets. But mistakes do happen. Rat poison is extremely palatable to dogs, as well as to rats, cats, and kids, so it's vital to keep it locked up.

The dog next door, Buddy, was poisoned in just such a way; he managed to jump against a not so very securely latched door, and eat two cakes of poison.

The symptoms of deadly rat poison may not show up for three to five days after ingestion. The poison is an anticoagulant, so it may be four or five days before you notice anything is wrong. By the time you notice the symptoms, your dog may bleed to death internally right before your eyes.

If you even suspect your pet has been exposed to rat poison, induce vomiting immediately, and get him to the veterinarian. The vet will probably begin vitamin K injections three times a day for a couple of days, to be followed by vitamin K pills for one to three weeks afterwards. This regimen saved the life of Buddy, who never showed a symptom from his unorthodox eating habits.

Porcupine Quills

The insatiably curious Siberian, if left to his own devices, may run afoul of a porcupine, a slow-moving denizen of the northern woods. Get to a veterinarian if possible. If you can't get to a vet, you can try to extract the quills with pliers. It's important to get out *all* of the quill, so you don't risk infection in your dog.

Seizures

Seizures are frequently a sign of epilepsy, although there may be other causes as well, such as sleep deprivation, food allergies, overused supplements, toxins like heavy metal and flea dips, hypoglycemia, and dehydration. Signs include staggering, head tilting, sudden blindness, snapping, jerking, or unaccountable aggressiveness. Seizures are frightening, but rarely life-threatening. After the seizure is over, the dog will usually come to you for reassurance and love.

During a seizure, the dog is not aware of himself or his surroundings. Remove dangerous objects, but try not to touch the dog. If a seizure continues for more than 30 minutes, it's an emergency. The dog should be taken to the veterinarian immediately. Devise a makeshift stretcher with a blanket. Keep a record of the length, frequency, and symptoms of all seizures.

Wounds

Major wounds may require stitches; you can handle minor ones yourself. Penetrating wounds in the abdomen or chest areas should be considered major emergencies.

Clean the wound carefully, removing any hair or debris in it. Hydrogen peroxide is no longer recommended to clean wounds, because it can damage tissues. Use commercial wound cleaner like Nolvasan or even soap and water. Wash the wound thoroughly, for at least 10 minutes (most people do not wash the wound thoroughly enough).

If the wound is a puncture-type wound or an abscess, contact your veterinarian.

Part V

Bringing Out the Sled Dog in Your Siberian

The 5th Wave   By Rich Tennant

ALONG WITH BEING VERY GOOD SLED DOGS, HUSKIES ARE KNOWN TO BE EXCELLENT SHOPPING CART DOGS

In this part . . .

If you haven't figured it out by now, Siberian Huskies were made for sledding. That's not to say that your Husky won't be perfectly content with his calmer home life. But whether you're just interested in discovering what your Husky's ancestors did or you'd like to see first-hand what he could do if you hitched him to a sled, this part is for you. If it's sledding you're interested in, it's sledding you'll get in the chapters in this part.

Chapter 16

Getting Your Husky into Sledding

*E*veryone associates the Siberian Husky with sled dog racing, a practice that developed during the Alaskan Gold Rush of 1896. It didn't become a formal institution, however, until 1908, the year of the first All Alaska Sweepstakes Race.

Pulling a sled is what Siberian Huskies were bred for. It comes more naturally to them than any other canine sport. So, if you want to make the most of your Husky's noble heritage, you can't go wrong in hooking him up to a sled or cart, like the proud Husky owner in Figure 16-1.

Sledding 101: The Basics of the Sport

In sled dog racing, the dogs are paired up on either side of a *gangline*. The line that connects the dog to the gangline is called the *tugline*. The *neckline,* a thin line attached to the dog's collar, keeps the dog close to the gangline. You will often see sled dogs leaping from one side of the gangline to the other as they try to avoid curves.

Professional teams have up to 20 dogs. The lead dogs are selected for their intelligence and willingness to lead (some nice dogs just prefer to follow along). Mushers are equal opportunity employers. Both male and female dogs are used as lead dogs.

If two lead dogs are used, they are called *co-leaders.* Most dogs appear to prefer having a co-leader than to run alone. Following the leader are the *point dogs.* Most mushers put their fastest dogs in this position, although sleds must obviously go at the speed of the slowest dog.

Dave and Bonnie Lundberg

The *swing dogs,* who follow the point dogs, are responsible for turning the sled and other dogs in the direction of the lead dogs. Swing dogs must be strong and determined. They are responsible for making sure the turning sled doesn't veer off course and crash into a tree. Point and swing dogs are often leader dogs in training.

The following pairs of dogs (if any) are called the *team dogs* and keep the entire group moving. Closest to the sled are the *wheel dogs,* who are the largest and most powerful dogs on the sled, pulling the most weight.

Keep in mind that the team I describe here is a deluxe team! You can mush with just one dog. And when you're first learning the ropes, that's by far the best plan.

When it comes to sled dog racing, probably the most difficult aspect is finding a place to train. You can't train on concrete or in a dense forest, so your options may be pretty limited. The best thing is to join a sled dog club that sponsors meets and has access to training areas.

Unless a dog team is properly socialized, and taught to respect its human leader, the team can become a pack, with its own leader, and its own rules. The human being must remain in control at all times. A team of Huskies is much stronger than any one person, so you need to use common sense and fair treatment to keep your natural position as leader.

In the warm, snowless off-season, dogs are conditioned on three- or four-wheeled training rigs.

In today's sled dog world, dogs generally compete in one of the following races: three dogs and three miles; six dogs and six miles; eight dogs and nine miles; and the unlimited class — up to 20 dogs at 14 miles or more. Recently, a team of 210 dogs was harnessed to a flatbed truck (with a sled in front). The dogs pulled it with no difficulty.

The premier event of sled dog racing is, of course, the Iditarod. It runs over 1,000 miles and is the longest sled dog race in the world. It was organized to honor the memory of Leonhard Seppala, who organized the 1925 run to Nome with diphtheria serum, saving the inhabitants from almost certain death. Its complete name is the Iditarod Trail Sleddog Race, and today it is worth well over $50,000 to the winning driver. See Chapter 17 for more on the Iditarod.

Nowadays, there are many international sled dog races. Chief among these, besides the Iditarod, is another Alaskan and Canadian event, the Yukon Quest. Like the Iditarod, it is a 1,000-mile run across rough terrain. Another event, the Fairbanks North American Championship covers 70 miles in three days, as does the Fur Rendezvous Sled Dog Race ("Rondy"), held every year in Anchorage.

The International Sled Dog Racing Association (ISDRA) sanctions these events. ISDRA also mandates safety regulations, trail conditions and required mushing equipment. The welfare of both dogs and drivers is paramount. Dogs must be certified healthy and free of contagious diseases. Dangerous equipment like choke collars and muzzles are forbidden, and the canine athletes are routinely tested for drugs. Even aspirin is illegal.

In the continental U.S., Idaho, New Hampshire, and Minnesota each host sled dog championships. Often, races for kids are offered, and many have torchlight parades, Mushers' Balls, and all sorts of thrilling Winter Carnival–like events.

"Gosh, they look thin!"

Like human long-distance runners and thoroughbred horses, a well conditioned racing dog is lean (but not mean). It's not that the dogs are poorly fed; in fact, most of them consume more calories per day than the average person. It's just that they burn off the calories they consume.

Using commercial dog food as a complete diet is out of the question for serious drivers. These foods may be adequate for a house dog, but they simply do not provide the nutritional value a racing animal needs. Commercial foods tend to be low in fat, which is good for sedentary pets but bad for the working Siberian. Fats provide quick energy for dogs. Racing dogs may eat a diet that contains 50 percent fat, 35 percent protein, and 15 percent carbohydrates. Mushers do sometimes use a base commercial diet, supplemented with ground meat, liver, oils, and fish.

Racing sled dogs are fed four or five times a day. They often dine on salmon and other rich, high-protein foods, to the tune of over 5,000 calories a day. Siberians get along with less than other racing sled dogs, some of whom consume nearly twice as much. This food frequently smells awful, by the way.

Racing dogs also drink an enormous amount of water. They do not eat snow. Eating snow is a dehydrating activity, because it takes the body more energy to melt the snow than the snow provides by way of water. You never see Eskimos eating snow, do you?

Serious mushers are always seeking a diet that will give their dogs a winning edge. Brian Patrick O'Donoghue, in his book *My Lead Dog Was a Lesbian,* tells of a horrific stew called "honey balls," a nightmarish concoction of raw hamburger, honey, corn oil, and bonemeal, all stirred up in the bathtub with a broken hockey stick. The resulting product was too awful to use.

Watching a sled race

If you get a chance, try to observe a sled race. It's an amazing event to watch, even if you don't feel the urge to try it yourself. Don't bring your own dogs, however, because they can be distracting to the canine athletes, especially if they break away and go charging into the middle of the course. You are free to take all the photos you like, but keep well away from the trail as the dogs rush past!

Ask permission of owners before petting their dogs, and don't give the animals any treats.

You will often have some time before the race to observe the animals being harnessed and readied for their task, so this is not a good time to talk to mushers about their hobby. However, once the race has begun, you can probably have a chat with the handlers, friends, and sled dog groupies about the joys of sled dog racing.

A mushing lexicon

Verbal commands are critical in the world of sled sports. The driver has no reins to guide the team; he relies on his voice and the common sense and obedience of his lead dog.

Mushers today say, "Hike!" instead of "Mush!", just like a quarterback. Sometimes they say, "Go!" The word "mush" is a corruption of the French "March!" meaning, "Get along! Walk on!" Some say that "mush" was felt to be too soft, and well, mushy a word for the drivers, who nevertheless, are still known as mushers. Go figure.

- ✔ **"Gee!":** Turn right! This term and "haw" both come from old draft-horse terminology.

- ✔ **"Haw!":** Turn left! Some people just say "left" or "right," but the nice thing about "gee" and "haw" is that they are the same all over the world, in every language.

- ✔ **"Tshckt!":** Keep going!

- ✔ **"Go by!" (or "on by!"):** Pass on, pay no attention to whatever is distracting you!

- ✔ **"Trail!":** Yield the right of way!

- ✔ **"Whoa!":** Stop! (More horse lingo.)

Mushing equipment

The sport of sled dog racing is not an inexpensive one. Here's a list of the basic equipment mushers need:

- ✔ **Sled:** Either a basket or toboggan type of sled will work. The former is better for beginners. Expect to spend $300 to $1,000 for a good sled. You can even get a fold-up sled for easy storage. These fold-up vehicles have no brake. You can also buy a cart; some carts can be used with or without snow.

- ✔ **X-back harness:** The x-back harness is just the traditional sled-pulling harness. You'll spend $15 to $20 for a good harness.

- ✔ **Gangline or towline:** The long rope that runs down the middle of the dog team. Tuglines are attached to it. A gangline or towline costs $10 to $15.

- ✔ **Sled bag:** At $25 to $30, a sled bag is not absolutely necessary to buy, especially for beginners. It's designed to carry gear.

  ✔ **Snow hook:** A kind of emergency brake, a snow hook is used like an anchor in the snow and costs about $10.

  ✔ **Booties:** These are worn by Huskies to keep their feet protected from ice or slush. They run about $1.50 each, unless you buy them in bulk, which you may want to do, because they do wear out and get lost.

  ✔ **Snubline:** A rope that attaches the sled to a tree or post while resting.

Getting a Sled Dog

If you are seriously interested in sled dogging, you should purchase a dog from a kennel specializing in breeding Siberians for sledding. But even this is a gamble, because kennels try to keep the best stock for themselves in order to improve their line. (The true qualities of a sled dog may not show up until he is about 18 months old.)

Still, sometimes kennels can be overstocked with males and may be able to sell you a very good sledding prospect. Even without a specially bred sled dog, however, you can still enjoy this exciting hobby. Most Huskies can happily learn to pull a sled.

A sledding or racing Siberian often looks a little different from his conformation counterpart. He is usually a bit rangier, with longer legs, and perhaps bigger feet. Many of the working or racing Siberians do not possess the classic close-set, inward-pointing ears of the conformation dog.

In addition to physical prowess, mushers look for several key mental elements in a good mushing dog: attitude, a good work ethic, trainability, and a desire to please.

Sledding for Fun

It's said that a dog comes by mushing ability half through heredity and half by training. But if your object is just to have fun rather than to race competitively, it's important to note that almost any Husky can be trained to pull a sled. You don't need to worry about getting a high-quality racing dog. (This is a good thing, because a premium trained racing dog can cost upwards of $5,000, if you can find one at all.)

If you're not sure whether you would like sledding, many organizations offer sled dog tours; you can get a package deal, which includes a sled, a team, and a guide.

If possible, find a mentor to help you get started. This can be as simple as contacting your local Siberian Husky Club or Sled Dog Club, and asking if someone will allow you to train with them. Most mushers are friendly and helpful people and will be glad to lend a helping hand to a neophyte.

You can teach your Husky to wear a pulling harness when he's about 5 months old, although some racing experts start earlier, using a soft harness designed to be attached to a small log. It's very important that your Husky learn to pull when wearing a harness and to heel when wearing a collar. Your job is to make sure he gets the connection. Stay behind the dog when teaching him to pull — don't lead him or walk along next to him. Start on a well-marked path — that will get him used to the idea of walking on a trail.

Serious training begins when the dog is about 1 year old, usually in the fall during cool weather. Most people try to place the pup in an established, harmonious team of dogs, so he can learn from example how to behave properly. Sled dogs must learn to get along with one another! The puppy's first jobs are to learn how to pay attention to his pulling, stay on the trail, socialize with the team, and listen to the musher (that's you). Start with short runs and gradually increase the length of your trips as your dog builds up his muscle and strength. (Fully grown racing dogs train from 10 to 90 miles every other day during racing season.)

Siberian Huskies actually run best when the temperature is 15 or 20 degrees below zero, so get out your mukluks!

Chapter 17

The Last Great Race: The Iditarod

· ·

· ·

*F*or most of us, the name *Husky* is synonymous with *sled dog,* and *sled dog* means *Iditarod.* The Iditarod is much more than a sporting event, however. It's a final test of stamina, loyalty, and courage. It's a commemoration of the Great Serum Run. And it's a glorious celebration of the great sport of sled dog racing. The Iditarod is also one of the few sporting events in which men and women compete equally.

The Start of the Iditarod

The 1,000-mile race we call the Iditarod was first run in 1973, the brain child of Dorothy G. Page, a native of Wasilla, Alaska. Page was worried by the fact that since snowmobiles had been invented, no one seemed to remember the Great Serum Run or any other feats of the famous sled dogs of the past.

She approached Joe Redington, and together they organized the first Iditarod Trail Race in 1967. It wasn't much compared to the Iditarod today — only 27 miles long. This sprint was run again in 1969.

The Pages and Redingtons raised money for the event by donating an acre of land and selling square-foot "lots" with official certificates. They actually managed to scare up $10,000 by this scheme, and eventually the purse swelled to $25,000. Today, the Iditarod is worth $550,000. Considering that it costs about $10,000 to run the race, this doesn't seem like a lot of money. There are also smaller prizes given out to the first mushers to reach certain points, awards for the best sled dog (the Golden Harness Award), and a Sportsmanship Prize.

That first year, mushers from all over Alaska (and two from Massachusetts) entered. The race was won by Isaac Okleasik, and the Iditarod was born.

Naturally, the Pages and Redingtons weren't going to be satisfied with a mere 27-mile dash; they had their eyes on bigger things. Unexpectedly, they got some help from the United States Army, which decided, for reasons of its own, to open the sled trail all the way to Nome in 1973, thus following the old Gold Trail from Anchorage to Nome.

The Iditarod Today

Today, the Iditarod begins in Anchorage on the first Saturday in March. Usually between 50 and 80 teams compete, although few have any chance of winning. For most, it's enough of an honor even to finish the famous race. In 2000, a record number of 81 drivers did so.

The Iditarod has seen mushers from Austria, Canada, France, Italy, Japan, Sweden, Norway, Great Britain, Russia, Germany, Czechoslovakia, Switzerland, and even Australia.

Not everyone with a sled and a bunch of dogs is eligible to run the Iditarod. First, there is an entry fee of $1,750 (the entry fee originally was $1,049, a dollar for every mile run). Then, only mushers with a proven track record can qualify; this includes those who have finished the Iditarod previously, or those who have completed at least two approved races within the previous two years. An approved race is a continuous run of at least 500 miles.

Each team is required to have between 12 and 16 dogs, 5 of which must be hitched to the gangline at the finish in Nome. Over the years, teams have become larger. With a big team, the musher can be 80 feet from the lead dog; that means a lot of yelling. Many Iditarod drivers use two lead dogs, but it's not unusual for someone to run the race with just one.

The race begins in downtown Anchorage. Most years, over 1,000 dogs compete for the prize. The contestants then run 8 or 10 miles to Eagle River. This is a chance for mushers to check out their dogs and equipment. A number of *joy riders* or *Iditariders* go along for this first leg. This is purely a ceremonial start. It doesn't count for overall time, and after the dogs get to the VFW Post in Eagle River, they're all loaded up in trucks and sent home for the night.

You can actually win a trip aboard a dog sled for the first leg of the Iditarod, thus becoming an *Iditarider*. The race uses auctioned bids to help support the teams. In fact, everyone who finishes the race (after the top 20, who get larger cash prizes) receives $1,049 for his efforts — a dollar for every mile run.

After the symbolic start in Anchorage, there's a restart in the Matanuska Valley at the old Wasilla Airport, about 40 miles north of Anchorage. After the mushers reach the checkpoint at Knik, they say goodbye to roads for the rest of the race. Between 9 and 12 days later, depending on weather conditions, the first of the mushers will reach Nome.

The slowest winning time was in 1974, when it took Carl Huntington well over 20 days to make the trek; the fastest time is owned by Doug Swingley, who finished in 9 days, 2 hours, 42 minutes, and 19 seconds in 1995. Swingley, from Montana, is the only non-Alaskan so far to win the race. He won the race again in 1999. Winners include members of both sexes, and all of them come from places with names like Red Devil, Knik, Trapper Creek, and Clam Gulch. So if you live in Dayton, I wouldn't count on winning the Iditarod anytime soon.

Mushers have to pass through 26 checkpoints between Anchorage and Nome. Food, straw (for dog bedding), and supplies for both dogs and racers are flown in by bush pilots (the so-called *Iditarod Air Force*), but mushers have to carry their own survival gear. The Iditarod organizers ship in as much as 200,000 pounds of food, provided by the mushers themselves, for the race.

The officially mandated gear includes a proper cold-weather sleeping bag, an ax, snowshoes, an operational cooker and pot, a veterinarian notebook, and two sets of dog booties per dog. (Over 2,009 booties are used in the average Iditarod.) Mushers also carry a harness repair kit, extra mittens, and emergency food for themselves and their dogs.

It is illegal to use most kinds of drugs on Iditarod dogs: anabolic steroids, analgesics, antihistamines, anti-inflammatory drugs, cough suppressants, and more are all forbidden. Some exceptions are made for topical ointments to be applied directly to the feet. Dogs are subject to urine and blood sampling at any point on the race.

About six hours ahead of the dog teams are the *trailbreakers,* who use special snow-machines to break the trail and carry supplies.

If you'd like to participate in the Iditarod yourself, you're more than welcome, even if you've never seen a dog sled. The Iditarod Trail Committee needs thousands of volunteers every year — veterinarians, trail breakers, logistic personnel, publicity people, fundraisers, people to staff the checkpoints and information centers, and so on.

Mushers are required to take a mandatory 24-hour stop during the race, at any time "most beneficial to the dogs." The checker at the rest point must be notified that the musher is taking his rest stop. In addition to the 24-hour stop, a musher must also take one eight-hour stop on the Yukon and one eight-hour stop at White Mountain.

Each checkpoint staff includes veterinarians. Veterinary checks are mandatory, and any tired or ill animals must be left behind. (The humans, however, are free to continue no matter how sick they are.) There are usually three vets per checkpoint, and the chief veterinarian has the authority to require that a tired or ill animal be dropped from the race. A *dropped* dog is permanently removed from the race and may not be replaced by another one. This rule, of course, is designed to prevent anyone from getting the idea that he can run his dogs till they drop and just replace them as they fall. Any driver who is cruel or abusive to his animals will be disqualified. Dropped dogs are shipped back to Anchorage, to the Hiland Mountain Correctional Center, where attentive and responsible inmates care for the animals until they can be returned to their owners. This plan works as a healing therapy for both prisoners and the dogs. Dangerously ill or injured dogs are sent by medevac to an emergency veterinary clinic.

Some mushers begin the race with more dogs than they plan to finish with; younger dogs in particular are often run only for the first part of the race.

The welfare of the dogs is a primary Iditarod concern; of the 57 "rules of the race," 26 apply directly to animal care. Animal care shelters are also provided along the trail.

A 50-pound Husky will consume over 5,000 calories per day during the Iditarod! Nearly all of the calories come from meat — fish, beef, caribou, and moose are favorites.

For several years in the early 1990s, someone named John Suter entered the Iditarod with a team largely composed of poodles. Of course, they didn't win, because poodles are singularly unsuited to running the Iditarod. (Their fur sticks to the snow, for one thing.) Still, rather surprisingly, Suter managed to finish the race three times. He went on a lot of talk shows afterwards. "There are five billion people in the world," he would say, "and only one of them mushes the Iditarod with a team of poodles." I suppose that is very true.

Iditarod dogs do not have to be Siberians or any purebred dog at all. Most, in fact, are Siberians mixed with other breeds by mushers hoping for just the right combination of speed and stamina for long-distance racing.

The first woman to win the Iditarod was Libby Riddles in 1985. She and her team plunged through a dangerous blizzard to victory. In that same year, favorite Susan Butcher lost most her team in an encounter with an enraged female moose. Moose sometimes stand in the middle of the mushing trail and attack the sledders. Two dogs were killed and another badly wounded; the distraught Butcher was of course forced to withdraw from the race. The next year, however, she went on to win — and repeated her victory three more times! One of those wins earned her the title of Woman Athlete of the Year.

Iditarod notables

- **Rick Swenson.** From Two River, Alaska, Swenson has competed in 20 Iditarods and has always finished in the top ten. He's won the race a record five times.

- **Dick Mackey.** In 1978, Mackey beat Swenson in an incredible photofinish, unbelievable in a race of this length. Dick's son, Rick, has also won the Iditarod. They both wore #13 on their winning rides. So far, they are the only father and son winners.

- **Norman Vaughan.** Vaughn has finished the race four times, although he hasn't won yet. He still has time — at age 88.

- **Libby Riddles.** Riddles was the first woman to win the Iditarod, in 1985.

- **Susan Butcher.** Butcher was the first woman to finish in the top ten. She has won four times.

- **Dr. Terry Adkins.** Adkins was the only veterinarian to race in the first Iditarod. He has completed the race 20 times, a record matched only by Rick Swenson.

- **Joe Runyan.** Runyan is the only musher to have won the Iditarod, the Alpirod (Europe's version of the Iditarod), and the Yukon Quest (another Alaskan-Canadian race, and the Iditarod's chief competitor).

Even the last-place finisher in the Iditarod does not go unnoticed. He or she wins the Red Lantern award. This award started as a joke but is now taken quite seriously. The Red Lantern is lit at 9:00 on the first Saturday in March in Nome, and placed at the Burl Arch, where the finish line is. It stays lit as long as anyone is still competing in the race. The Red Lantern Award is a symbol of courage, sportsmanship, and stick-to-it-iveness. In fact, there's a Red Lantern Banquet for the late finishers.

Only the top finishers manage to complete the race in nine or ten days; it often goes on as long as two weeks. Mushers race during the night, as well as during the day; still, the dogs get between 12 and 14 hours of sleep per day, not necessarily all at once. The driver isn't so lucky. While the dogs are sleeping, he is preparing their food, fixing the harnesses, and wondering why he got started in dog racing in the first place.

When the race is over, a gigantic all-city party is held in Nome, including basketball tournaments, dart games, and the Ice Golf Classic.

Part VI
The Part of Tens

"Okay, let's get into something a little more theoretical."

In this part . . .

This wouldn't be a book ...*For Dummies* without the Part of Tens. If you don't have much time, the chapters in this part are perfect for you. They provide lots of information in a small amount of space — everything from why you should own a Husky to how to raise the one you have. I also point out some common household hazards that Huskies can fall victim to and let you know how to travel with your Husky so that both of you are happy. In a rush? Read on!

Chapter 18

Ten Reasons to Have a Siberian Husky

. . . .

In This Chapter

▶ Figuring out what makes Siberians so special

▶ Seeing whether you're the right person for a Husky

. . . .

*I*f you're not sure whether a Siberian Husky is the dog for you, in this chapter you'll find ten great reasons to own one of these wonderful dogs.

Huskies Always Smile

That cheerful, devil-may-care look reveals something special about the Siberian Husky's personality and his relationship to you. Huskies are good-natured and willing to please. Plus, they're human-oriented, which means that they are happiest when they are with you. They look to you for companionship, guidance, and love. This is one of the qualities that makes them great pets — their very willingness to share their life with yours.

The Husky's smile also reminds us that dogs need to be happy — and it doesn't take a whole lot to keep them that way. Siberian Huskies don't require expensive dog beds, high-priced toys, and expensive vacations to the Riviera. A comfortable pillow at your feet, a chew toy, and frequent trips to the great outdoors is a Husky's idea of paradise.

The key to all these pleasures is you. Your Husky doesn't want to sleep alone, play alone, or run alone. But with you at his side, he'll keep that happy, cheerful smile.

Huskies Make Terrific Exercise Partners

Because Siberians must have adequate amounts of exercise, they are perfect pets for the human athlete. As long as the weather is cool enough, your Siberian will go charging happily (on a leash, please) at your side.

And if you are not a human marathoner, well, having a Siberian is a great way to get you started — or at least enough to get your heart rate going. A Siberian Husky can turn the most dedicated couch potato into an avid exerciser. Exercise not only keeps both of you fit, but it also helps keep a dog's mind entertained and his body physically tired. This is a great combination for the hours your Husky must spend by himself. A tired dog is a nondestructive dog, and nondestructive dogs make for happy owners.

A Siberian Husky Can Pull You Wherever You Want to Go

This is one of the many things that make a Siberian unique. A Pekinese can't pull you. A Basset Hound won't. But with a Husky, a whole new world of sport can open up to you. In the summer, hop on your inline skates, and start going uphill as well as down.

In the winter, grab your sled or skis; a Siberian is just the ticket. Not only will you find this entertaining, but so will your dog. Siberians are bred to pull — it's in their blood. All you need to do is follow happily along.

Allowing your Husky to pull you is also a great way to make friends — or at least to get people to pay attention to you. And you can join a club of like-minded folk and make even more friends.

Siberians Have No Doggie Odor

Compare a Husky to a hound, and you'll realize just how lucky you are. Their odorless state makes it possible to keep your dog inside all the time without giving him a bath every week. This is an important consideration for people who are sensitive to such things.

Huskies Are Educational

You will learn more from your Siberian than he will ever learn from you. Dogs teach you the following wonderful virtues:

- **Neatness:** If you don't put your things away, the dog will eat them.
- **Patience:** Training a Siberian gives you practice in this important virtue. Rome wasn't built in a day, and you can't teach a Siberian to fetch in 5 minutes.
- **Tolerance:** You will learn what you can expect from a dog, as well as what you can't.
- **Medical skills:** All experienced dog owners develop skills in handling medical emergencies. You never know when this may come in handy.

Huskies Provide Social Mobility

Although others have nothing more exciting to brag about than their child's last birthday party or toilet training triumphs, you can regale the office with any of the following tales:

- "What My Dog Ate Last Night When I Had My Back Turned for 5 Minutes"
- "What My Dog Dragged into the House That I Thought I Had Buried"
- "What Happened When I Went on a Sledding Trip with the Dogs and Somehow Got Lost"

And so on. Besides, your beautiful Siberian Husky is much better looking than any of their kids, and everybody knows it.

Huskies Are Great with Children

Unlike many other breeds, Huskies are tolerant of kids. They are sturdy enough to enjoy roughhousing, and forgiving enough to endure being fallen upon. It's also a plus that Huskies are non-protective. Many an unfortunate accident has occurred when a dog has bitten a neighbor's child because he thought the kid was attacking his owner's child (whom he views as his own), when all that was happening was normal child wrestling. You won't have to worry about your Husky doing something like that. Huskies welcome new children into the family circle readily.

Huskies Will Make You a Better Citizen

How can a Husky make you a better citizen? Well, a strong America is a prosperous America. And a prosperous America is one in which the consumer supports the economy. The Husky owner *really* supports the American economy. Here's how: First, he buys the Husky (thus reducing the loss of some poor hobby breeder). Then he buys the dog food (helping the farmer and pet food industry). Then he buys the leashes, collars, and bowls (helping manufacturing). Then he buys the book about Siberian Huskies (like this one) and helps the author and the publishing industry. Then he buys the computer to get online to get to the Husky Web sites and chat groups (helping the techies). Then he decides to take the dog on vacation and buys a new van to load up all this stuff (helping the automotive industry). Then he actually goes on vacation (helping the tourist industry). And on and on. . . . Don't you feel better about yourself and all the ways you're helping just by owning a great dog?

Siberians Remind You What Really Matters in Life

In other words, they help you prioritize. Life before Huskies may have been taken up with mundane matters like housekeeping. You can forget all that now. Not only do you have better things to do — like playing with the dog — but the obliging Siberian makes perfect housekeeping impossible anyway. So why bother with it?

Siberians teach you that what's really important is having fun, going places together, keeping healthy and strong, and giving and getting love. This brings us to the most important element of all.

Huskies Love You Unconditionally

Huskies don't put bounds, parameters, or limits on their affection. They don't care if you've put on a little weight recently or gotten a bit gray. They don't care if you're having a bad hair day or have bad breath. They don't care what kind of car you drive, clothes you wear, or accessories you sport. They don't care if you're poor. They don't mind if you're in a wheelchair, or deaf, or blind, or have epilepsy. They don't judge you by your race, religion, or sexual orientation. They don't care if you've been in jail.

They ask no questions, tell no lies, and make no judgments. They don't give up on you. They forgive you if you're short-tempered or absent-minded. They feel for you when you're down. They try to cheer you up without prying into your secrets.

And they not only love you, but they love everyone you love, too. Your Husky will be a friend to your entire family and all your acquaintances. He won't complain about your mother-in-law or sneer at Uncle Marvin.

Please do the same for your Husky. Don't give up on him. Care for him when he gets old and sick. Forgive him if he rips up the couch or digs a hole in the yard. Give him the same love and tolerance he gives you. After all, it's only fair.

Chapter 19

Ten Tips for Raising a Siberian Husky

● ●

In This Chapter

▶ Keeping in mind some important tips for raising a Husky

▶ Knowing what it takes to be a responsible Husky owner

● ●

Raising a Siberian Husky takes time, love, and above all, patience. In this chapter, I give you some quick tips for raising a Husky. Remember, it's all worth it in the end.

Learn about the Breed

Take the time to read everything you can about Siberian Husky history and care. The more you know, the better owner you will be. Subscribe to dog and breed magazines that will give you hints on training, nutrition, and fun activities with your dogs. Join a local Siberian Husky club. You will not only meet new friends and have more fun, but you'll also develop a supportive network to help you out when and if you run into training difficulties or health problems with your dog.

Join an online e-mail list or chat group. It's free and informative, and you never know whom you'll meet. Go to Husky events like sled racing. Or get involved in obedience, tracking, dog showing, or agility competitions.

Take the time to learn something about canine health, especially problems that are particularly pertinent to Siberians, like eye diseases.

Spay or Neuter Your Dog

Unless you are actively involved in showing or breeding Siberians, there is no excuse not to spay or neuter your pet. Doing so will make the dog a healthier, happier pet. Males will be much less apt to wander, and females will be less apt to draw the entire neighborhood to your backyard.

More importantly, both sexes will be healthier. Problems like testicular cancer and pyometra are killer diseases that affect unaltered animals.

By neutering your dog, you will have the satisfaction of knowing that you are not contributing to the problem of unwanted dogs in this country. You are also setting a good example to other people. After all, if *you* don't neuter your non-show dog, why should anyone else neuter theirs?

And bearing puppies is a life-threatening endeavor. Would you want to risk the life of your beautiful Siberian bitch just because you think she'll have cute puppies? Puppies are also a lot of work and expense. I heard of one recently who needed a $3,000 operation. Are you willing to pay that kind of money? How much do you know about your dog's bloodlines and the genetic diseases he may carry? Are you willing to submit your dog to eye tests and hip x-rays?

Be a responsible pet owner, and have your dog neutered or spayed. And you won't have to worry about the potential problems with breeding your dog.

Give Your Husky Plenty to Do

Siberian Huskies are extremely intelligent animals who get bored quickly. The best way to solve the problem is to become your dog's best friend (after all, he's already yours). Give him lots of interesting toys and plenty of exercise.

Best of all, take time from your own schedule to fit in with his. Go hiking together, play ball, take up sledding, or just run around like crazy together in the backyard. You may even consider getting a second Siberian for your dog to play with.

A dog with plenty of fun and companionship is his life is going to be happier, healthier, and a lot less apt to rip the furniture to shreds the minute you step out of the house.

Make Sure Your Dog Has a Secure, Fenced Yard

Siberians love the outdoors, but it's not a safe world out there. Loose dogs can get hit by cars, poisoned by chemicals, and tortured by kids. They can tangle with skunks, roll in tree sap, trample the neighbor's garden, kill a farmer's livestock, and run deer to death. They can catch diseases, get caught in traps, drown in rivers, and be killed by bigger, meaner dogs. They can get lost or stolen. They can come back to you with one eye, three legs, and pregnant. Or they may never come back at all.

Because you don't want any of this to happen, provide your dog with a comfortable and safe yard of his own. Be sure the fence is high enough that he can't jump over it and well secured at the bottom so he can't dig under it.

The yard is a great place for your Husky to play, but when you must be away from home, keep your dog in the house where he won't annoy the neighbors or be too much of a temptation to would-be thieves and mischievous children. I knew a dog who was let out of his fenced yard by some kids because they wanted to play with him; he was killed by a car. Keep a lock on your fence gate, just in case.

Make Sure Your Husky Gets Regular Veterinary Checkups

Make your vet your best friend. Find one you trust, one who gives careful consideration to your dog's needs and your own questions. Choose a vet who is close to where you live, has convenient office hours, loves dogs, and takes his time with you. Find a vet who has a clean facility, a courteous and friendly staff, and reasonable charges. Choose a vet who has someone to cover for him when he's away.

Keep your Siberian in the pink by taking him to your veterinarian regularly. Even apparently healthy dogs need a yearly checkup. Your Siberian should be up-to-date on all his vaccinations according to the protocol you and your vet have set.

Have your Husky's teeth cleaned on a regular basis, especially as he ages.

Feed Your Husky High-Quality Food

If you feed your dog a commercial dog food, choose one that has no meat or grain by-products. Avoid foods with artificial dyes, artificial preservatives, and artificial sweeteners.

If you decide to feed your dog a homemade diet, do the research to make sure he is getting what he needs. Don't just throw him the leftovers every day.

Feed your dog a healthy variety of food to keep him interested and to give his immune system a good workout. The same food day in and day out is boring, and invites allergies and immunodepressant diseases.

Keep your dog fit and trim by providing the correct amount of nutrients and exercise.

Groom Your Siberian Often

Keep that gorgeous coat in condition (and the hairballs out of the house) by brushing your Siberian thoroughly and regularly. You'll not only keep his coat looking nice, but you'll be helping his skin remain healthy. Good brushing also aids the circulatory system by acting like a massage. Regular grooming keeps you alert as to your Husky's current body condition; you'll notice lumps, cuts, scabs, and sore places.

Brushing your dog also makes him feel good — and bonds the two of you together.

When grooming, don't overlook his ears, eyes, teeth, and nails.

Train Your Siberian Early

Although old dogs *can* learn new tricks, it is true that young ones learn them more easily. And while you may not care if your dog is up to David Letterman's standards, it's nice to have your Husky come, sit, heel, and stay on command. If you can train him to fetch the paper and make coffee, so much the better.

Young dogs want to please you, and if you train him to get off the couch, not jump up on people, and refrain from tearing the trash into shreds when he's 8 weeks old, your life will go easier. Never allow a puppy to do anything (like nipping) that you wouldn't allow your older dog to do.

Socialize Your Siberian

Your Husky should be friends with the world. Your puppy should meet a whole bunch of human beings both on walks and in his home. Let him get acquainted with children and elderly people, people on bikes and people in wheelchairs, people with uniforms and people with Poodles. Let him meet people of various races.

He should also get acquainted with other animals. Siberians generally like other dogs of their own size, but smaller dogs, cats, and rabbits may arouse a different response. Unless and until you are absolutely sure your dog will not chase small animals, keep him securely away from them.

Use Positive Reinforcement Rather than Punishment

Never strike or brutalize your dog. Siberians respond much better to rewards of food, praise, and play. Hitting a dog makes him fear you and hate training. It may elicit a similar response.

Love, patience, and kindness always reap their rewards by producing the similar effect in the dog.

Chapter 20

Ten Hazards for a Siberian Husky

*T*housands of pets in the United States die unnecessary deaths every year. Some are run over by cars, and many others are poisoned, electrocuted, or strangled in their own homes. Still, a reasonable degree of foresight can prevent any of this from happening to you and your pets. Dogs are very much like small children, curious, innocent creatures who are at the mercy of electricity, household chemicals, and weird plants. Your benign looking house can quickly turn into a chamber of horrors for an unsuspecting puppy. So in this chapter, I let you know about ten potential hazards for your Husky. Then it's up to you to dog-proof your home to keep him safe.

Electricity

The ordinary 110-volt circuitry in your house can easily kill your dog. Siberians don't seem to be aware of this simple fact, however, and they enjoy pulling on electrical cords and dragging whatever is attached to them, usually lamps, to the floor. When the item is on the floor, the light bulb is available for swallowing. Puppies especially are very fond of eating light bulbs. All electrical cords should be attached to the baseboard where they are inconspicuous or removed completely from your Husky's reach.

Extension cords that trail across the center of the floor are very tempting to dogs. Safe Living/Smart Products makes a pet-safe extension cord. It's called the Smart Cord and sells for $14.95. It contains an advanced internal monitoring system that stops electrical flow in $\frac{1}{40}$ of a second. Even if your Husky's teeth sink into it, he won't get shocked. The Smart Cord also provides built-in fire protection. These cords may be purchased in most hardware or appliance stores.

Rat Poison

Rat and mouse poisons are highly toxic to dogs as well as to rodents. Most of them are anticoagulants and interfere with the blood's clotting ability. If your dog ingests the poison, he can bleed to death internally. Unfortunately, the dog may exhibit no signs for three to five days after ingestion. So by the time you realize it, it may be too late.

If you have a problem with rats and mice, avoid using poisons at all cost.

Household Cleaning Agents

Evidence has been accumulating that some popular household cleaners may be dangerous for dogs. They contain phenol or phenol derivatives, which have been implicated in liver and kidney damage. Phenols are slow-acting toxins that may affect your dog so gradually that you don't know what's happening. They are especially dangerous around puppies. Some experts recommend disinfecting with rubbing alcohol instead of products containing phenol; rubbing alcohol works fast and has no side effects.

Caustics like drain cleaners, automatic dishwashing detergents, and toilet bowl cleaners are also extremely dangerous to dogs.

Make sure you keep all household cleaners in a place where your dog can't get to them. And don't just assume that he can't get under your kitchen sink. Dogs have been known to get cupboard doors open. A high shelf in a pantry is a better bet.

Medicine Chest Menace

The American Veterinary Medical Association (AVMA) says that 70 percent of pet poisonings are due to the ingestion of drugs. Curious dogs often get into both over-the-counter and prescription drugs, and they can easily end up dying.

Child-proof bottles are not dog-proof. A Husky can chew his way through a plastic bottle faster than you can get it out of his mouth. Keep medications locked up, and unless specifically advised by your vet, never give your pet human medication. Tylenol and ibuprofen (Advil, Nuprin, Motrin) are particularly bad for dogs. Tylenol is toxic to a dog's liver. Ibuprofen is extremely toxic to dogs, even in low doses. And even when dogs and people take the same drugs, dosages can vary considerably. Don't gamble with your pet's life.

Hazardous Plants

Poisonous and otherwise dangerous house plants include cactus, English ivy, dumb cane (dieffenbachia), wax begonias, yellow calla, peace lily, and philodendron. Both philodendron and dieffenbachia, both of the Araceae family of plants, can cause intense pain and allergic reaction; the latter can swell tissues in the mouth to the point of choking the dog. Dieffenbachia induces kidney failure. Clinical signs of Araceae poisoning include salivation, head shaking, pawing at the mouth, and vomiting or diarrhea. If your dog is exhibiting any of these symptoms, get him to the vet, and bring a leaf from the suspect plant with you.

Household plants aren't the only plant hazard for your dog. Some common poisonous yard, garden, and forest plants include the following:

- Azalea and rhododendron
- Boxwood
- Daffodils
- Delphiniums
- Caladium
- English ivy
- Holly
- Rhubarb

- Skunk cabbage
- Tulip bulbs
- Tomato and avocado leaves
- Mushrooms
- Honeysuckle
- Dutchman's breeches
- Mayapple
- Buttercup
- Foxglove
- Bleeding heart
- Horse chestnut
- Elephant's ear
- Lily-of-the-valley
- Wisteria
- Morning glory
- Monkshood
- Daphne
- Mother-in-law's tongue
- Nightshade

Holiday Leftovers

Gluttony is a deadly sin for pets, at least as far as turkey skin and fat go. They can give dogs a bad case of pancreatitis. Be generous, and give your dog a nice plate of lean turkey breast instead of the skin or fat. And never give a dog cooked chicken or turkey bones — they can get stuck or splinter in the dog's esophagus, stomach, or bowel.

Throw the bones away, if possible, in a large jar with a screwed-on lid. That will keep the smells in and save your trash from being ravaged by the neighborhood cats and dogs, who don't need any turkey bones stuck in their throats either.

Most Huskies are excellent counter-cruisers and can lift a whole cooked turkey right off the old carving board when no one is looking. Watch out!

Turkey stuffing sometimes contains onions, which are poisonous to dogs. Apple seeds, green potato skins, rhubarb, moldy cheese, and cherry pits are also bad for dogs. Although your dog isn't likely to gobble down rhubarb, you never really know.

Garage Doors

Automatic garage doors can be extremely dangerous for your pet. A dear friend of mine lost her Golden Retriever puppy when he was accidentally caught in just such a door. Thankfully, most modern units have emergency safety devices built into them, which will reverse the door if it strikes something. Regardless, always be careful and check under the garage door before (and *during*) closing it.

Antifreeze

Without a doubt, antifreeze is the most dangerous item in your garage. Autumn, when people are changing their radiator fluid, is the time of greatest danger. Antifreeze is apparently sweet and pleasant-tasting, but the main ingredient of many brands, ethylene glycol, is deadly poison to dogs, cats, and children. Its metabolites attack and destroy the kidneys, and the final results are coma and death. Unfortunately, when dogs start drinking the stuff, they don't stop.

Because antifreeze is a necessary fact of life for those of us in the colder climates, try using one based on propylene glycol, rather than ethylene glycol. A propylene-glycol-based antifreeze is somewhat more expensive, but it's worth it. Propylene glycol affects the central nervous system, but not the kidneys. *Tufts Veterinary Newsletter* estimates that a medium-sized dog would need to ingest about 20 ounces of propylene glycol before getting seriously ill, while only 2 ounces of the more deadly ethylene glycol can kill. Propylene glycol is less tasty to dogs than is its deadly cousin. ***Remember:*** Even though propylene glycol is considerably less toxic that ethylene glycol, it is *still* a poison.

Most commercially sold antifreeze is 95 percent ethylene glycol. The safer alternative, propylene glycol antifreezes, includes Sierra (Safe Brands Corporation) and Sta-Clean (Sta-Clean Products).

The best solution when it comes to antifreeze is prevention. Keep all antifreeze locked away from anywhere your Husky may possibly go. And, no matter what kind of antifreeze you use, clean up any spills immediately. You can use cat litter to absorb most of the liquid; follow up with rags. And dispose of the stuff carefully. Although antifreeze is biodegradable, it takes a couple of months to degrade. Rinse the area of the spill thoroughly with water.

Lawn Chemicals

Pets and chemicals don't mix. We Americans pour, shake, powder, rake in, and dump 300 million pounds of pesticides on our lawns every year. This stuff is not good for your pets — or your kids! Most of these chemicals are not water-soluble, which means that they're going to be in your yard for a long, long time. They're also poisonous.

So, if your lawn could double as a chemistry lab experiment, keep your dogs away from it. Pesticides come in two basic kinds: organophosphates and carbamates. Both types have similar toxic effects. If your dog does inadvertently walk on freshly applied chemicals, wash his little tootsies with a gentle shampoo as soon as possible.

Consider using organic, rather than chemical treatments for your lawn, like flea-eating nematodes and the seeds from the Asian neem tree. Both help rid your lawn of fleas and other pests naturally. The environment will appreciate it. Always dispose of yard-product containers safely away from pets and children. If you're out to get slugs, make sure the slug bait is safely enclosed.

Swimming Pools

The family swimming pool can be a death trap to your pet. Although many Huskies enjoy swimming, be sure that you never leave your dog alone — even for five minutes — in the pool. A good rule is, if you wouldn't trust the toddler, then don't trust the dog.

If you do allow your Husky to use the pool, always show him how to find the stairs. Sometimes dogs get confused about which way is out. They should be trained to enter and exit the pool by the stairs only.

Winter covers for pools can be dangerous. Unless you have a Loop-Lock-type cover, make every effort to keep your dog and your covered pool strictly separated. Dogs cannot distinguish pool covers from solid ground until it is too late. And if they walk on the pool cover, they can get trapped and drown.

You can purchase a life vest for your dog; they come in various sizes, and are really handy, especially if you and your dog will be traveling to a lake or going boating.

Chapter 21

Ten Tips for Traveling with (Or without) Your Husky

....

In This Chapter

▶ Keeping your Husky safe and happy when you travel with him

▶ Looking into your options if you can't bring your dog along

....

Siberians are born to be on the move; just lying around the house isn't for them. With proper planning, you can expand your own travel plans to include your dog. Why travel solo when your best friend is just panting to go along for the ride?

In this chapter, you get some quick tips for traveling with your dog, whether by plane, train, or automobile. I also give you some great suggestions for things to do if you can't bring your Husky with you. Planning a trip? Look no further.

Go for a Walk

Walking is a great exercise — and a great means of getting around — for both you and your Husky. When you go for walks or hikes with your Siberian, keep him attached to you with a leash at all times. Urban areas pose many hazards for dogs. Even well-behaved dogs may leap into traffic because of an irresistible squirrel, child, pile of garbage, or worse. And in rural areas, unleashed dogs encounter skunks, snakes, rabid raccoons, horse manure, and other choice goodies more often than one would wish. Our Mugwump is a genius at finding excrement and rolling delightedly in it.

If you are a hiker, consider getting a lightweight nylon backpack for your dog. Then the dog can haul his own food and water.

If you happen to be, by choice or necessity, a night walker, you may want to buy a Leashlight, which is a combination 16-foot retractable lead and flashlight. It's a tremendous convenience for those creepy, dark alleys. And it's sold by Black & Decker for around $35.

Include Your Husky on Your Bike Rides

Many Siberians enjoy tagging along while their owners ride their bikes. Because allowing your dog to run free can be dangerous, you can purchase some nifty devices like the Springer or Canine Cruiser, which attach the dog to the bike while preventing him from getting too close and getting hurt. These products cost around $30.

Use your head about bike riding with your dog. Make frequent stops, don't go too fast, and don't go too far. Dogs will exert every ounce of energy to keep up with you, and they can die of heatstroke or exhaustion in their gallant efforts. We human beings are by nature tropical beasts, but the Siberian is an arctic one. The balmy spring days we find so enjoyable are a little too hot for your Siberian to work hard. Some compromise is essential. Be alert and keep an eye on your friend.

Bring Your Siberian in the Car

Your Siberian's car trip should begin before yours does. Most dogs love to ride, but the excitement of the trip can have unfortunate consequences. Before you leave, exercise your dog to tire him out — or at least to calm him down.

If you are a tense or aggressive driver, your attitude will transfer to your dog. Then you'll both be on edge.

Keep your car at a cool and comfortable temperature — for the Siberian. Dogs tend to get very excited or anxious in a car, and what seems comfy for you may be unbearably hot for them. Open the window a crack and get some nice fresh air. This will help you both avoid the dreaded car trip vomit.

Keep car windows a few inches open when you have to leave your pet in the car, even briefly, on warm days. It may be a pleasant 80 degrees outside, but the temperature inside your vehicle can hit a lethal 140 degrees really fast. Puppies are especially vulnerable to heat stress. A good rule is to never leave your dog in a closed car if the temperature outside is over 60 degrees or you are parked in the sun.

You can buy a folding plastic barrier (it looks like a miniature baby gate) for your car windows. This helps circulate the air if you absolutely must leave your Husky in the car. Still, be sure to park in the shade. And don't be gone long (more than a few minutes), if the outside temperature is above 60 degrees.

Fasten Your Husky's Seat Belt

As a rule, your dog should ride safely in the back seat, with proper doggy seat belts. Some countries, like Germany, actually require dogs to have seat belts. Several varieties are on the market. They safely restrain your dog, keeping both you and him safe. Having a Husky leap into your lap while you're trying to negotiate a difficult turn is not as much fun as it sounds. Unanticipated sharp stops can also hurl a dog through the windshield.

You can also buy barriers to insert between the front and back seat. These barriers are adjustable both vertically and horizontally and are pressure-mounted for quick installation. Some versions are netlike, which is fine if don't think your dog will chew them to pieces.

Dogs love to ride in the back of pickups, but it's usually not a safe way for them to travel. Dogs will jump out of trucks, or worse, they can be thrown out and get severely hurt or killed. If your Husky must ride in the back of a truck, you can get a dog restraint. These are designed to be used in conjunction with a harness, *not* a collar. Remember, though, this restraint does nothing to prevent debris from being blown into your pet's eyes, a very real danger. Alternatively, and more safely, you can secure the dog's crate in the cargo area. Consider a cargo liner; Rearguard makes one that fastens with Velcro.

Dogs, especially when excited, pant and drool a lot and can quickly become dehydrated. To reduce chances of dehydration, bring along a canteen with a plastic dish attached. Many companies make special traveling water and food containers, some of which are soft sided for easy handling and storage. There's a product called Pet Galley that holds about 1 gallon of water and 7 cups of food. Freeze the water first to keep it extra cool for your pet.

Bringing your own water is especially important for puppies. Young animals are very sensitive to water changes and can acquire a bad case of diarrhea from drinking strange water. And believe me, puppy diarrhea is the last thing you want to deal with while on a vacation.

Find a Pet-Friendly Hotel

According to a survey taken by the American Animal Hospital Association, 41 percent of pet owners take their pets along on a vacation, at least sometimes. Some hotels allow pets, but you need to inquire first. Expect to put down a deposit, because hotels take a dim view of having their carpets and furniture eaten or urinated upon by pets.

Even a dog who never chews anything at home may suddenly develop a tremendous taste for curtains when away. Most hotels will not allow you to leave your pet alone in the room and require that he be kept crated at all times, even when you are there.

It's very important for dogs everywhere to make a good impression on the hotel management and staff. People make decisions about welcoming dogs based on the behavior of those who have gone before. Be sure to pick up after your dog every time. It's disturbing, but the number of hotels who accept dogs has dropped by 25 percent in recent years. If your dog is not well behaved in every way, it's best to leave him at home.

Take Public Transportation

Some municipalities allow you to bring your Siberian on a bus, even if he's not a certified guide or service dog. Some places merely require the dog to be restrained on a leash or confined in a crate. A few cities just stipulate that the dog should be "well behaved," while using public transport, whereas others add size requirements. Some cities want dogs to be muzzled. Sometimes the pets must pay a fare. Some cities employ the "one dog per bus or car" rule. Be sure to check with the city you're visiting to see what its policies are in this regard.

Fly with Your Husky

If you're thinking about flying with your dog, call the airlines and compare pet policies. The USDA-APHIS produces an excellent brochure entitled "Traveling by Air with your Pet." You can call 301-734-7833 to get a copy. The ASPCA also has a booklet entitled "Traveling with Your Pet."

Many airlines and state health officials require health certificates issued by a licensed veterinarian within ten days of the scheduled flight, so have your pet checked out within that time.

U.S. territories and many foreign countries have quarantines or special health regulations. Check with your travel agent, the airline, or the appropriate consulate for specific information about your destination.

Dogs must be at least 8 weeks old and weaned at the time of flight. It's best not to ship elderly animals. And you should never ship a bitch who is in heat.

If possible, schedule a direct, nonstop flight, which is less stressful for your pet and will reduce his chances of being lost. Try to schedule flights during less-busy times. Don't have your pet sedated before a flight if at all possible; tranquilizers can wreak havoc on a dog's temperature regulatory systems. Check with your veterinarian and get his advice.

Crate your dog in an approved container, and attach all necessary instructions to it. Approved containers are big enough to allow the dog to sit, lie down, stand, and turn around. The floor of the container must be solid and covered with absorbent lining or litter. Pegboard flooring is not allowed. Most airlines require that wheels on the container be removed or made immobile prior to the flight. Kennels must be ventilated. Be sure to buy a crate that is airline-approved.

Put one of your Husky's favorite toys in the kennel with him. Items with your scent will keep your dog comfortable and happy.

Make sure your pet has a flat, buckle collar with identification tags firmly attached. Never use a choke chain. Include your name and a phone number where you or a friend can actually be reached during the pet's flight time. Also provide food, water, or medical information. Food and water dishes must be securely attached.

The words *live animal* must be written clearly on the crate. Include arrows or the words "this end up" to make sure your pet doesn't get transported upside down! You should also print directions reading, "keep away from hot sun and extreme cold" — and hope somebody pays attention. Secure the crate firmly, but do not lock it. It's more likely that someone will need to reach your pet to help than it is that your pet will be stolen from the crate.

Bring along a current photo of your pet in case he gets lost. This will be immensely helpful in relocating him. Believe me, just saying, "He's a Siberian Husky" will not create an instant mental image in the mind of most people. I once had my Basset Hound mistaken for a Pit Bull.

Get Great Husky Photos

While you're on vacation, you will certainly not want to miss getting great photographs of your dogs. With a snowy background, experts recommend using low-sensitivity film ISO 50 or ISO 100, which promote clarity and good color saturation. Select a shutter speed of 1/500 or less for action photos. A telephoto lens is pretty much a must at racing events.

For close-ups, shoot the photo just below eye level, and get as close as you can.

Pay attention to the background! You don't want your best shots ruined by the sudden intrusion of a stranger's foot.

Find a Reputable Pet-Sitter

If your Husky can't actually go with you, he would probably prefer a pet-sitter to a kennel. Most animals resent being hauled off to a pet motel, even the luxury kind with heated pools and exercise classes.

A good pet-sitter should have references and be animal knowledgeable. Make sure you discuss fees in advance, and allow the pet and the sitter to meet beforehand. If your Husky (or the pet-sitter) has a negative response, try a different sitter.

Before you leave, make sure your pet-sitter has all the information she needs about food, medication, and your itinerary.

Locate a Good Boarding Kennel

If you would feel more comfortable sending your dog to a kennel, ask for recommendations from your vet, groomer, and friends. Many vets and groomers operate boarding facilities themselves. Whatever option you choose, your pet will board much more successfully if he has been crate-trained at home. Animals unused to confinement can really suffer at a kennel, where restraint is usually necessary for at least part of the day.

Inspect the place before you board, and ask questions. Provide the kennel management with your itinerary and where you can be reached, your veterinarian's number, and a complete health record for your dog. Give them a big clear photo of your dog also, in case he gets lost somehow while you're gone. Leave the name of a local person who can pick up the dog in case you can't.

Before you leave your dog in a kennel, visit yourself and look for and ask about the following:

✔ **Is the kennel clean?**

✔ **Is the kennel heated and cooled according to the season?**

✔ **Is there a vet on call?**

✔ **Does the kennel employ veterinary technicians on its staff?**

✔ **Are there both indoor and outdoor runs?**

✔ **Is the kennel secure?** With the Siberian's propensity for escaping and taking off for the far hills, this should be a prime consideration. If your Husky is an escape artist, let the kennel manager know in advance.

✔ **Is the indoor area well ventilated?**

✔ **What kind of bedding is provided?** Most kennels allow you to bring your dog's own bed for him, if you like.

✔ **How are the animals separated?** Good kennels do not allow nose-to-nose contact between animals, both for fear of spreading disease and to prevent fence fighting.

✔ **Does the kennel have adequate quarantine facilities?** This is an important consideration if a boarded dog develops symptoms of a contagious disease.

✔ **Can you pick up your pet on Sunday?** Many boarding kennels are closed on Sunday, and pets are unavailable for pickup. Sunday, of course, is the very day when most people return from trips and want to pick up their pets.

✔ **Is the kennel accredited by the American Boarding Kennel Association (ABKA)?**

Appendix A

Glossary

agouti: The "wild" color. Guard hairs are banded with black at the tips and roots, with bands of yellow in the middle. Agouti is also the name for a wild rodent.

alpha: The dominant member of a dog or wolf pack, or the human in a dog-human relationship.

bi-eyes: One blue eye, one brown eye.

bitch: A female dog.

Canis lupus: The gray, or northern, wolf.

Canis lupus familiaris: The domestic dog. Includes Siberian Huskies, Chihuahuas, Labrador Retrievers, and all other domestic dogs.

chinchilla factor: The guard coat hairs banded with white, producing a silvery effect.

Chukchis: Native people of extreme northeastern Siberia; the first breeders of the Siberian Husky.

dam: The mother dog.

dewclaw: An extra, unneeded claw on the inside of the Husky's rear leg. It should be removed shortly after birth.

dog: A male dog.

forging: Pulling ahead on the leash.

guard hairs: Long, smooth guards that grow through and conceal the undercoat.

Husky: A term, derived from a derogatory slang word for Eskimo, for any of several northern dog breeds.

hypothermia: Excessive loss of body heat; a serious chill.

Iditarod: A Gold Rush city of interior Alaska; the great sled race that takes place every March in that state.

Irish: Colloquial term for a Siberian with a mask, white legs, and a white underside.

monochrome: A hair of one solid color.

Obsessive-Compulsive Disorder (OCD): A condition in which a dog manifests repeated, destructive, or annoying behaviors like whirling or paw-licking.

parti-color: An eye with patches of two or more colors. Sometimes referred to as *pinto* or *split.*

sable: Guard hairs banded with red near the roots, but tipped with black.

scissors bite: The correct bite in Huskies. The outer side of the lower incisors touches the inner side of the upper incisors.

sickle tail: Carried up and out in a semicircle.

sire: The father dog.

snipy: A pointy, weak muzzle, lacking breadth and depth.

snow nose: A normally black nose that acquires a pink streak in winter.

stop: The step up from the muzzle to the back of the skull; indentation between the eyes where the nasal bones and cranium meet.

taiga: A moist, subarctic forest at the edge of the tundra, composed mostly of firs and spruce.

topline: A dog's outline from just behind the shoulders to the tail set.

tundra: A level, treeless plain characteristic of arctic regions; its subsoil is permanently frozen.

undercoat: The soft dense hair that supports the outercoat.

vaccine titer: A measure of the level of disease-fighting antibodies present in the blood.

withers: Top of the shoulders.

Appendix B

Resources

Publications

The Siberian Husky Club of America (SHCA) publishes a variety of materials that are helpful for Husky owners. Check out the following:

- *A Partnership for Life: Learning to Understand Your Siberian Husky*
- *Your Siberian Husky: Its Hips and Its Eyes*
- *The SHCA Information Booklet*
- *The Siberian Husky Club of America, Inc. Newsletter*

You can find information on how to get these materials at the SHCA Web site (www.shca.org) or by contacting the SHCA Corresponding Secretary, Fain Zimmerman at 210 Madera Drive, Victoria, TX 77905-0611 or by e-mail at sledog@tisd.net.

Also check out *The Siberian Quarterly,* an excellent resource for Husky enthusiasts. For information on subscriptions, visit them on the Web at www.hoflin.com/Magazines/The%20Siberian%20Quarterly.html or contact them at *The Siberian Quarterly,* Hofflin Publishing, Inc., 4401 Zephyr Street, Wheat Ridge, CO 80033 (telephone: 303-420-2222).

Siberian Rescue Organizations

Siberian Husky Club of America
National Rescue Chairman
Gerry Dalakian
telephone: 908-782-2089
e-mail: gericksibe@aol.com

Siberian Husky Rescue Site
Web site: www.siberianrescue.com

Mushing Organizations

International Sled Dog Racing Association
HC 86, Box 3380
Merrifield, MN 56465
Web site: www.isdra.org

Mush with Pride
P.O. Box 84915
Fairbanks, AK 99709-4915

Organizations

American Kennel Club
5580 Centerview Drive
Raleigh, NC 27606
telephone: 919-233-9767
Web site: www.akc.org

Siberian Husky Club of America, Inc.
Fain Zimmerman, Corresponding Secretary
210 Madera Drive
Victoria, TX 77905-0611
e-mail: Sledog@tisd.net
Web site: www.shca.org

International Siberian Husky Club
Liz Deye, Recording Secretary
35687 Blackfoot Street NW
Cambridge, MN 55008
telephone: 612-689-4984

Yankee Siberian Husky Club, Inc.
Tamara Davis, Membership Chairperson
13 Titus Lane
Boxford, MA 01921

Mushing/Sledding Equipment

Adanac
4108 Highway 93N
Kalispell, MT 59901
telephone: 406-752-2929
sleds, harnesses, equipment

Alaska Feed Company
1600 College Road
Fairbanks, AK 99709
telephone: 907-451-5570
harnesses, ganglines, picket cables, collars, skijor belts

Alpine Outfitters
P.O. Box 245
Roy, WA 98580
telephone: 206-843-2767
stock and custom harnesses, modular cablelines

Arctic Star Dog Sled Company
Johnn Molburg
RR#4 Box 381
Tyrone, PA 16686
telephone: 814-684-3594
sleds

Black Ice Dog Sledding Company
3620 Yancy Ave
New Germany, MN 55367
telephone: 320-485-4825
sleds, wheeled rigs, harnesses, ganglines, skijoring

Frank and Nettie Hall
5875 McCrum Road
Jackson, MI 49201
telephone: 517-782-1786
fax: 517-782-0191
dog sleds and rigs, harnesses, ganglines, books

Kaleb's Kart Co.
5770 Wildwood Rd.
Neillsville, WI 54456
telephone: 715-743-3864
skijoring and other mushing equipment

Kema Sleds & Equipment
Mile 2.2 Wasilla-Fishhook Road
P.O. Box 870415
Wasilla, AK 99687
telephone: 907-376-5523
sleds, harnesses, ganglines, rope, snaps

Kiva Outfitters
1256C Poplar Avenue
Sunnydale, CA 94086-8619
telephone: 408-733-7919
carts, rigs, sleds, clothing, collectibles, books

Konari Outfitters, Ltd.
52 Seymour Street
Middlebury, VT 05753
telephone: 802-388-7447
harnesses, books, sledding gear

Kondos Outdoors
626 Kawishiwi Trail
Ely, MN 55731
telephone: 218-365-4189
harnesses, sprint and long-distance sled bags, rope

Lead Dog Supplies
2269 Lisa Lane
Fairbanks, AK 99712
telephone: 907-488-4135
arctic headlamps, ganglines, picket lines, aluminum brakes

Never Summer Sled Dog Equipment
P6750 Glade Road
Loveland, CO 80538
telephone: 970-622-8658
equipment for mushing, skijoring, and weightpulling

Nordkyn Outfitters
5903 316th Street East
Eatonville, WA 98328
telephone: 253-847-4128
sleds, lines, bags, collars, harnesses, carts

Pet-Tech International
2144 Primrose Ave
Vista, CA 92083
telephone: 619-599-9759
3- and 4-wheeled rigs

The Real Alaska Mushing Company
471 Fleshamn St
Fairbanks, AK 99712
telephone: 907-457-8555
complete line of sled dog equipment

Resha Sled Dog Equipment
HC1, Box 101
Lewis Run, PA 16738
telephone: 814-362-3048
sledding, weight pulling, freighting, and skijoring equipment

Risdon Rigs
P.O. Box 127
Laingsburg, MI 48848
telephone: 517-651-6960
sleds, wheeled rigs, harnesses, snow hooks, dog bags

Sawtooth Mountain Sled Works, Inc.
237 County Road
Grand Marais, MN 55604
telephone: 218-387-2106
sleds and bags

Boarding and Pet-Sitting

To get a list of accredited boarding kennels, contact the follow organizations:

American Boarding Kennel Association
4575 Galley Road, Suite 400A
Colorado Springs, CO 80915
telephone: 719-591-1113
Web site: www.abka.com

National Association of Professional Pet Sitters (NAPPS)
1030 15th Street NW, Suite 870
Washington, DC 20005
telephone: 202-393-3317
Web site: www.petsitters.org

Pet Sitters International
418 East King Street
King, NC 27021-9163
telephone: 336-983-9222
Web site: www.petsit.com

Index

FOR

DUMMIES®

The easy way to get more done and have more fun

PERSONAL FINANCE

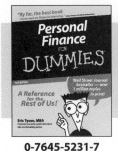

0-7645-5231-7

Investing

0-7645-2431-3

Home Buying

0-7645-5331-3

Also available:

Estate Planning For Dummies
(0-7645-5501-4)

401(k)s For Dummies
(0-7645-5468-9)

Frugal Living For Dummies
(0-7645-5403-4)

Microsoft Money "X" For Dummies
(0-7645-1689-2)

Mutual Funds For Dummies
(0-7645-5329-1)

Personal Bankruptcy For Dummies
(0-7645-5498-0)

Quicken "X" For Dummies
(0-7645-1666-3)

Stock Investing For Dummies
(0-7645-5411-5)

Taxes For Dummies 2003
(0-7645-5475-1)

BUSINESS & CAREERS

Accounting

0-7645-5314-3

Grant Writing

0-7645-5307-0

Resumes

0-7645-5471-9

Also available:

Business Plans Kit For Dummies
(0-7645-5365-8)

Consulting For Dummies
(0-7645-5034-9)

Cool Careers For Dummies
(0-7645-5345-3)

Human Resources Kit For Dummies
(0-7645-5131-0)

Managing For Dummies
(1-5688-4858-7)

QuickBooks All-in-One Desk Reference For Dummies
(0-7645-1963-8)

Selling For Dummies
(0-7645-5363-1)

Small Business Kit For Dummies
(0-7645-5093-4)

Starting an eBay Business For Dummies
(0-7645-1547-0)

HEALTH, SPORTS & FITNESS

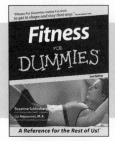

Fitness

0-7645-5167-1

Golf

0-7645-5146-9

Diabetes

0-7645-5154-X

Also available:

Controlling Cholesterol For Dummies
(0-7645-5440-9)

Dieting For Dummies
(0-7645-5126-4)

High Blood Pressure For Dummies
(0-7645-5424-7)

Martial Arts For Dummies
(0-7645-5358-5)

Menopause For Dummies
(0-7645-5458-1)

Nutrition For Dummies
(0-7645-5180-9)

Power Yoga For Dummies
(0-7645-5342-9)

Thyroid For Dummies
(0-7645-5385-2)

Weight Training For Dummies
(0-7645-5168-X)

Yoga For Dummies
(0-7645-5117-5)

Available wherever books are sold.
Go to www.dummies.com or call 1-877-762-2974 to order direct.

WILEY

FOR DUMMIES®

A world of resources to help you grow

HOME, GARDEN & HOBBIES

Feng Shui FOR DUMMIES
A Reference for the Rest of Us!
0-7645-5295-3

Gardening FOR DUMMIES
A Reference for the Rest of Us!
0-7645-5130-2

Guitar FOR DUMMIES
A Reference for the Rest of Us!
0-7645-5106-X

Also available:

Auto Repair For Dummies
(0-7645-5089-6)

Chess For Dummies
(0-7645-5003-9)

Home Maintenance For Dummies
(0-7645-5215-5)

Organizing For Dummies
(0-7645-5300-3)

Piano For Dummies
(0-7645-5105-1)

Poker For Dummies
(0-7645-5232-5)

Quilting For Dummies
(0-7645-5118-3)

Rock Guitar For Dummies
(0-7645-5356-9)

Roses For Dummies
(0-7645-5202-3)

Sewing For Dummies
(0-7645-5137-X)

FOOD & WINE

Cooking FOR DUMMIES
A Reference for the Rest of Us!
0-7645-5250-3

Cookies FOR DUMMIES
A Reference for the Rest of Us!
0-7645-5390-9

Wine FOR DUMMIES
A Reference for the Rest of Us!
0-7645-5114-0

Also available:

Bartending For Dummies
(0-7645-5051-9)

Chinese Cooking For Dummies
(0-7645-5247-3)

Christmas Cooking For Dummies
(0-7645-5407-7)

Diabetes Cookbook For Dummies
(0-7645-5230-9)

Grilling For Dummies
(0-7645-5076-4)

Low-Fat Cooking For Dummies
(0-7645-5035-7)

Slow Cookers For Dummies
(0-7645-5240-6)

TRAVEL

Italy FOR DUMMIES
A Travel Guide for the Rest of Us!
0-7645-5453-0

Hawaii FOR DUMMIES
A Travel Guide for the Rest of Us!
0-7645-5438-7

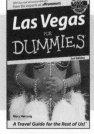

Las Vegas FOR DUMMIES
A Travel Guide for the Rest of Us!
0-7645-5448-4

Also available:

America's National Parks For Dummies
(0-7645-6204-5)

Caribbean For Dummies
(0-7645-5445-X)

Cruise Vacations For Dummies 2003
(0-7645-5459-X)

Europe For Dummies
(0-7645-5456-5)

Ireland For Dummies
(0-7645-6199-5)

France For Dummies
(0-7645-6292-4)

London For Dummies
(0-7645-5416-6)

Mexico's Beach Resorts For Dummies
(0-7645-6262-2)

Paris For Dummies
(0-7645-5494-8)

RV Vacations For Dummies
(0-7645-5443-3)

Walt Disney World & Orlando For Dummies
(0-7645-5444-1)

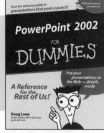
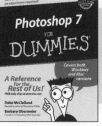

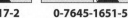

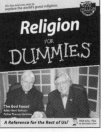

Notes

Notes